Georgia O'Keeffe

Titles in the series Critical Lives present the work of leading cultural figures of the modern period. Each book explores the life of the artist, writer, philosopher or architect in question and relates it to their major works.

In the same series

Georgia O'Keeffe

WITHDRAWN

Nancy J. Scott

REAKTION BOOKS

To the memory of my mother, Lelia, and the pioneer grandmothers
I never knew, women who devoted themselves to education and the
cultivation of heart and mind

Published by Reaktion Books Ltd
Unit 32, Waterside
44–48 Wharf Road
London N1 7UX, UK
www.reaktionbooks.co.uk

First published 2015
Copyright © Nancy J. Scott 2015

Printed and bound in Great Britain by Bell & Bain, Glasgow

A catalogue record for this book is available from the British Library

ISBN 978 1 78023 428 1

Contents

Alfred Stieglitz, *Georgia O'Keeffe*, 1918, platinum/palladium print.

Introduction: Pioneer, Independent Spirit, Visionary

Art became Georgia O'Keeffe's lodestar from her earliest childhood, as she navigated towards her goal, both in and out of art schools. American pragmatism and love of the tangible, the cleanly sculpted line and the technical mastery of colour informed her art making. She first trained to be an art teacher, and in later years – though she never taught again after 1918 – demonstrated her didactic manner in terse but distilled ways of seeing. She articulated her artistic priority clearly: 'I think I'd rather let the painting work for itself than help it with the word.'[1]

The artist taught her public to 'take time to see', admonishing those 'busy New Yorkers' who never stopped to look at a flower. Engrossed by the worlds within flora, O'Keeffe unfurled purple petunias and calla lilies, and magnified the simple stalk of corn, taking her gaze down to the 'fine little lake of dew' nestling at the core of the plant. She wrote spare, poetic statements on nature, her meditation and 'the forms in my head' that she always identified as the source of her daring abstractions. In one evocative passage in a letter of 1917 from O'Keeffe to Alfred Stieglitz she wrote of 'the space that is watching the starlight' – 'that space that is between what they call heaven and earth – out there in what they call the night'.[2] This liminal space, a seeming nothingness, became the centre of her creative invention.

Georgia Totto O'Keeffe's story is one that not only is rooted in the American prairie, where she was born on a Wisconsin dairy farm on 15 November 1887, but also reflects the pioneer daring of the mid-nineteenth-century Dutch, Hungarian and Irish immigrant generations that formed her ancestry. She followed a peripatetic pathway to later success in New York, first studying and teaching art in both public schools and colleges. Her exhibition life as an artist began in a hastily arranged, experimental group show in May 1916, when the renowned photographer and gallery impresario Alfred Stieglitz (1864–1946) first showed her recent charcoal abstractions at 291 Fifth Avenue. O'Keeffe's art emerged precisely at the time that American women gained the right to vote, signalling her own struggle to make her voice heard through artistic expression.

The reality of the harsh winters in Wisconsin gave her grandmothers' and mother's generation of pioneer women the strict resilience of making-do, learning basic life skills and surviving unforeseen crises, whether due to climate or in times of illness and death in the family. Her upbringing and childhood on a farm cultivated an independence that was both powerful and inborn. O'Keeffe's gaze favoured wide-open spaces – her love of the wind-blown prairie in Texas and, later, the high desert vistas of New Mexico. Like the nineteenth-century pioneers moving west, O'Keeffe sought out an extraordinary landscape, what many thought a desolate land. She stamped her vision of the land with the imprint of strength and endurance: 'the desert even tho' it is vast and empty and untouchable – knows no kindness with all its beauty.'[3]

O'Keeffe's art articulated both a modernist expressive vision, 'filling space in a beautiful way' based on her study of Asian composition with Arthur Wesley Dow at Columbia University. Her paintings and abstract designs avoided the human figure, and she certainly never wanted to become a portraitist (though drawings of family members exist from her early training). Instead, she described her process in her own way: 'There are people who have made me see shapes . . . I have painted portraits that to me are almost photographic. I remember hesitating to show the paintings, they looked so real to me. But they have passed into the world as abstractions – no one seeing what they are.'[4]

Her innovative and sensuous embrace of nature imparted a powerful organic expression to the simple still-life, once associated with women's art. As she established her presence in New York with yearly exhibitions, beginning in 1923, her studies of flowers, shells and stones became sites of powerful meditation, and controversy. She then expanded her view of the landscape to enlarge the crosses and relics of the southwest, starting in the summer of 1929, ultimately defining a new iconography of skull, pelvis and floating antlers, ethereally and mysteriously elevated above the land, against the vast sky.[5]

O'Keeffe was regarded as a woman artist of the first rank in America painting in an abstract style from 1915, and her reputation had solidified by the 1940s when she first showed her work in retrospective exhibitions in Chicago in 1943 ('the most famous woman painter in the world' exclaimed the *Chicago Tribune*) and at the Museum of Modern Art in New York in 1946, the first woman artist to be so honoured there.[6]

Her commitment to equal rights for women emerged from early friendships, influences and reading, and her support for the ideas of the suffrage movement also came early, although the artist rarely involved herself directly in activism. As she attained prominence, O'Keeffe gave a speech before the National Woman's Party in 1926. Later, in 1944, she wrote a personal letter to Eleanor Roosevelt, arguing a point on forthcoming legislation in her direct manner of speech: 'women do not have it [legal equality] and I believe we are considered – half the people.'[7]

After the Second World War ended, art historians, curators and critics grappled with the emergence of Abstract Expressionism, and plotted the genealogy of the 'triumph of American painting'. Only in the mid-1960s did O'Keeffe begin to receive accolades as a pioneer of Color Field and Minimalist painting. As her 79th birthday approached, in May 1966 her painting *Pelvis Series – Red with Yellow* spread across the cover of *Artforum*, marking the occasion of her retrospective, originating at the Amon Carter Museum of Western Art in Texas.[8]

By 1967 O'Keeffe's reputation at last had moved past the issues of her gender. An astute art historical essay described O'Keeffe as 'a thoroughly representative American artist of the first rank with a vision that helps to define just where our art has been and where it might be going'. The author, a curator, asserted that O'Keeffe's name, 'engraved on the cornerstone of American art', and her actual contributions had been obscured by her fame.[9] This evaluation of her work's evolution no longer depended on the 'first woman' category of her past achievements.

Then came feminism and the energy of a new generation of women who embraced O'Keeffe as their matriarch. To the present day her work receives active reassessment and attracts new generations who claim an allegiance with, or find direction from, her life and art.[10] O'Keeffe enjoyed young people, and the consequent attention to her defining retrospective at the Whitney Museum of American Art in autumn 1970, but had no time for the assertive new feminisms nor its art. As the Whitney exhibition *Georgia O'Keeffe: Abstraction* (2009) demonstrated, O'Keeffe had a distinct role in advancing the growth of abstract formal language in painting from the first generation of American modernism. Her legacy has passed on now to the Georgia O'Keeffe Museum in Santa Fe, opened to the public in 1997, which has owned and maintained her Abiquiu home since its designation in 1998 as a National Historic Landmark. The spirit of O'Keeffe, vibrant in northern New Mexico, reverberates across America and has extended to Hawaii, Japan and Europe in travelling exhibitions over the past two decades. An auction sale of November 2014, which set a new high for a woman artist when her painting *Jimson Weed* (1932) fetched over $44 million with buyer's premium, anchored the artist's continuing star power.

Through the release in 2006 of the extensive O'Keeffe–Stieglitz correspondence stored at the Beinecke Rare Book and Manuscript Library in the Yale Collection of American Literature, her paintings have gained a wider documented context. The rich resources and enormous correspondence provide the foundation for many of the themes of this book. Listening carefully to O'Keeffe's voice remains a priority in thinking about her art. The letters privilege an intimate view into her world, against which polemical interpretation, criticism and theory must be balanced.

The letters also reveal the art in life. Her constant attention to design is found in the spiral form in the letter 'I'; her idiosyncratic punctuation, with wavy dashes across the page; her deployment of an ink pen. All serve to shape the content, not only words. To the collector Dr Albert Barnes she described the quotidian pleasure of meeting a new friend when she invoked 'that American quality' of educator John Dewey: 'one of the things that gives me a lift off the earth – like a grand cold sunny day'.[11]

Stieglitz and O'Keeffe fell in love through their letters, keeping up a constant correspondence between Texas and New York in the period 1916–18. Whether O'Keeffe represented the untutored naive imagination of the child or the adult sensuality of a woman, all that she represented was amplified in Stieglitz's imagination, and ultimately in his photography, and advocacy for her art.

Thus it is a constant challenge to disentangle the independent O'Keeffe from representations of her, and the subjective lens employed by Stieglitz to interpret her creative world. The artist chose to join Stieglitz in New York in 1918, at the age of 29. Yet soon her independent spirit sought release from the straitjacket of 'words, words, words' that pelted down upon her painting. From the beginning of their love affair, Stieglitz's photographic images chronicled virtually every pore of his beloved, and trumpeted her art, albeit often in sexist terms. The images of her represented his own rebirth and return of his creative work to its highest commitment. O'Keeffe, first his youthful mistress and muse, became a scandal and 'newspaper personality' in 1921, before *her* art had a chance before the public. The artist's struggle to remain herself in the light of sensational publicity took years. Over time, this woman, who joined the suffrage generation and gained the vote, expressed herself vividly in colour and line, hiked to the summit of the Blue Ridge Mountains in Virginia and rode horseback up Mount Wheeler in New Mexico, still found that her intention and origins were often thwarted by the written word. Inspired by Stieglitz's memorable images, gallery monologues and intimate revelations, his gallery audience absorbed the 'idea' of O'Keeffe. Since she herself could not yet realize the full import of her experimentation, she depended upon Stieglitz's approval and support, yet chafed at his domination. Stieglitz never wavered in his conscious advocacy to nurture the creative arts in America or to promote O'Keeffe's career. In many ways, she owed her public success to him, yet in many ways he also owed the second half of his creative life to her.

The contradictions of O'Keeffe's strong personality are many. The minimalist O'Keeffe, who preferred to live in as bare a room as possible and who declared that she 'gave away everything of value' before moving to New Mexico in 1949, saved every letter and kept many of Stieglitz's photographs of her in New Mexico. In 1976, on publishing her autobiographical text, she scarcely acknowledged Stieglitz, yet she then allowed 51 of the remarkable O'Keeffe portrait photographs, including many of the nudes, to be displayed at the Metropolitan Museum of Art in 1978 and to honour his art. There in the introductory essay to the catalogue

Georgia O'Keeffe, letter to Dr Albert Barnes, 18 December 1930.

Georgia O'Keeffe, *Ranchos Church, New Mexico*, 1930–31, oil on canvas.

she wrote an unforgettable phrase about Stieglitz's impact: 'It was as if something hot, dark, and destructive was hitched to the highest, brightest star.'[12]

The painting *Ranchos Church, New Mexico* serves as telling metaphor for O'Keeffe's distilled vision in New Mexico, where she painted the adobe church, San Francisco de Asis Mission Church, in several versions over two summers. Viewed from the back, the church's apse and buttresses take on a lively, sculpted form, shaped by her expressive style. 'I had to create an equivalent for what I felt about what I was looking at', she wrote, about a building she called 'one of the most beautiful . . . left in the United States by the early Spaniards'.[13]

The goal of O'Keeffe's art is best formulated by words she once wrote to the novelist Sherwood Anderson: 'Making your unknown known is the important thing – and keeping the unknown always beyond you – catching crystallizing your simpler clearer vision of life.'[14] O'Keeffe's art articulates her pioneer innovation, pursuing motifs in nature to a meditative simplicity. The perception of the sensuous forms in flowers, the body in thrall to nature's storms or sunsets, the liminal space between the earth and starry skies: all found shape and colour from her creative unknown.

1

Family Untied:
An Artistic Education

In the account of her life and art published in 1976, O'Keeffe wrote an interdiction to her readers: 'Where I was born and where and how I have lived is unimportant. It is what I have done with where I have been that should be of interest.'[1]

Georgia O'Keeffe had every reason to wish that parts of her past might be erased, deemed forgettable. Nevertheless, she had pleasant childhood memories of growing up on a Wisconsin farm: sunlight on a quilt, an account of her visual memory from her earliest months, the first satisfying drawing of a man with his feet in the air, crafting her dollhouses, her great-grandparents' portraits in the family home. All served to sketch in a usable past, that of a farm girl growing up on the prairie in the Midwest in the late nineteenth century. In reconstructed accounts of her childhood, as the oldest daughter the young Georgia enjoyed the benefits of the 'O'Keeffe neighborhood' where her 'Papa had a prize farm; there was no better one in Sun Prairie'.[2] She claimed to have had no complaints about her childhood 'before the age of twelve', but just as she wished to erase her former teachers' styles and motifs in 1915, she hoped to bury the traces of the misfortunes that befell her family.

At the time of Georgia O'Keeffe's birth in 1887 in Wisconsin, European immigration had already begun to transform the American heartland, stretching from Ohio to Minnesota and the Great Plains beyond. The rich agricultural land of dairy farms, creamery and cheese production farmed by the first German and Scandinavian waves of settlers also promised a fresh start to the Irish, Dutch and Hungarian émigré cultures that would mix in O'Keeffe's own lineage. Her maternal grandfather George Victor Totto (1820–1895), a Hungarian count and revolutionary who faced death or exile in his home country after the rebellion of 1848, when he was rumoured to have been an aide-de-camp to the exiled governor Lajos Kossuth, took flight to America. When he first landed in New York, Totto stayed at an inn in lower Manhattan, but settled in Sauk City, Wisconsin, a Midwestern town first anchored by Hungarian émigrés. There he registered by 1852 with the Freethinkers' Congregation.

Her mother's maiden name, the aristocratic surname Totto, descended to Georgia Totto O'Keeffe. Though she never knew her absent grandfather Totto, who left his family in Wisconsin in 1876 for his native Budapest, she inherited a certain natural aristocratic bearing. '[She was] dignified, haughty without meaning to be', wrote a school friend.[3]

O'Keeffe's maternal grandmother, Isabella Wyckoff, hailed from a proud line of Dutch settlers in New York who had arrived in America in 1637, and one Wyckoff ancestor, Edward Fuller, had in fact come on the *Mayflower*. By the mid-1840s Charles Wyckoff, O'Keeffe's great-grandfather, owned an inn on Warren Street in New York. There his daughter Isabella first met George Totto, and Charles Wyckoff followed with his family to Wisconsin to open an inn. The adventurous Isabella kept a tiny diary, beginning with the bold statement 'I Came West. April 1854.'[4]

Isabella Wyckoff and George Totto married in May 1855 after the unexpected death of Isabella's father during a cholera epidemic, and built a log cabin on the prairie. Isabella would eventually bear six children, four girls and two boys – the third girl, born in 1864, was named Ida Ten Eyck Totto, and the youngest boy, George Totto, after his father. But in 1876, when the child George was just ten years old, his aristocratic father decided to leave America and his growing family and return to his ancestral land. He may have intended to reclaim his lost property, perhaps the Totto castle near Budapest, but whether or not this was realistic it perhaps masked other issues. He never returned to America and died, reportedly impoverished and blind, at age 75. The city-born Isabella reared her children in the university town and state capital, Madison.[5] She inherited the family portraits of Wyckoff's grandparents, Abraham and Isabella, and benefited from the assistance of her younger sister Jennie (Jane Varney), widowed in California, who moved in to help bring up the children.[6] Isabella's children did not work the land; rather, the Wyckoff-Tottos were able to rent out their 200 acres to the hard-working O'Keeffes, their Irish neighbours who owned the adjoining property of similar size. The hard work and management fell to the O'Keeffe brothers, Peter, Boniface and Bernard, and particularly the third son, Francis Calixtus O'Keeffe (1853–1918), known as Frank, who returned from the West to till the land.

Isabella's third child, Ida Ten Eyck Totto (1864–1916), her middle name emphasizing her Dutch maternal line, had been brought up to expect the best. She hoped to study to become a doctor, and kept a diary like her mother, recording her bookish interests.[7] When Ida accepted the proposal of the hard-working Irish bachelor Frank O'Keeffe, ten years her senior, she became the young bride who dutifully secured family property. When she married Frank at the age of twenty, the home service was Episcopalian, a distinct echo of her father's heritage; she had last seen him when she was thirteen. Ida yoked her future to the land's prosperity in a marriage alliance evocative of a Jane Austen narrative. Frank had worked the land for almost a decade, though in his youth he had explored the Dakotas, a thrilling adventure that signalled to the young Georgia that 'deep down' she was like her father: 'When he wanted to see the country, he just got up and went', she recalled.[8]

Frank and Ida became the parents of six children: following their marriage on 19 February 1884, their first son, Francis Calixtus Jr, was born in 1885, and their first daughter, the artist Georgia O'Keeffe, arrived on 15 November 1887 on the family farm in Sun Prairie.[9] Ida's aunt, Jennie, moved in with the family to assist with her great-nieces and -nephews as a disciplinary matriarch, and the family ancestral portraits followed. The young Ida became strict, insisting on excellent behaviour and reports from her children. Georgia recalled the inspiring qualities of both her grandmothers; each painted watercolours and her O'Keeffe grandmother in particular made still-life studies worthy of display. Catherine Mary O'Keeffe wore her hair in a 'wide brown braid coiled round her head' and lived nearby in the house where her sons were born. She also possessed beautiful sewing skills, a trait O'Keeffe shared. Her Totto grandmother, Isabella, 'tall, dignified', had a 'beautiful bearing' and 'masses of white hair'.[10]

O'Keeffe's family traits from both sides, of good humour, whimsy, a love of reading, hard-working stamina, determination and an imperious attitude, all became explicit in the artist, and can be traced back not only to the Dutch forebears and Hungarian aristocracy, but to the Irish spirit of the O'Keeffes. Pierce O'Keeffe, the artist's paternal grandfather and patriarch of the clan in America, came directly to Wisconsin from County Cork in Ireland when his wool business foundered in 1848, even though he survived the devastating potato famine that was then raging. Pierce O'Keeffe's Irish family arrived in the same year that Totto fled Hungary. These distinct cultures may have blended in the pioneers, but the Catholic and Protestant backgrounds never lost their identity in America. The marriage of O'Keeffe's parents was an economic necessity linked to stern affection, and the plot of land fused the uneasy bond between her Irish Catholic father and Protestant mother. In later years O'Keeffe, who was not raised in the Catholic Church, acknowledged, 'I always felt sympathetic to the Catholic Church.'

Clockwise from left: Ida O'Keeffe, Catherine O'Keeffe Klenert, Alexis O'Keeffe, Anita O'Keeffe Young, Eleanor Jane Young and Catherine Klenert Krueger, *c.* 1930.

As she recalled in an interview, 'the Catholic Church was a pleasure to me.' In contrast, when taken to the Congregational church by her Protestant aunt, she felt 'nothing attractive about that at all'. With her usual firm tone, O'Keeffe concluded: 'A child learns a lot about religions.'[11]

From the Totto–O'Keeffe marriage, 400 acres of rich land came under the O'Keeffe name, and in 1898 Frank O'Keeffe acquired more acreage when his youngest brother Bernard died from tuberculosis. Bernard had willed his property to Frank for 'one dollar, with affection', which increased the farm to over 600 acres.[12] The family considered itself prosperous and settled. Tuberculosis, however, remained the curse hanging over the O'Keeffe generations, and Frank O'Keeffe saw the dread disease and harsh winters take his brothers one by one. Illness would inevitably, tragically, follow the family, with the later consequence of poverty.

In a revelatory letter to Alfred Stieglitz in 1916, O'Keeffe confessed: 'talking about my family always makes me mad.' She described the many strands of the melting pot of her heritage:

'Irish – English – Scotch – Hungarian – and Dutch – or maybe
we aren't any more peculiar and mixed up than other folks', she
concluded.[13] O'Keeffe's recollections of Totto's story when she
was 96 had clearly acquired the colour of myth after a century's
passing. For an article in *Interview* in 1983, when Andy Warhol
asked her if she credited her Irish genes with her longevity, she
responded: 'We grew up thinking we were Hungarians.'[14]

Her grandmother Isabella Totto, left adrift by her husband's
abandonment in 1876, never knew his precise fate in Hungary.
The daughter Ida enjoyed prosperity with Frank O'Keeffe, but any
dream of her supposedly wealthy father returning from abroad
ended with his death in 1895. Ida showed the first signs of illness as
early as 1903, as O'Keeffe later wrote: 'My mother began dying to
me the Christmas after I was sixteen.'[15] Wealth and fame did return
to the family through the talents of her daughters, but Ida O'Keeffe
did not live to enjoy this unanticipated fortune.

In the large family, O'Keeffe's older brother Francis (1885–1959),
tall and dark-haired, was the favourite, as she always told the story.
She considered herself an ugly child, comparing herself with the
sisters who came just after: Ida (1889–1961), Anita (1891–1985),
Catherine (1895–1987) and Claudia (1899–1984). All the O'Keeffe girls
sought a professional education, initially in nursing or teaching,
and a friend later recalled that 'the five girls all turned out to
be exceptional individuals.'[16] The oldest boy, Francis, studied
architecture at Columbia University, lived in New York in the
1920s and eventually pursued business development in Cuba,
where he died in 1959. The younger brother, Alexis Wyckoff
O'Keeffe (1892–1930), born between Anita and Catherine, never
overcame the lingering repercussions of illness and trench warfare
during the First World War in France.[17]

In the fertile Wisconsin farmland, Georgia O'Keeffe as a young
girl played with her siblings and friends around her father's dairy
farm, excelling at running and climbing trees. The quiet child also

spent endless hours playing with her dolls, making their clothes and a collapsible doll's house. Although she told one friend that she had 'no complaints' about her first twelve years, she later seemed to despise the idea that they were idyllic. The artist denied that the idea of happiness was ever important to her, preferring that she be remembered always as 'interested'.[18] In a long letter describing her family, she described herself to Stieglitz as 'a damnable independent – self-sufficient young woman'. She wrote: 'I can't help feeling independent – wanting to be free from everyone.'[19]

Despite her mother's strong influence, O'Keeffe identified with her Irish side, remembering her father's 'wonderful black curly hair with big waves'.[20] Of her father, she wrote to Stieglitz: 'I am very like him – so like him that some members of the family [said] – You are so much alike that you are afraid of one another.' She continued: 'he was very much fonder of my mother than she of him – Still he and I agreed more frequently . . . though I always felt he was much fonder of – my nice sister.' Here she meant Ida, 'the nicest girl I know', and just two years younger. It was Ida who encouraged Georgia to resume painting in 1912 by enrolling in summer school classes at the University of Virginia.[21]

Her ill-fated younger brother Alexis inherited their father's bright blue eyes and black curly locks. She wrote: 'I've always been very fond of him – I am yet.' She described him as 'fresh and free – the kind that fills a room to bursting'. About Claudia, the youngest, who came to live with her in Texas at the age of seventeen after their mother's death, O'Keeffe wrote that she had 'snappy black eyes – smooth shiny hair – very dark brown'. O'Keeffe drew precise pencil portraits of Francis, Ida and Claudia during her year at the School of the Art Institute of Chicago in 1905–6, and made a small oval oil portrait of Claudia aged six with those very deep brown eyes.[22] O'Keeffe herself inherited her mother's dark brown hair, but her eyes mixed the reflected light in 'grayish' irises, as friends described them; others saw 'blue-green'.

One interviewer focused on 'her expressive eyes, their gray-blue-green irises speckled with "good luck" spots'.[23] At school she acquired the nickname Patsy, or Pat, due to her Irish surname.

Her mother's overarching commitment to her children centred on education. Ida's planning meant that her first daughter gained privileges the others would not have. After spending her first years from the age of five at the tiny one-room schoolhouse near the farm, young Georgia was sent off to parochial school at age thirteen, for her eighth grade year.[24] But in fact, as she entered adolescence, her budding artistic talent was already meriting attention. During her one year at the Sacred Heart Academy in Madison, she excelled academically, despite her spelling. While under the nuns' tutelage, Georgia earned a gold pin for her deportment, gained the school prize in ancient history and generally felt pleased with her art class. She later bristled, however, at the memory of a 'terrible scolding' by a nun of her drawing of a baby's hand that was too small, with too-dark lines: 'I wasn't convinced that she was right, but I said to myself that I would never have that happen again.' It was during this formative time that she startled herself by telling a girl named Lena, 'the washwoman's daughter', that she wanted to be an artist.[25]

But O'Keeffe did not remain at any high school for more than one or two years. The artist later spoke of her education with disdain: 'I never did like school.' Disruptions and transitions surely contributed to this dislike. In 1902 Georgia and Francis were shifted to a high school in Milwaukee, where they lived with Aunt Lola Totto, the younger sister of Ida, while O'Keeffe's next-younger sisters, Ida and Anita, attended the Sacred Heart Academy in their turn.

Then, in 1903, her father Frank decided to uproot the entire family. After the fierce winter of 1899 when Claudia, the last child, was born while temperatures plummeted to well below freezing, he became deeply concerned about the threat of tuberculosis, and his last brother died the following summer. He and Ida sold the extensive family acreage at a handsome profit, reported as $12,000,[26] and moved the clan to the warmer clime of Williamsburg, Virginia. There they purchased a spacious home, Wheatland, on 9 acres of land called Peacock Hill, which became a gathering place for the seven children and friends, but reflected an overly optimistic view of the family's economic resources.[27] O'Keeffe's last two years of high school, from 1903 to 1905, were spent at a girl's boarding school, Chatham Episcopal Institute (now Chatham Hall), 200 miles from the new home in Virginia, while her brother Francis attended the College of William and Mary, near their home in Williamsburg.

Though Frank O'Keeffe hoped to establish himself in a new business, he soon found that his northern ways, not to mention his relative inexperience, impeded his first grain and feed supply store in the South. Georgia, benefiting from the last years of the O'Keeffe prosperity, found at Chatham a culture of Southern belles, but also important encouragement.[28] At her third school in four years, sixteen years old, she encountered a vast divide in dress and manners. A fellow student later wrote: 'The most unusual thing about her was the absolute plainness of her attire . . . this strong minded girl knew what suited her and would not be changed.'[29] At first, O'Keeffe planned to study music, and practised the piano diligently for several hours each day, performing a Grieg piece for the school recital in 1904.[30] Fortunately the head of the school, Elizabeth Willis, was also the art teacher, and recognized O'Keeffe's abilities. Soon the young artist flourished in her art, and was called 'Queen of the Studio' by her fellow students; 'her easel stood in the center of the floor and was the high spot of interest.'[31] At the Chatham graduation in 1905, having done the bare minimum to pass the required spelling test, young Georgia O'Keeffe gained several more art prizes to her credit. She also became the arts editor of the *Mortar Board*, the school yearbook, created its black pen drawings, and wrote the traditional class prophecy, sketching out the future for her fellow students. O'Keeffe wrote of her own

Georgia O'Keeffe, 1903, photographer unknown.

future that she 'still would be at Chatham twenty years later trying to pass spelling'. The couplet under her photo in the yearbook read: 'A girl who would be different in habit, style, and dress / A girl who doesn't give a cent for men – and boys still less.'[32]

Highly recommended by Elizabeth Willis, O'Keeffe soon left home to enrol at the School of the Art Institute of Chicago, in a first year of college-level art training. There she lived with her aunt 'Ollie' (Auletta Totto), Ida's eldest sister, and her uncle Charles. Ollie, born in 1856, had worked for years as the sole woman proofreader for the *Milwaukee Sentinel*, and possessed a 'fierce independence, abundant authority and a trace of hauteur'; she was another powerful female influence in O'Keeffe's formative world.[33] She lived to the age of 103, setting a family goal for her nieces, as Catherine later teased Georgia.

At the School of the Art Institute of Chicago in 1905, the basis for 'art . . . [was] the study of the human figure'.[34] O'Keeffe's year-long study included her first exposure to the curriculum of anatomy and the life class, which met once a week, and the study of anatomy and drawing from plaster casts continued daily. This practice never unfolded as a vital part of O'Keeffe's painting, and she called the life class 'a suffering'. For the first time, she encountered a (nearly) nude model. She recalled her embarrassment with candour, aged eighteen, 'a little girl with a big black ribbon bow on my braid': 'Out walked a very handsome, lean, dark-skinned, well-made man . . . naked except for a loincloth.'[35] This liberal exposure of female students to the male anatomy was relatively new. Just two decades earlier, in 1886, Thomas Eakins had been sacked from his position as director of the Pennsylvania Academy of Fine Arts for over-emphasis on the study of the nude.

At Chicago, O'Keeffe gained new technical skills in John Vanderpoel's drawing classes, and between the fall and spring semesters her class rating rose from fifth place to first, Vanderpoel rating her work 'exceptionally fine'.[36] During the spring semester in 1906, ten-year-old Catherine, convalescing after illness, arrived in Chicago to live with her sister and the aunts. O'Keeffe's watercolour of Catherine depicts her in a red coat, seated on a colourful couch, with intersecting patterns of rug and oriental fabric.[37] But then the art training ended abruptly. During the summer of 1906, in Virginia's coastal heat and humidity, O'Keeffe contracted a severe case of typhoid fever. The debilitating recovery, during which her hair fell out, caused her to stay close to home rather than returning to school that autumn. To Stieglitz in 1916, at the beginning of their correspondence, she confided: 'I was very sick when I was eighteen – and I have forgotten lots of things that happened a year or two before and after.'[38] Fear of illness subsequently bred a kind of panic that caused her to change course abruptly, as did any sort of weight loss. During the influenza epidemic of the winter of 1918, she would suddenly give up a teaching position as head of the Art Department in West Texas that she had held for two years.

Her recovery from typhoid meant a year at home, during which she helped with her younger siblings as the family's finances dwindled. O'Keeffe had inherited her mother's love of books, and she recalled the 'high point of the first summer in Williamsburg' when she read Washington Irving's *The Alhambra*, a book in her mother's library that perhaps stimulated her future interest in Spain, which she saw for the first time only in the 1950s.[39] But again, and fortunately, Mrs Willis's counsel prevailed, and the Chatham art teacher persuaded the O'Keeffe parents that their talented daughter should continue her art schooling.

Thus it was that O'Keeffe arrived at the Art Student League in New York in autumn 1907, with 'soft and curly hair' that had just grown back, very unlike the fashion of the time.[40] It may be that the League represented a less expensive alternative than returning to the School of the Art Institute of Chicago.[41] Certainly New York opened great possibilities and her year at the League became a memorable period of validation and exposure to new trends in the art world. While enrolled there, O'Keeffe studied under William Merritt Chase (1849–1916), the American Impressionist. She credited him warmly with the rigorous requirement that the students produce a painting a day, and he led her to a new focus on still-life. Photographs of the flamboyant bewhiskered Chase, with his monocle and waxed moustache, confirm O'Keeffe's memory.[42] Meanwhile, she made quite an impression on her fellow students: 'the pretty curly-haired art student . . . not only the toast of the school and a prize winner but had also the distinction of being painted by all the star pupils at the Art League . . . Speicher's first bow to the public was a portrait of O'Keeffe'.[43]

In her dutiful absorption of Chase's teaching, O'Keeffe began to perfect techniques of dark, lustrous, metallic painted surfaces alongside the fine detail of rabbit fur. She won a prize for her work, and *Untitled (Dead Rabbit with Copper Pot)* (1908) remains a unique surviving marker of this early period, the beginning of her professional work.[44] The early confidence gained from Chase's class led to a summer scholarship at the Amitola Art Camp on the eastern shores of Lake George, New York. During that summer of 1908, far from home, she experienced for the first time the serene calm of the lake – coincidentally just opposite Stieglitz's family enclave, a substantial part of her future creative life after 1918. The lake's residual emotional power of moody mists and fog that often clung to the surrounding mountains infused her first summer landscapes. O'Keeffe's realist art of the 1920s is richly rooted amid the spring flower gardens, the cornstalks of summer and autumnal foliage of the 'Queen of Lakes' in the Adirondack Mountains.

Equally momentous, 1908 was the year when O'Keeffe first crossed the threshold at 291 Fifth Avenue to see an art exhibition arranged by Alfred Stieglitz.[45] There on the walls were drawings by the French sculptor Auguste Rodin, arranged for '291' through the good offices of the photographer Edward Steichen (1879–1973). For O'Keeffe and fellow students from the League, the drawings of the great sculptor represented a provocation, and her professor, Chase, encouraged his students to visit the gallery and see this outrage. As for herself, she saw the Rodin figures and nudes as 'a lot of scribbles'. Her memories of 1908 recalled a talkative Stieglitz, wound up by the students to an ardent defence of the new, creative force in Rodin, and her recollections resonate with her suppressed ambition at this moment. Earlier that January day, she had taken time to pose for her portrait by fellow student Eugene Speicher, who brimmed with confidence about his future success and assured her that she need not worry about taking time away from her painting.[46] The O'Keeffe portrait is a stand-in for her in a photograph of League alumni taken by Arnold Newman in 1950. Speicher sits a few feet away from his creation of 1908, which hangs beneath a bronze sculpture. Only one woman artist, Peggy Bacon, appears there, since the best-known artist from the League was too busy to return to New York.

In O'Keeffe's autobiography of 1976, she omitted the difficult years of leaving her art behind, tending the family and her ill mother. Rather she jumped directly from her year at the League in 1908 to her remarkable autumn of innovative abstractions in 1915. Though O'Keeffe would 'not admit to personal tragedies', a League friend, later a writer and critic, divulged: 'she had to give up the thing she loved best, painting, in order to fit into the narrow hemmed-in existence which circumstances made for her.'[47] O'Keeffe declared after her summer art retreat at Lake George that she was 'through with art as a career'.[48]

She returned home to face a disheartening situation. During this important year for her artistic growth, the family sold Wheatland House and bought a smaller eighteenth-century colonial home on Travis Street; there Mrs O'Keeffe began to take in boarders from the college.[49] Within the year, her father had built a new house of concrete blocks on the remaining acreage near Wheatland. The family's third house in five years reflected Frank O'Keeffe's most recent business venture, manufacturing building blocks crafted from James River crushed shells. This practical notion hardly sold; in a historic city of colonial brick structures, it was not a popular idea. Worse, O'Keeffe's mother Ida had contracted tuberculosis, and had been moved to a sanatorium in western Virginia. O'Keeffe referred elliptically to this difficult period in her early life when she moved in with her father to help the younger ones: 'Mama was away for a couple of years.'[50] On her return, O'Keeffe's mother moved to the more salubrious mountains of Charlottesville, site of the University of Virginia, where she set up a boarding house and rented rooms to university students to make ends meet.

O'Keeffe could not pursue her career until she returned to Chicago in 1911, where she found work in an advertising firm, designing embroidery and lace and learning to work quickly. This job ended abruptly, however, when she contracted measles, and had to rest her eyes as part of the cure. Her teacher Mrs Willis yet again providentially stepped in after O'Keeffe's second major illness to request that the young artist teach in her place in the summer session of 1911.

The family's residence near the University of Virginia brought O'Keeffe back to art in the summer of 1912. Her sister Ida convinced her to join an art class at the university, and there a reluctant O'Keeffe met Alon Bement (1875–1954), who taught at Teachers College, Columbia University, with Arthur Wesley Dow (1857–1922). A student of the remarkable global artist and teacher, Bement espoused the techniques published in Dow's book *Composition* (1899) with its richly illustrated examples, derived from his extensive knowledge of Asian art. Bement also emphasized the idea of making art while listening to music, seeking analogies with musical harmony. O'Keeffe had played the piano and the violin, like her father, and felt a natural sympathy with musical rhythms and tone. With Bement, O'Keeffe continued to teach the summer art classes as his teaching assistant at the university until 1916, remembering that he 'gave me some very good advice'.[51] He encouraged her to read Kandinsky's treatise *On the Spiritual in Art*, which famously articulated the expressive power of non-objective forms and colour in painting. Alfred Stieglitz had translated and printed a brief excerpt from Kandinsky in *Camera Work* in 1912, emphasizing the potential of 'expression' in visual art.

During that first summer, O'Keeffe learned of a public school teaching position in Amarillo, Texas, where the Western adventure tales of her mother's childhood readings beckoned (*The Adventures of Kit Carson* were among those she recalled). Her Chatham friend, Alice Beretta, directed O'Keeffe to the teaching position. Seeking independence and responding to the allure of the frontier, she landed a job that lasted for the academic years 1912–14, an 'improbable position' as 'supervisor of art in grades one through eight'.[52] Few of O'Keeffe's letters from this period survive, though she continued to receive letters from a student and suitor from the League, George

Dannenberg. Dannenberg's art study in Paris marked a sharp contrast to her own circumstances. Pollitzer detailed the artist's struggles with a recalcitrant administration over standardized books for teaching art, and Wagner notes that she 'stood her ground', insisting that 'creative design must take priority', so that teachers could be free to select their resources.[53] It is generally agreed that the Armory Show of 1913, first on view in New York and later in Chicago and Boston, ushered in the far-reaching impact of modernism to America. O'Keeffe missed it while teaching art to children, out of sheer necessity, in the Panhandle of Texas.

By the winter term of 1914, with needed aid from Aunt Ollie, O'Keeffe sought further artistic training in New York – her first full year of higher education since 1907–8.[54] Given Bement's influence, she wanted to study with Arthur Wesley Dow at Teachers College. She gave Dow credit for her understanding of a new pathway towards modernism when she stated decisively: 'It was Arthur Dow who affected my start, who helped me to find something of my own.'[55] The art classes prepared her for a better position as a college-level art instructor, one of the few secure options entirely open to a 'self-sufficient young woman'.

Her abiding commitment to the Asian art of design and composition, the Japanese design concepts advocated by Dow, all led O'Keeffe to her goal in art: 'to fill space in a beautiful way'.[56] As for Bement, O'Keeffe wrote to Anita Pollitzer that her interest in 'arting' grew from her summer's work with Dow's pupil. And certainly his influence was important: it was Bement who first recommended that she read Floyd Dell's feminist essays *Women as World Builders* (1913), which profiled contemporary women's lives.[57]

Dow's practical manual *Composition* incorporated Asian principles of design and became a widely consulted book, in print for more than twenty editions. By 1903, when Dow travelled to India, China and Japan, his understanding of non-Western design and art had become a primary thrust of his teaching. In composing shapes within the visual field, O'Keeffe's search for abstraction drew upon Dow's principles. By the time O'Keeffe met her supportive new friend Anita Pollitzer in the class of Charles Martin, also at Teachers College, it was the well-travelled, published artist Dow who ruled the department, and guided her on her path to innovative art. He espoused the 'trinity of power' that hinged upon line, colour and *notan* (literally: lightness–darkness), so fundamental to O'Keeffe and generations of students. A final parallel with O'Keeffe's future painting came from Dow's early interest in painting the Grand Canyon on trips there in 1911, and his espousal of the study of photography as early as 1907 at Teachers College.

Though Georgia O'Keeffe spent her years of schooling in five different cities and three states, her good fortune came from having a remarkable talent that the family, and her teachers, recognized and supported early on. In contrast, her sister Catherine left home at eighteen in 1913, trained as a nurse in Madison (Wisconsin), and graduated there in 1918. She never saw her parents again. Anita, still living at home in Charlottesville in 1915 aged 25 with her two sisters, Ida and young Claudia, watched as their increasingly ill mother could not afford to feed the boarders. Anita eloped with a college sweetheart, Robert R. Young. Their long marriage together took them to the heights of financial prosperity and wealth, including mansions in Newport and Palm Beach, where they enjoyed a friendship with the Duke and Duchess of Windsor in the 1930s.

What remained of O'Keeffe's immediate family disintegrated when Ida Totto O'Keeffe died in May 1916 in Charlottesville, Virginia. She was buried in the Episcopalian cemetery in Wisconsin. Claudia, at the age of seventeen, took the train to Texas alone to join her older sister at West Texas State Normal College, where Georgia O'Keeffe had just been appointed head of the drawing department. Catherine O'Keeffe Klenert tersely stated twice in an interview in 1977: 'our home was broken up.'[58]

Frank O'Keeffe, who died in a fall from a roof project at Petersburg, Virginia, two years later, was buried in the Catholic cemetery in Wisconsin alongside his brothers. At the time of her father's funeral in 1918, O'Keeffe did not return, and Claudia, having started teacher training in Texas, wrote to Georgia that: 'universal joy loomed up before me and also universal and personal sorrow' as she learned of her father's death on 11 November 1918, Armistice Day.[59] By that time, O'Keeffe had left Texas for New York, propelled to begin her new artistic life. The entire O'Keeffe family had scattered, each forced to find employment and to make their own way.

2

Breakthrough:
'Charcoal Landscapes'

Anita Pollitzer, a vibrant young student from Charleston, South
Carolina, met Georgia O'Keeffe in classes at Teachers College in
1914. She admired the elusive, reclusive artist who dressed like no
one else, and often worked behind a screen, shooing away those
who wanted to watch her work. Pollitzer noted the 'coat suit of
excellent material' and the 'crisply-starched white blouses that she
herself had made', which seemed to mask O'Keeffe's austere living
circumstances.[1]

O'Keeffe rented a room at $4 per week while studying at
Columbia University, placing red geraniums on the fire escape in
the otherwise bare space.[2] Pollitzer's background as the youngest
child of a prosperous Southern Jewish family contrasted sharply
with O'Keeffe's situation. When Pollitzer arrived in New York aged
twenty, full of high spirits and primed to pursue her art, she also
devoted herself to the cause of women's suffrage. O'Keeffe shared
all the same enthusiasms, but Aunt Ollie provided only for the
academic year 1914–15. What the young women saw and read,
the daring exhibitions the two so enjoyed at 291 Fifth Avenue,
all became grist for their subsequent letters once O'Keeffe had
to leave to teach summer school in Virginia.

The Pollitzer–O'Keeffe letters document the most fertile period
of O'Keeffe's youthful progression towards abstraction, told in her
own words. The diary-like exchange allows a glimpse of her artistic
process, and makes her voice audible so that one can hear her

excitement. From Pollitzer's side, there emerges a discerning judgement of O'Keeffe's new means of expression, and constant support.[3]

O'Keeffe, seven years older than Pollitzer and ever the older sister, appears to have enjoyed the admiration that the petite twenty-year-old accorded her, as well as her infectious enthusiasm, later recalling her as an energetic friend who was constantly in a whirl.[4] Pollitzer and O'Keeffe had found what inspired them most in the arts at Alfred Stieglitz's gallery at 291 Fifth Avenue.

Stieglitz, the energy centre of all that expressed modernity in the New York art scene by the time O'Keeffe and Pollitzer became friends, had established his own reputation as the defining photographer of the age in Europe by the late 1880s, when he was in his late twenties. On his return to New York in 1890, he became the impresario of a gallery known as '291', which had a relentless driving force, championed photography as a fine art and acted as chief 'midwife' to emerging artists of the avant-garde.[5] Though he focused first on pictorialist photography, he then brought over early showings of works on paper by the most extraordinary artists active in France, from Rodin to Picasso.

Stieglitz's own photographic work had begun to languish at the time he was pushing hardest for putting on view the 'experiments' of American moderns. His young associate, the photographer Edward Steichen, emerged as a vital conduit, bringing the work of artists such as Rodin and Matisse into the gallery. Stieglitz also cultivated knowledge of new talent in Paris through his friendship with Leo and Gertrude Stein, and a visit to Paris in 1910.

In the centre of the small gallery of 291 stood its iconic brass bowl, signifying its place as cauldron and laboratory for experimental tendencies in twentieth-century art, an investigation based upon Stieglitz's own photography and the gallery's origins in showing photography. There before the famous Armory Show of 1913, Stieglitz displayed the earliest works of Cézanne, Matisse and

Edward J. Steichen, *Alfred Stieglitz at 291*, 1915, coated gum bichromate over platinum print.

Picasso shown in America. Major first viewings of African tribal art as aesthetic objects, rather than ethnographic curiosities, followed in 1914, and that winter the new charcoal Cubist *papiers collés*, drawings by Picasso and Braque, also went on view. A sculpture exhibition of the works of Constantin Brancusi, his first in America, came that spring, another introduction for American modernists.

Earlier, in 1909, Stieglitz had experimented with another new idea closer to home, and showed the latest tendencies in American abstract painting in the exhibition *Younger American Artists*, which included works by Arthur Dove, John Marin and Marsden Hartley. His success extended the 291 aesthetic over time to the nurture and growth of an American avant-garde – and the notion that these Americans artists should be evaluated against the fine art of photography. All the Americans named above became the core members of the Stieglitz circle for decades to come. Certainly there were important others: Oscar Bluemner, Alfred Maurer, Stanton Macdonald-Wright and Max Weber also showed their work at 291; some fought and many fell out with Stieglitz. By 1925, when the photographer celebrated twenty years of the 291 spirit, long after 291 Fifth Avenue had closed in 1917, the core group solidified as 'Seven Americans': Marin, Hartley, Dove, Paul Strand and O'Keeffe, and on occasion, Charles Demuth.[6]

As a student, O'Keeffe began to frequent the gallery during her year at Teachers College, when she returned to New York in autumn 1914, but she studied its artists in *Camera Work* both before and after her time there. The production of *Camera Work* meant that the avant-garde ideas circulated far beyond Stieglitz's tiny rooms. This photography art periodical was founded in 1903, and functioned as the house publication of Stieglitz's gallery, its cover designed by Steichen. O'Keeffe's ecstasy over the strong impression made by Picasso came first during the winter of the Picasso and Braque exhibition.[7] The de luxe publication featured carefully printed photographs and sepia-toned reproductions of works of painting and sculpture in thematic sections, including recent reviews of exhibitions and excerpted essays by renowned avant-garde authors.

Stieglitz not only created a unique environment to study the latest art in New York, he fought for photography as a fine art, and extended that to make beauty from the era of 'strange brazen human emptiness' that emerged with the commercialism, over-building and vertical expansion of the city in the early twentieth century. O'Keeffe wrote: 'He gave a flight to the spirit and faith in their own way to more people – particularly young people – than anyone I have known.'[8]

In the midst of New York's vital mix of culture, political and generational issues as well as a zeal for all things 291, 'Patsy' O'Keeffe and Anita Pollitzer discussed art, literature and politics avidly. Especially important was the issue of women's suffrage, well before the ratification of the Nineteenth Amendment in 1920; Anita reported plans to walk with a parade of ten of thousands in late October 1915.[9] The vehicle of letter writing became an energized conversation that flowed between the dynamic young women once they departed from New York at the end of the semester. O'Keeffe returned to Virginia, where she again taught with Bement in the summer school. Her bright, empathetic friend Anita effectively worked as coach and critic from a distance, and represented a lifeline to New York when the autumn term began.

O'Keeffe's voice in the letters rings true as an evocation of the free place in her creative life that the mature woman envied. The letters reveal an unvarnished view of her, sometimes silly or preachy: Anita once protested about O'Keeffe's 'little sermons . . . about self control'. These also reveal the young artist's edginess, wondering if she was a 'lunatic' for making such art, exulting when she felt that she had hit the mark. More critically, the letters exchanged with Pollitzer provide the documentation

Anita Pollitzer with W. J. Jameson, chairman of the National Finance Committee of the Democratic Party, checking the Tennessee vote tally on ratification of the Nineteenth Amendment, August 1920.

of O'Keeffe's breakthrough into making abstract works of art on paper.[10] The artist later spoke with regret of the lost freedom of her generative early years when the 'forms in her head' flowed quickly onto paper. The lively exchange with Anita Pollitzer brings to life the immeasurable spark that artistic energy in New York generated for 'Patsy', as well as the splendid isolation of her job in South Carolina in the autumn of 1915, before she became 'O'Keeffe'.

The first letters in 1915 from Pollitzer to O'Keeffe began tentatively. They address one another as 'Miss' – or, as O'Keeffe called Anita at first, 'litttle [*sic*] Pollitzer'. At the summer's end, O'Keeffe thanks Anita for calling her Pat (a version of her Irish nickname at school), saying 'I like it.'[11] Their first unfinished business was to give a book as a gift to one of their favourite professors at Teachers College, Charles Martin. This led Pollitzer to trek downtown to ask, perhaps, if Mr Stieglitz would be willing to sell her a back issue of *Camera Work*. She reported to O'Keeffe: 'Mr S said – "let me pick out the most wonderful one we have."' Anita then described her treasure, 'an old Rodin number – the most exquisite thing you can imagine . . . magnificent nudes with colour touched in'. She concluded: 'It was three dollars but worth a million.'[12] And she then bought two. O'Keeffe immediately asked to borrow Pollitzer's copy. The Rodin drawings illustrated there came from the exhibition O'Keeffe first saw at 291 in 1908. Now her training with Bement and Dow unconditionally directed her towards modernism, a 'turning point in her conception of drawing . . . drawing was the central creative medium at the heart of all kinds of art'.[13]

O'Keeffe's immediate attachment to nature, her determination to make 'her own fun in living', following the ideas imparted by Dow, led to her uncanny confidence to begin working from the forms in her head. The early teachings yoked to an independent spirit, infused with the art she could see in New York, lay behind the breakthrough that led to her first completely abstract charcoals, works of energized angles and rhythms that she began to send to Pollitzer in small batches through the early autumn. O'Keeffe absorbed the rich visual world developing rapidly around her.

In the Virginia summer school session of 1915, her first after Dow's teaching, O'Keeffe became an unselfconscious innovator, working and experimenting, as she compressed her emotion or mood into 'the yellow and red ball' in the corner of a wild blue picture.[14] She said of this work in 1915: 'It is only a human document', but she had seized upon a core element of modernist Expressionism, the rendering of interior feeling in abstract form. Then there was also a growing romantic interest between herself and Arthur Macmahon, a studious, young Columbia doctoral student who was already a professor. They first met when O'Keeffe was teaching in Virginia during the summer school of 1914, saw one another at Columbia University in New York and kept up a correspondence (though far less regularly than the many notes to Pollitzer). O'Keeffe's oblique and humorous references to 'Political Science' continually crop up in her virtual diary by mail with Anita. An abstract, colourful pastel (*Special No. 32*) swirls colour into a spiral as she recollected her sense memory of 'tramping' with Macmahon, 'dabbling our feet in the water . . . red from the red clay . . . [where] the motion of the water had such a fine rhthm [*sic*]'.[15]

In the late summer of 1915 O'Keeffe made the difficult decision to leave Virginia, and not to return to school in New York. At the high point of her newly blossoming romance with the doctoral student, she chose the new job. About her dilemma, Georgia wrote to Anita: 'I think I will go to South Carolina . . . you see – I have to make a living.'[16] Her decision came abruptly as Arthur Macmahon chided her in mid-September: 'You exasperating girl! You say you are sewing your head off against your departure but you don't say where you are going.'[17] The bare facts of her confession to Anita, and the necessity to sew new clothing for the autumn, indicate that O'Keeffe's pressures at home in Virginia had mounted. Anita's privileged family position and Arthur's steady New York professorial life supported by his mother indicated a freedom that was in stark contrast to the O'Keeffe family's deteriorating sense of security.

About the Virginia climate and summers O'Keeffe would later complain, with no small measure of underlying sadness: 'Everything is wonderful heavy dark green – and the green is all so very clean –

but I hate it.'[18] Moving further south, she decided that the schedule offered by Columbia College compensated for her feeling that she was 'in a shoe that doesn't fit'. Anita's responded: 'you're not jailed in Columbia for life, remember.'[19]

For O'Keeffe, the semester teaching in a Methodist women's college led to intense reflection, reading and much time to absorb the latest *Camera Work* and art periodicals from New York, as well as the other books that friends supplied. Ultimately, isolation provided O'Keeffe with the calm turning moment to evaluate her past decade of peripatetic training and teaching. Soon she made the fateful decision to trust her own instincts in the new work, as she boldly wrote to Anita: 'I am starting all over new – Have put everything I have ever done away.'[20]

An excerpt in *Camera Work* gave her remote access to Gertrude Stein's essay on Picasso, written in Paris. She recalled first seeing an early Arthur Dove abstraction in Arthur Jerome Eddy's *Cubists and Post-Impressionism* (1914), a book recommended by her University of Virginia teacher Alon Bement.[21] From the many letters exchanged

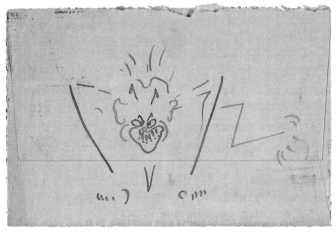

'I'm going to work like a tiger', Georgia O'Keeffe to Anita Pollitzer, Columbia College, South Carolina, November 1915.

with Pollitzer, it is clear that O'Keeffe studied the important artists of her era, first seen in New York, from a distance.

In October 1915, feeling more at peace with the world because the 'undergrowth in the woods has turned bright', O'Keeffe pondered: 'What is Art any way?' She blamed her feelings of 'muddle' on a new direction, her first mention of new works – the 'charcoal landscapes' that satisfied her the most. 'I decided I wasn't going to cater to what any one else might like – why should I?' she asked Anita.[22]

Pollitzer first received O'Keeffe's October efforts of works on paper in a mailing tube, and became her first critic. Anita described the works back to her as she wrote, referencing the black and white designs. When Georgia decided her colours were too distracting, she simplified the means, just as the charcoal prototypes of Picasso and Braque had been references. Her love of colour literally pushed to the edges, she described placing flowers out of view:

> I have an enormous bunch of dark red and pink cosmos . . .
> I can only know they are there with my left eye – . . . They give
> me a curious feeling of satisfaction – . . . and put a wonderful
> bunch of zinnias in the closet.[23]

Instead, the Marin cover of *291* sent to her by Alfred Stieglitz, on Anita's request, became a focal point. She wrote to thank Stieglitz: 'I always want it where I can see it in my room.'[24] O'Keeffe distilled the energy of New York, made immanent in Marin's swaying, twisting skyscrapers, and at the same time she studied the vanguard drawings of Picasso in charcoal (*Nude Woman, Cadaqués*, 1910), also visible in the pages of *Camera Work*.

In November O'Keeffe declared her intention to work harder, and imagined herself as a devilish tiger caricature on the envelope to Anita.[25] As Thanksgiving drew near, Arthur Macmahon wrote with excitement that he needed to make a professional trip to Chapel Hill, North Carolina, and might be able to visit to South

Carolina too.[26] In fact, his visit to O'Keeffe over the Thanksgiving holidays seems to have brought their much-anticipated reunion to a closer happiness than the pair had experienced, or would again. Macmahon's attentions broke through O'Keeffe's reserve to ignite her new energy for abstraction.

Upon leaving, as he journeyed north on a 'wholly disagreeable and trying day' of travel to Chapel Hill, Macmahon concluded: 'I have felt your sweetness about me all the time.'[27] To Anita, O'Keeffe wrote in turn: 'He has the nicest way of saying things, and making you feel that he loves you – all way round – not just in spots.'[28] At the end of this 'nicest' letter, Macmahon left off for the first time his usual 'Sincerely Arthur' – signing only 'Arthur'. He did not quite say all that might have been. Painting consumed her.

The visit infused O'Keeffe with a bright energy, expressed to Pollitzer as 'the world looks all new to me.' She worked on the paper directly 'crawling around on the floor till I have cramps in my feet'. She described her state of art making in a letter of mid-December:

> Did you ever have something to say and feel as if the whole side of the wall wouldn't be big enough to say it on and then sit down on the floor and try to get it on to a piece of charcoal paper . . . and try to put into words what you have been trying to say with just marks – and then – wonder what it all is anyway – [29]

The results were the abstract charcoals that she decided within days to send to the receptive Anita, continuing: 'I hope you love me a little tonight – I seem to want everybody in the world to.' Anita replied as if she were in the room urging on her friend: 'Use two sides of the wall if necessary, Pat, I could feel the cramps in your feet . . . Keep at it. Cezanne [*sic*] & Van Gogh and Gauguin were all raving lunatics. – but they didn't mind a little thing like that.'[30]

Anita rendered her reactions to her friend's earliest radical designs and drawings; she was both generous and clear in her earlier appraisals, drawing quick sketches for reference in letters back to O'Keeffe, tacking up the drawings and watercolours that O'Keeffe would mail to her in paper tubes. At the end of her 'disgustingly gay' holiday season in the pre-war New York of 1915, Pollitzer was 'reveling in music music music' (a Fritz Kreisler performance of Brahms, and Wagner at Carnegie Hall). Still she wrote nightly summaries to O'Keeffe, including details of a dinner and dance at the St Regis Hotel in a fancy gown – 'pretty giddy', she related, at '3:30 in the morning!'[31]

O'Keeffe sent a Christmas telegram to Macmahon in New York, and his to her is dated 24 December 1915: 'When you turn listen and I'll shout Merry Greetings Georgia.'[32] A longer letter of the same day describes what he will do on Christmas Day – an imaginary walk with Georgia, retrospectively tracing their time together: 'lots of South Carolina sunshine . . . Oh it was a happy walk I had tomorrow with you.' Switching tone, Macmahon concluded on a more practical note, true to his nature: 'I suppose you, like the rest of us in academic life, welcome the holidays because they give you uninterrupted opportunity to work. So you'll be painting your head off.'[33]

And so she did. It is perhaps no surprise that O'Keeffe's sudden decision to send Pollitzer a new batch of charcoal abstractions expressed her high note of pleasure and tender affection, created in an isolated concentration. Her product resulted in work fed by the aesthetic of 291, encouraged through Stieglitz's 'laboratory' for art and egged on by Pollitzer. Her younger friend received the package of O'Keeffe's art, rolled up, from the mail on Friday, 31 December, and she remembered this for the next five decades: 'This was the day before the New Year of 1916.'[34]

Anita opened her amazing report, addressed to Patsy, late that same evening, 'Astounded and awfully happy were my feelings today when I opened the batch of drawings.' Pollitzer had first studied O'Keeffe's works in the school studio alone, before she concluded that the artist had 'gotten past the personal stage into the big sort of emotions . . . but it's your version of it . . . [if] I'd been told that xz did them I'd have liked them as much as if I'd been told Picasso did them.' Before making the fateful decision to visit Stieglitz, she attended a stage play of *Peter Pan*, 'with them under my arm'. Then she confessed: 'I had to do, I'm glad I did it, it was the only thing to do.' Anita knew she had to defy O'Keeffe's express request if she were to show the work to anyone. Nonetheless, the energetic 21-year-old took O'Keeffe's daring new work in charcoal directly to the man they both admired and idealized, the fighter for new art, Alfred Stieglitz.

Stieglitz's search for innovative art, made by a woman, was confirmed at last by Pollitzer's intuition. Anita relayed a sense of his extraordinary reception when she wrote to Georgia late into the night on New Year's Eve:

> I went with your feelings & your emotions tied up & showed them to a giant of a man who reacted – I unrolled them – I had them all there . . . He looked Pat – and thoroughly absorbed & got them – he looked again – the room was quiet – One small light – His hair was mussed – It was a long while before his lips opened [Finally a woman on paper!] – Then he smiled at me & yelled 'Walkowitz come here' . . . Then he said to me- 'Why they're genuinely fine things – you say a woman did these – She's an unusual woman. – She's broad minded. She's bigger than most women, but she's got the sensitive emotion. – I'd know she was a woman – Look at that line.[35]

There is continuing debate about whether Pollitzer, or someone else later, added in pencil the famous phrase supposedly uttered by Stieglitz: 'Finally a woman on paper.' It has been much questioned, and turned into a legendary moment.[36] Nearing midnight, at the end of an exciting day, Anita gave O'Keeffe the concluding words from Stieglitz: 'They're the purest, finest, sincerest things that have entered 291 in a long while . . . I wouldn't mind showing them in one of these rooms one bit – perhaps I shall.' Anita kept the charcoal drawings close by that night, and reminded O'Keeffe: 'I think you wrote to me once – I would rather have Stieglitz like something I'd done than anyone else. It's come true – I've written you only what I plainly remember.'[37]

There was no turning back from Anita's fateful decision. After the drama of her actions on New Year's Eve, and Stieglitz's stunning reaction, the New Year seemed full of possibility for the young artist. O'Keeffe weighed the outcome: 'There seems to be nothing for me to say except thank you – very calmly and quietly. I could hardly believe my eyes.' She continued: 'Of course I would rather have something hang in 291 than any place in New York . . . but what sounds best to me is that he liked them . . . I would be interested in knowing what people get out of them – if they get anything – Wouldn't that be a great experiment'. Her intertwined emotions about her art and Macmahon kindled the inarticulate intensity and visual passion of the work: 'I am *living* in Columbia . . . balancing on the edge of loving like I imagine we never love but once.'[38]

Yet O'Keeffe sought adventure. Modernity, the possibility of her art being on view at 291, all gathered to propel her ambitious pursuit. The feminist slant of the influential Dell book, a work that Macmahon urged her to read, confirmed her inclination: 'The woman who finds her work will find her love.'[39] And she still needed to make a living; she had begun to consider a new job in Texas by mid-January. Alon Bement, to whom Pollitzer had also shown her breakthrough drawings, supplied a recommendation letter for the new position.

'Kick up your heels in the air!' she squealed to Anita, 'I just had a telegram . . . this morning telling me my election [to go to Texas] is certain.'[40] By late February Georgia had decided to accept the post in Canyon, Texas, but she was required to finish her training at Teachers College, a requirement that became a welcome reprieve. Her beau, who had written wistful 'congratulations on the Texas appointment', now changed gears to telegraph with great relief: 'Fear too good to be true/cheers if you're coming.'[41] After giving her notice at Columbia College, she wrote to Anita: 'Two hundred dollars short of what I need to finance me . . . I'll go without it – because I'm going – Im [sic] chasing it.'[42]

The first letters between Stieglitz and O'Keeffe were exchanged in January 1916. According to the only other eyewitness present at the unrolling of the O'Keeffe charcoals, the artist Abraham Walkowitz, Stieglitz had talked the entire walk home from 291 that evening: 'never interested in names. It was the work that he talked about . . . at last a woman was sensitively seeing and expressing in visual form her own relation to the universe.'[43] O'Keeffe plainly put it to Stieglitz in her note: 'what is it you see in my drawings?' And he, guarded, kindly replied:

My dear Miss O'Keeffe: What am I to say? It is impossible for me to put into words what I saw and felt in your drawings . . . I might give you what I received from them if you and I were to meet and talk about life . . . they gave me much joy . . . a real surprise [and] . . . I felt they were a genuine expression of yourself.

Stieglitz left open the most enticing possibility of all: 'I would like to show them', and ended: 'The future is rather hazy, but the present is very positive and very delightful.'[44]

O'Keeffe stumbled over her first reply: 'I don't exactly get your meaning', but she pressed on, 'I am so glad they surprised – that they gave you joy. I am glad I could give you once what 291 has given me many times.'[45]

And so began the first notes of what slowly grew into a love affair, and the tumultuous shared creativity of dual careers. As O'Keeffe wondered at what Stieglitz 'really thought' about her work, the two initiated a correspondence that would stretch over 30 years, and amount to more than 25,000 pages of writing between them, over 5,000 separate letters, notes and telegrams, the rich documentation that O'Keeffe fiercely guarded after Stieglitz's death, for her 98 years and beyond.[46]

On 3 May 1916 O'Keeffe received a telegram containing long-dreaded news. Her mother had died the day before, on 2 May, and so ended the long struggle with tuberculosis. Ida Totto O'Keeffe's collapse at 52 years of age left the family without an anchor. The young artist wrote almost immediately to Stieglitz: 'then the telegram was there', referring to the bleak news from Virginia.[47]

The independent Miss O'Keeffe left by train immediately, and while en route to Charlottesville began to unburden herself to the patriarchal mentor Stieglitz: 'You must not feel sorry for me . . . Just talk to me.' On O'Keeffe's return from Charlottesville (she did not attend her mother's burial in Wisconsin), she went back to Teachers College, and resumed writing to Stieglitz. First came 'a very bad dream about Mama . . . my hands were on her face'. Then between bouts of sleeplessness and inertia, she fell ill with tonsillitis.[48]

Stieglitz carried on thinking about her work: 'Had I known how . . . I would have written or phoned. I wanted to hang them [your drawings] primarily for myself.' O'Keeffe in turn sent her phone number to Stieglitz on her return (8 May), indicating that she was well aware he planned to show her work: 'If you put up my things let me know . . . I might like to see them first.'[49] These exchanges from the letters prove that their own myth making exaggerated O'Keeffe's surprise; she knew perfectly well that Stieglitz intended to show her work.

According to the tales later spun out by both parties, O'Keeffe rushed to 291, ready to argue with Stieglitz to take down the drawings. Decades later, she remembered on film: 'You try arguing with him and see where you get.'[50] Stieglitz's own recollection turned on his persuasion, telling the young artist: 'You have no more right to withhold these pictures than to withdraw a child from the world.'[51] Her experimentation in the isolated furore of work in South Carolina, her 'messages' to Arthur Macmahon, became her debut work in New York. On 23 May, just three weeks after Ida O'Keeffe's death, Georgia O'Keeffe's first exhibition opened in a public gallery with ten of her abstract charcoals, at 291. Her work was paired with two other experimental artists, Charles Duncan and René Lafferty, all three working in abstraction. Stieglitz introduced the work as being 'of intense interest from a psychoanalytical point of view'.[52]

Drawing XIII represented the best of the lot for Stieglitz, and he twice wrote to O'Keeffe that he wanted to keep it forever, calling it 'The one I want most . . . by far the finest – the most expressive.'[53] His sexualized reading of her abstract charcoals of 1915 hastened his response. In the tumultuous month of May 1916 he decided that he should demonstrate to the New York art world that '291 had never before seen woman express herself so frankly on paper'.[54]

Drawing XIII stands apart in its synthesis of rising Expressionist form, filtered through John Marin's architectural renderings of a frenetic Manhattan and layered with memories of Van Gogh's *Cypresses*.[55] In short, the young artist incorporated diverse threads of avant-garde art on view in New York, all channelled through her avowed practice to draw upon forms in her head. Her interest in the power of charcoal as a starting point for expressive line surely links back to the mark-making delineation of Picasso's and Braque's early Cubist charcoals and *papiers collés*, which had been on view at 291 the winter before. Picasso's drawing

Georgia O'Keeffe, *Drawing XIII*, 1915, charcoal on paper.

Standing Nude, Cadaqués (1910), a breakthrough sketch for Cubist figuration, was an early Stieglitz acquisition, and O'Keeffe commented on the work in the joint exhibition of 1914–15, one year before her own evolution in charcoal.[56]

At the time of O'Keeffe's first showing, however, the press reaction wavered in the face of what remained difficult non-figurative art, presented without explanation, 'tacked up on the walls'. Stieglitz's presentation of the trio together created a context that could only highlight the unusual nature of O'Keeffe's generative organic imagery. One critic puzzled over what seemed 'the innermost unfolding of a girl's being, like the germinating of a flower'.[57] Confusion reigned, as another notice deciphered 'a conflagration & . . . [a] stalagmite state'.[58]

O'Keeffe surrendered her own subjectivity to the verbally enthralling Stieglitz. His words and perception of her imagery 'from the womb', often delivered as ongoing monologues in the gallery, trained a bright light on her work. But in her view, the images derived from distinctly different sources, as she wrote to him on 1 February: 'things I wanted to express'. Stieglitz's imagination projected only a gendered view.

The spare, calligraphic ink painting *Blue Lines x*, which Stieglitz had installed on the walls of 291 late in 1916, provides a clear example of the different lenses the pair brought to the work. O'Keeffe casually referenced the work's origins from the previous spring, as she had looked out over her windowsill, seeing blue and purple in the night: 'I was sick in New York – the dark buildings going up.'[59] She began her first sketch for *Blue Lines x* from the building profiles, what would later be titled *Two Lines* (or *Two Lives*). Her prosaic reality had been long forgotten, lost in the letters and usurped by Stieglitz's reaction to her 'little blue streaks'.[60] 'My heart stood still', he wrote after first opening her package at Lake George and discovering its 'whiteness' or purity.[61] Quickly his interpretation flowed into an anthropomorphic view, as he

Georgia O'Keeffe, *Blue Lines X*, spring 1916, blue watercolour on paper.

re-named the work, and the press took it from there: '*Two Lives* [*sic*], a man's and a woman's distinct yet invisibly joined together by mutual attraction, grow out of the earth like two graceful saplings, side by side.'[62] Pollitzer, who was shocked to discover the work hanging near Stieglitz's desk, also saw the *Blue Lines X* as 'your two *dependent on each other* yet perfectly separate individual lines of fine dark blue'.[63] The stunning rise of lines that swell, detour and diminish to an elegant lifting of the brush remains evocative of O'Keeffe's early abstract power.

Over the summer in Virginia, O'Keeffe gradually regained her strength, and wrote to Stieglitz about her camping adventures: 'Everything I have done this summer has been green and blue.'[64] Anita received considerably richer detail on the hiking escapades with the *Blue I–III* series: 'I'm glad blue is your color . . . Where did you keep the rest of yourself while you were doing it? I shall keep that a while – *on my wall*.'[65] O'Keeffe's letters about her summer outdoor adventures, one written from a town named Craggy, North Carolina, dispel any doubt about the artist's full embrace of nature. She reports to Stieglitz of camping out on 'wonderful nights out under the stars' in the Blue Ridge Mountains, on the way to West Texas.[66] And O'Keeffe sketched watercolours (*Tent Door at Night*) even as she chose to sleep on bare rock, enduring cold temperatures to be closer to the top of the mountain and the sky. Stieglitz replied, capitalizing his nouns, since his German habits remained intact: 'A climb in the Night to see Dawn light up the World!'[67] Hiking through the mountains in Virginia and North Carolina, O'Keeffe began to recoup the fierce natural self that would gain full expression on the plains of Texas.

3

Painting in Canyon:
'Between Heaven and Earth'

On a clear starry night in 1917, O'Keeffe ended a letter to Alfred
Stieglitz in New York with the poetry of visual transport: 'I send
you the space that is watching the starlight and the empty quiet
plains.'[1] The letter directly evoked her feeling before the stark
prairie landscape she so loved in Canyon, Texas. All the threads
of her first desires to launch a career in making art had begun to
come together. Her work in abstraction had been shown for the
first time in the 291 Gallery she had admired from afar. After her
mother's death, the return to Virginia and ensuing 'blue' summer,
her journey across America to the prairie landscape of the
Panhandle, all paradoxically brought her closer to Stieglitz.
His long letters and mailings of recent periodicals and favourite
books soon arrived in the dusty prairie town of Canyon, piling
up the instruction and art world overview that uniquely he could
impart. It was while teaching in Canyon at West Texas State Normal
College that many of O'Keeffe's important pictorial inventions
originated, including a new watercolour series based on her
excitement over the expansive landscape.

Already acquainted with the vast Texas plain after two years of
teaching in Amarillo, Georgia O'Keeffe knew of the extraordinary
geology of the area, notably the Palo Duro Canyon, a 120-mile-long
crevice that punctuated the flat horizon. O'Keeffe caught up with
Anita Pollitzer upon arriving, describing her first evening trip to the
post office ecstatically: 'I walked into the sunset.' But she anticipated

Claudia O'Keeffe in Canyon, Texas, 1917, photographer unknown.

trouble with the locals, since she had already experienced a hard battle over the freedom to choose art textbooks in Amarillo. Writing both to Pollitzer and to Stieglitz after fewer than twelve hours: '*Think* quick for me – of a bad word to apply to them – the *little* things they forced on me . . . I feel it's a pity to disfigure such wonderful country with people of any kind.' And her feeling about the nature around her was no less intense: 'The plains – the wonderful great big sky – makes me want to breathe so deep that I'll break.'[2] After only two weeks in Canyon, she began to take long walks before breakfast and spent her free time watching the sky.

Sunsets and skies full of lightning flashes quickly infused her painting motifs. For a lightning storm, she developed an arc of zigzag shapes to invoke the flashes across the dark prairie. Then she experimented with organically vibrating watercolours, a sun-streaked horizon with primary colours rising up to encircle Venus, the evening star, the first planet to appear at night. Her letters translated her nature perceptions into *Evening Star, I–VI*: 'That evening star fascinated me . . . I had nothing but to walk into nowhere and the wide sunset space with the star.'[3]

Three separate studies, starting with a charcoal design, depict *Train at Night in the Desert*. Each shows an enormous cloud of steam dwarfing a tiny black engine that becomes an inverted teardrop; the watercolours show tints of blue, yellow and peach tones, increasing in light and volume. O'Keeffe was transfixed by the sight at the break of dawn:

> This morning I got up and while it was starlight . . . I walked northeast – A train was coming a long way off – just a light with a trail of smoke – white – I walked toward it – The sun and the train got to me at the same time – It's great to see that terrifically black thing coming at you in the big frosty stillness – and such wonderful smoke . . .[4]

In October of the same year, her seventeen-year-old sister Claudia arrived abruptly from Virginia.[5] Delighted by the Texas Panhandle landscape, yet apprehensive of 'those darned educators' and oppressed by a room wallpapered with pink roses, O'Keeffe quickly left her first lodging.[6] She then managed to persuade the Shirleys (Douglas – a physics professor known as D.A. – and his wife, Willena) to allow her to rent an upstairs room that faced east with an unobstructed view of the rising sun and, within weeks, to accommodate her sister too. The severe iron bed and wooden crate offered simple furnishings that suited her. The Shirleys' daughter remembered the artist as 'as different as they come', and that Miss O'Keeffe 'spent much time drawing on the floor'.[7]

Given the recent upheaval in her family, O'Keeffe shouldered the responsibility of acting as guardian to her youngest sister, Claudia. Claudie, as the family knew her, enrolled as a seventeen-year-old in West Texas State Normal College.[8] O'Keeffe wrote about her sister, who loved horseback riding and guns, in late November: 'No I'm not going to shield her from anything – and she is that kind that can't be anything but free – She is queer – and about as independent as they are made . . . I don't see any reason why I shouldn't take care of her if I can.'[9]

Claudie brought out an unbridled instinct in O'Keeffe for shooting contests and walking on the plains, though she pushed the limits. O'Keeffe worried aloud to Stieglitz about her sister's excited state; the artist soon regarded her new parenting responsibility with unease. Claudie went shooting and brought back her catch, mostly prairie owl and jackrabbits, for amusement. O'Keeffe moaned to Stieglitz: 'last night the sister was hunting for my paint brushes to clean her gun – put my pallet [sic] on the bed – then sat on it.'[10]

O'Keeffe found the fierce weather of the Texas Panhandle compelling: harsh windstorms, blue northers (a sudden drop in temperature brought by deep-blue northern clouds), the canyon

Georgia O'Keeffe (far right) and friends in Palo Duro Canyon, Texas, *c.* 1912–13, photographer unknown.

Georgia O'Keeffe, *Train at Night in the Desert*, 1916, watercolour and pencil on paper.

and its valleys with wide-open vistas, and flat landscape everywhere surmounted by sky. The locals reported that she once walked the 12 miles to the brilliantly coloured Palo Duro Canyon, which plunges from the horizontal line of the plains to a depth of 335 metres (1,100 feet). She rose early to celebrate the dawn, or would sit on a fence, gazing out over the prairie at sunset. O'Keeffe enjoyed the attentions of young suitors, but her priority became the drive out to see the canyon in the 'wonderful lavender moonlight'. Though the young O'Keeffe loved dancing, the young men of the Canyon period never quite seemed to understand her, and she managed to elude them all.

The West Texas State Normal College bulletin from 1917 lists 'Miss O'Keefe' (*sic*) as head of the Department of Drawing. Rebuilt and opened only the previous April after a devastating fire in 1914, the College had new facilities, including a swimming pool, serving 300 students. Though the artist represented the arts, the actual curriculum centred on drawing and various applied design training for teachers to work in Texas schools.

On her first day of preparation for the new school year O'Keeffe received 'the biggest letter I ever got . . . the size of the plains' from Stieglitz.[11] Both Stieglitz and Pollitzer came to her aid, posting new books and materials for her teaching. She informed Anita of the recently rebuilt school: 'Books are scarce here.' Her request to Anita reveals her continued reliance on the *Composition* of her professor, Arthur Wesley Dow, and she specified that the study of photographs should include 'textiles – greek pottery and persian plates' for design classes.[12] An archival photograph of her classroom shows how artfully she installed non-Western designs and provided pottery for still-life study. She established a reinvigorated arts curriculum: among the ten courses listed in the roster of the College bulletin of 1917 are 'drawing, industrial art, costume design, interior decoration and methods of teaching art in the public schools'.[13]

For the advanced design and drawing courses, O'Keeffe chose the latest books on art from New York. Willard Huntington Wright's *Modern Painting* (1915), which features a colour image of Cézanne's *Mont Sainte-Victoire*, became a reliable source.[14] She also gave the students Clive Bell's *Art*, the definitive Bloomsbury formulation on Cézanne and the significant form. But her foundation came from her training with Dow at Teachers College and her practical nature:

> I got very interested in teaching . . . What I enjoyed was teaching people who had no interest in becoming artists. Dow's teaching had been based on the idea that the same principles applied no matter what sort of work you were doing – pottery, making wallets, anything.[15]

O'Keeffe's most visible mark on the West Texas college was her lecture before the faculty in January 1917. When she turned her attention to prepare a lecture on 'Modern Art – to give it in an interesting ¾ of an hour to folks who know nothing about any kind of art', she appears to have had a case of nerves: 'I have been laboring on Aesthetics–Wright–Bell–De Zayas–Eddy – All I could find . . . have been slaving on it since in November – even read a lots of Caffins [*sic*] – lots of stupid stuff.'[16] She also describes practising a dry run of the talk with a prosecuting attorney educated at Yale: 'a fair sample of the mind Id [*sic*] have to tackle in Faculty Circle'. She wrote to Anita: 'and it was a great success – They kept me going all through the time allotted . . . and an hour after it was time to go home.'[17]

Stieglitz continued to send bulky letters, books and periodicals. And 'astounded to say the least', she found Wright's *Creative Will* and seven back issues of *Camera Work* dropped on her porch.[18] Stieglitz's obsessive mailings are best captured in his gift of the book *Faust*, which he sent in October 1916. With an intellectual flourish, his words dwell on his precocity, 'When I was NINE I discovered

Faust. / It gave me quiet then', and his fascination with the book that grew with him. To her, he inscribed: 'To one who without knowing it has given me much at a time when I needed Faust.'[19] For this precocious, sensitive and increasingly melancholy man educated in German culture, O'Keeffe was becoming his innocent Gretchen, the 'Eternal Feminine' of the cursed Faust's pursuit.

Stieglitz nurtured his new protégé, who read Faust with great interest in the shade of some tumbleweeds on an autumn afternoon; he assured her that he had never given such an important book to anyone, 'man or woman'.[20] In her absence from New York, in the autumn of 1916 he included her works on paper in a group show with Marin, Hartley and Walkowitz. O'Keeffe, delighted to think of her work besides the 'blue Marin', continued to send the latest examples of her works on paper both to Pollitzer and to Stieglitz, the latter more often. He then overstepped his bounds, asking O'Keeffe if she minded that '[I] send you one hundred dollars & we own together three more outside of the one "ours" already. – Will you?'[21] This elicited her spirited response: 'I cannot let you buy – no, that's not the word – I cannot let you give me anything in exchange for your share in – my children.' She ended with a flourish: 'If I find myself wanting a hundred dollars someday I'll tell you . . . I return the check tomorrow.'[22]

The letters from Stieglitz to O'Keeffe in Texas arrived every few days, and document the busy round of his daily events at 291; they comprise a valuable resource on his New York friends and connections, at the gallery and beyond. One evening he met Marcel Duchamp when he attended an elegant dinner party at the home of avant-garde collectors Louise and Walter Arensberg. Stieglitz described their art collection: 'splendid examples of Matisse, Picassos, Duchamp, a Cézanne watercolour & a Cézanne lithograph – several Brancusis – in marble, wood, & bronze'. Such images had hung on the walls of his tiny rooms at 291, and O'Keeffe had seen much similar work there. But more, he related

GEORGIE O'KEEFE
Drawing.

'Miss Georgie O'Keefe, Head of Drawing', faculty page from the West Texas State Normal College yearbook *Le Mirage*, 1918.

to O'Keeffe in Canyon the (now-historic) privilege of visiting the site of incubation of Duchamp's *Large Glass*, noting: 'It's all worked with fine wire & lead . . . very perfect workmanship – He has a beautiful soul – he loves the age of machinery – its significance, orderliness – precision.'[23]

O'Keeffe, seeking modern expression in the arts, had been enlivened about all things 291, and wrote to Stieglitz on another occasion: 'I wonder if you know how much finer life has seemed to me through knowing you – a little.'[24] She gradually came to trust that he would shepherd her career. One night on the plains, her tone became both poetic and intimate as she described the liminal space where light emerges at a great distance. This very image was breathed into the luminous orb that became her nature abstraction *Light Coming on the Plains*: 'that space that is between what they call heaven and earth – out there in what they call the night – is as much as anything. So I send you the space that is watching the starlight and the empty quiet plains.'[25]

With the American entry into the war against Germany in April 1917, and plunging financial markets that deteriorated his wife's family brewery fortunes, Stieglitz could no longer keep 291 going. In despair, in spring 1917 he decided to close the gallery, and as his last hurrah he installed in May a solo exhibition of O'Keeffe's recent Texas watercolours on paper. His own installation photos vividly portray O'Keeffe's progression to new motifs. The works traced her movement from New York to North Carolina, and her important first year in Canyon. The *Blue i–iii* series that Anita had critiqued at 60th Street now hung near the *Tent at Night* from North Carolina, and then came the blue ink drawing *Blue Lines x*, first sketched of building profiles from her New York window. From the Canyon experiences and vistas, the *Train at Night in the Desert* was placed next to the charcoal study for *Special No. 21 (Palo Duro Canyon)*. This charcoal study for *Train*, the first work O'Keeffe ever sold from the gallery, was one she remembered into her nineties.[26] O'Keeffe's interest in the Kandinsky-inspired synaesthesia of expressive harmonies surfaced in her new pursuit of colour. She once wrote to Pollitzer: 'You asked me about music – I like it better than anything in the world – Color gives me the same thrill once in a long long time.'[27] While in South Carolina colour had distracted her, now the new work exhibited in New York reflected the colour gradations of earth awakening, light arriving and heat fading in the warmth of sunsets. Colour became dominant

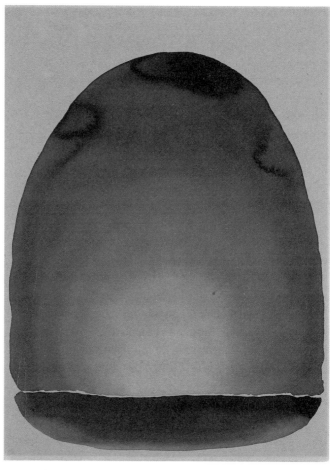

Georgia O'Keeffe, *Light Coming on the Plains, II*, 1917, watercolour on paper.

in all the work from Texas, whether in the canyon, prairie or evening star series.

The drawing *Special No. 12* is photographed in this placement opposite the memorial first made for Ida O'Keeffe, *Abstraction*, a slender white Plasticine sculpture. This represents Stieglitz's interpretation, even though Georgia never clarified its origins as a mourning figure, nor did she tell him why she made this work. His interest in it as phallic form became a point of further interpretative revelations through his photographs, and through installation.

William Murrell, a singular critical voice at this point in O'Keeffe's nascent career, reached for an old-fashioned word, 'magnalities', to describe her sense of self, a consciousness 'active in the mystic and musical drawings of Georgia O'Keeffe', a sense of oneself lost in the wholeness of nature. In her charcoals and new watercolours, the critic found the Sublime and 'an inner harmony'; 'Of all things earthly, it is only in music that one finds any analogy to the emotional content of these drawings . . . to the gigantic, swirling rhythms and exquisite tendernesses.' The Murrell article was the single commentary on O'Keeffe republished by Stieglitz in the last issue of *Camera Work,* in spring 1917.[28]

This review pleased O'Keeffe enormously; it allowed her also to share her new (strange) work with one of her fellow teachers at the College, and to show the installation photographs of her works to her students. But another early critic wrote: 'Miss O'Keefe, [*sic*] independently of technical abilities quite out of the common, has found expression in delicately veiled symbolism for "what every woman knows" but what women heretofore have kept to themselves, either instinctively or through a universal conspiracy of silence.'[29] This too gives a sense of the inner expression that Stieglitz extolled in her work.

Once O'Keeffe was free from her teaching duties at the end of May, she made the impulsive decision to take the long train trip back to New York for a few days to see the exhibition, the last show that would hang on the walls of 291. She sent an inchoate letter to Stieglitz, but did not tell him of her arrival: 'Your little girl – a piece of fast-burning wood'. She ended the note: 'I feel like a fire-cracker.'[30]

Stieglitz was thunderstruck to see her in the gallery where her small exhibition had already been taken down; he hung it again for her. The sad ending of her relationship with Arthur Macmahon, 'balancing on the edge of loving', came at the end of Georgia's New York trip in May 1917. O'Keeffe spent a day at Coney Island with Paul Strand, and especially Stieglitz – one of 'the most wonderful days of my life'.[31] Yet it was Macmahon who accompanied her to the train, and wrote just after her departure: 'I think that I have never been more profoundly depressed . . . [you] going away some two thousand miles – how much of me was going with you. I shall believe in you always.'[32]

After seeing O'Keeffe off, Macmahon dutifully conveyed her portfolio to the small gallery of such vast reputation, where he found his unlikely rival, the 53-year-old Stieglitz, in the darkroom with the first images of the O'Keeffe portrait, images that would define the second half of his photographic career. Macmahon wrote to her:

> In the water-tank, developed but as yet unprinted, Stieglitz had photographs he took of you. I thought they were very wonderful. Perhaps I was thinking more of you than of photographic techniques. Stieglitz was talking of you when he showed them to me; – the things in you which make you wonderful.[33]

O'Keeffe replied to Anita's later query: 'Arthur? . . . I sort of felt that I have gone on past . . . I had a great letter a few days ago – The greatest he ever wrote me.' But she concluded: 'Stieglitz – Well – it was him I went to see – Just had to go Anita – and Im so glad I went. 291 is closing.'[34]

Writing during the long train ride back to Texas, she composed a cold, winter image of herself that was both predictive, provocative and opposite to the 'fire-cracker' of early May: 'I seemed to be headed for something – just like a sled tearing downhill.'[35]

Because of the interception of a German cable and the threat of a wartime invasion through Mexico, newspaper headlines in Texas raised war fever, rattling the draft-eligible boys: 'Germany Seeks Alliance with Mexico and Japan to Open War upon the United States'.[36] O'Keeffe wrestled with the fear of war spreading to America, and wondered over the 'use of Art' during this same spring. Her students began to volunteer and leave in droves.[37]

Among the young men leaving Canyon to serve was Ted Reid (James Warren Reid, 1895–1983), who is listed in the 1918 yearbook *Le Mirage* from West Texas State Normal College. Reid joined a troop called Guenther's Soldiers, bearing the motto 'Service is Sweet'. He was the student who had come closest to claiming O'Keeffe's heart, and his call to serve brought the danger even closer.

Reid was 'one kind of cowboy', 'tall and thin – muscles like iron', according to O'Keeffe. He had trailed her briefly, but his attachment and her reciprocated interest flouted convention because he was her student.[38] Rumours swirled, and the friendship was abruptly broken off when Reid first contemplated service at the Rio Grande. The British code-breaking of the infamous Zimmerman telegram revealed that Germany had proposed an invasion of the u.s. through Mexico, and Mexico in turn hoped to reclaim southwestern states.

O'Keeffe, who expressed her pacifist attitudes for decades afterwards, had seen her own brother Alexis, nicknamed Tex, called up for service at the age of 25. She visited him briefly at Fort Sheridan, near Chicago in Illinois, on her way back to Texas in early June 1917, and was able to visit him again during her Thanksgiving break in late November, when his troop was camped in Waco, Texas, just before the unit was dispatched to Europe. She reported to Stieglitz: 'What it is all doing to them is astounding to me . . . It seems as though I never felt a real honest need of Art before – it never seemed *necessary*'.[39]

On 5 February 1918 the transport steamship *Tuscania*, carrying more than 2,000 troops including Alexis, was torpedoed by a German submarine off the coast of Ireland.[40] The disaster was widely reported, and the ship was the last of the Anchor Line to be destroyed by submarine attacks.[41] The German U-boat torpedoes resulted in the deaths of 150 soldiers, and only the bravery of British sailors and the nearby fleet saved the rest. Though Alexis survived and recuperated briefly in Ireland, he subsequently fought in the trenches in France, was gassed and caught influenza. Their younger sister Catherine remembered that he took a full year to recuperate, but his health was broken and he died in January 1930 at the untimely age of 38.

Even before these events, the stress of the war and worry over her brother's prospects caused O'Keeffe's strong views on the war to break through her already dissolving civility with the Canyon locals. She protested against the sale of Christmas cards picturing the Statue of Liberty and ending with unusual Christmas wishes: 'And wipe Germany off the map'. She endured negative reactions – 'even faculty folks got after me about it . . . They couldn't understand how or why anyone would object for any but pro-German reasons.'[42] Just as her close friendship with Ted Reid had earlier caused trouble, her resistance to war-related jingoism led to more friction with the town people.

Her strong personality mirrored her great passion for the stark landscape, its sunsets, wild weather, sandstorms and biting cold that could suddenly sweep down on the plains. But if there was drama in the fierce weather on the flat level land of the Panhandle, more awaited her in the sudden crevice opening to the Palo Duro Canyon. O'Keeffe described the experience of climbing there as 'merciless'. The site is a powerful upheaval of geologic forces that gives the ranching town of Canyon its name. The flat prairie with mirages on the road yields to one of the most remarkable coloured rock canyons of the continental United States, apart from the Grand Canyon in Arizona, more than 700 miles to the west. The detail of O'Keeffe's extensive Canyon letters again renders a written parallel to what became her art.

To Stieglitz, she related a 'wonderful day' of a spring visit to the canyon, but a 'wobbly little girl writing' at the end of a daring trek. Hiking with new friends, she described wading in an icy cold stream, lying in the sand near big cedars – not atypically, she left the group to take 'a long walk by myself – following cow trails through the cedars'. But up the cliffs they climbed, and those 'awful places' were 'tremendous'. She returned to this topic while revealing her increasing reliance on Stieglitz:

> so much afraid – And you feel like something that protects me – something I want to be very close to – like I had to shrink back – so many times today – against the wall of rock going straight up beside me – and in front . . . a misstep and I'd roll down forever – and the dirt and rocks crumbled and rolled down and there was nothing to hold to . . . I couldn't stand still by the wall of rock – or I'd never get to the top – I must keep moving – being so afraid made it all the finer.[43]

This remarkable letter concludes with a visual memory that traces the origin of O'Keeffe's series on the Palo Duro Canyon: 'When we came out – way off on the edge of the earth against the sunset were a lot of cattle in a string – We could see daylight under them – on the edge of the earth.'[44]

To Pollitzer, she wrote about almost the same view, though here emphasizing her stamina: 'out to the canyon all afternoon – till late at night – wonderful color', and concluding with a slight condescension to their teacher: 'I can understand Pa Dow painting his pretty color canyons.'[45] She had already begun to move towards an abstracted aesthetic suggesting the bubbling lava-like energy of the earth. A score of drawings resulted from these climbs, defining cliff edges and the plunge into the earth, as well as a close-up view into the sloping rock faces and valley beyond. Finally, in *Special No. 21* O'Keeffe created a design of organic pod forms and tumbling rocks between two curved slopes, indicating that the canyon's descent moves past a representation of place. Rather it is the hot colour and composition that convey the intensity of the earth's ancient formation. The expressive space of the reddish-orange canyon is visible behind O'Keeffe in the Stieglitz photograph of her in several related poses, of 1918 (see page 6).[46]

At the same time, her candid letters to Stieglitz often reveal how many young men asked to drive her out to the canyon, and in a provocative way she perhaps wanted her mentor to know. Her easy acceptance of herself as 'little girl' accentuated her distance in age from Stieglitz, as did his inscription to her as 'the Little Girl of the Texas Plains' in the last issue of *Camera Work* he sent, signing himself as the 'Old Man of 291'.[47]

The influenza epidemic of the frigid winter of 1917–18 and only secondarily the war furore caused O'Keeffe to leave the much-loved Texas Panhandle landscape in February 1918. Her leave-taking from Canyon was as abrupt and self-willed as her departure exactly two years earlier from her Columbia College position. Her doctor in Amarillo, 'Dr Mac', strongly advised her to go south, to get away from the intense cold and the stubborn illness that came on after Christmas, the 'queer feeling in my head and slow walking'. She was taking a serum dose that Dr Mac had advised her to give herself, and Stieglitz sent her a copy of a book on Van Gogh that she 'read mostly to forget how sick I felt'.[48] Then came the news of the sinking of her brother Alexis's transport. The weather on 8 February was 'a yellow Hell of tearing biting cold wind – fairly blinding with dust'; on 14 February she wrote to Stieglitz: 'I'm on the way . . . I had quit work and was on the way to San Antonio.'[49] If O'Keeffe's transition from New York through the Virginia summer after her mother's death in May 1916 paralleled a period of depression, her leave-taking from Canyon reverberated with feelings of desperation. No one in Canyon knew why she had left, and her sister Claudia had gone to Spur, Texas, to start her student teaching.[50]

Leah Harris, a friend of both O'Keeffe sisters and a nutritionist in Randall County, West Texas, offered her family home in San Antonio, and travelled with O'Keeffe to the warmer climate of South Texas. Both young women were intermittently ill even in San Antonio, each needing care for a time. Then they moved to Waring, a tiny town outside San Antonio, along the Guadalupe River in the Texas Hill Country, a dramatically different landscape of high cypresses and grassy meadows distinct from the Panhandle prairie. The women were determined to restore the neglected family farm in Waring, and despite their flu symptoms camped out one night in late March in front of the decrepit house. O'Keeffe pottered about for a time planting, and imagined that at the very least she could farm, ready to take on whatever life threw at her. The instability of her situation, and the country at war, all combined to throw her art into limbo. This last chapter of her Texas artistic growth and inspiration in the landscape turned to indecision. Stieglitz stage-managed a dance of confusion from New York that involved Paul Strand. After long anguishing talks, he sent his unlikely rival to bring O'Keeffe back to New York.

The entire year of 1917 featured her correspondence with this talented young photographer sponsored by Alfred Stieglitz. Strand and O'Keeffe represented the new rising generation; they were both younger artists whom Stieglitz had discovered and exhibited. Strand sent to O'Keeffe examples of his early photographic abstractions, such as *Abstraction: Porch Shadows* and *Bowls* (1915–16), which she admired greatly. And she in turn painted watercolour abstractions that recalled her thought forms of Strand.[51] These daring washes, darkened puddles of an abstracted standing form amid bright primary colours, strongly echo the forms in Kandinsky's *Garden of Love* (1913), purchased by Stieglitz from the Armory Show for his collection in 1913.

Strand had travelled through Texas in 1915, visiting sites of manual labour and rural poverty, impelled by the vision of his

most famous teacher, the social realist photographer Lewis Hine.
Thus it was to Strand that Stieglitz turned; he knew Texas, and
Stieglitz persuaded him to take on the risky strategy. Events
came to a head in May 1918. Stieglitz related to O'Keeffe the
tenor of his conversations, which lasted for 'twenty-nine–thirty'
hours straight': with his wife about their marital issues and
their daughter Kitty, then eleven hours of talk with Strand, all
concentrated on 'The question of your coming East'.[52] After
the obsessive marathon, Stieglitz became even more desperate to
act quickly because O'Keeffe and her friend had had an intruder
on the Harris family property, whom Leah had waved away with
a gun.[53]

Her letters signalled to Stieglitz that she had coped, even if she
had not recovered, but for him ill health always sent up warning
flares. The older man, still sending O'Keeffe 'big fat letters',
obsessively in love with 'Canyon' (the code name for O'Keeffe),[54]
asked his younger rival to go halfway across the country and
bring her back. Stieglitz admitted to her: 'It's queer how it was
decided that Strand go.'[55] Despite O'Keeffe's correspondence with
Strand, and Stieglitz's interception of the letters, there was a
remarkable letter from O'Keeffe written only to Stieglitz just before
Christmas 1917 that surely had sustained his hope. Wondering
'what you are to me – it's like father, mother, brother, sister, best
man and woman friend, all mixed up in one', the artist concluded:
'I love you greatly.'[56]

Strand arrived in Texas, but he did not capture O'Keeffe and
put her on the train immediately; in fact, he stayed more than a
month. But her letters suggest that he did not betray Stieglitz, or
perhaps she was dissembling: 'You can't imagine anything funnier
than the combination of Leah, Strand and myself'; she and Leah
found Paul 'so slow . . . we can hardly realize it's true'.[57] Yet the
youthful group cavorted in the Hill Country for a few weeks, Strand
photographing her friend Leah in the nude, while O'Keeffe painted

Paul Strand, *Georgia O'Keeffe*, 1918, photograph, platinum print.

nude studies in graphite and watercolour, all the while writing to
Stieglitz of her confusion.

O'Keeffe recalled at the end of her life: 'I liked everything about
Texas', exclaiming: 'I didn't even mind the dust, although sometimes
when I came back from a walk I'd be the color of the road.' Most
of the Texan works are in watercolour or graphite; her harvesting
of the motifs instilled by the Canyon period would bear fruit in her
coming oil abstractions made in New York. Her memory of a bus
ride early one morning links the sun to the defining wonder that

Texas symbolized for her: 'we saw the most extraordinary sunrise. When we got to Canyon, I thought maybe that was something I could paint. It was what started me painting again. I worked in watercolor, because I never had the time for oils.'[58]

4

A Portrait: Woman

On 3 June 1918 O'Keeffe dispatched a lengthy telegram to Stieglitz
from Texas: 'Starting for New York tonight', it began. It continued:
'If I had let anybody or anything get in my way I wouldn't be going.
It has to be this way . . . I don't know anything. Think I see straight
yet see nothing. O'Keeffe.'[1] When at last Georgia O'Keeffe and Paul
Strand arrived at the Pennsylvania Station after the long trip across
the country from San Antonio through New Orleans, it was early
Sunday morning in New York, 9 June 1918. Stieglitz was waiting.
She ran to kiss Stieglitz immediately while Strand stood apart,
a moment that Stieglitz remembered in detail for years.

Strand had realized his fate during the long month in San
Antonio. He had written disarmingly to Stieglitz of O'Keeffe's
needs and his confusion from Texas: 'if it were to be – But it isn't
– which I knew long ago'.[2] Left standing by himself on the station
platform, Strand soon made plans to leave for army service with
'nothing else to look forward to particularly', and soon faced
induction with conscientious objector status.[3] The First World
War raged on, with O'Keeffe's brother Alexis still stationed in the
trenches in northern Europe.[4] Elizabeth Stieglitz, Alfred's niece and
co-conspirator who had urged O'Keeffe to return, promised the
young artist a loan of her attic rooms atop the family's brownstone
on the corner of East 59th Street. Georgia O'Keeffe chose not only
Stieglitz and the city, but a daring leap towards a professional life
as an artist.

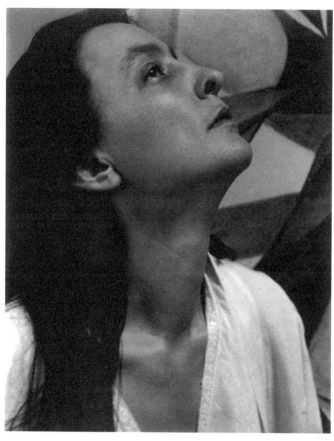

Alfred Stieglitz, *Georgia O'Keeffe*, 1919–21, palladium print.

Feverish and pallid with the residual flu, still hampered by a cough, the young woman was put to bed in the brightly painted orange and yellow room under the skylight. Strand conveyed how perilously close O'Keeffe had come to tuberculosis, and Stieglitz pressed his brother into service. Dr Leopold (Lee) Stieglitz and wife Lizzie were the parents of the lively Elizabeth, and all lived in the brownstone, where Lee enjoyed a prosperous Manhattan clientele. By the end of June, with Stieglitz actually learning to cook eggs and Arthur Dove supplying fresh produce from Connecticut, O'Keeffe's fever and chills vanished, and her health returned. Stieglitz asked her what was the most important thing she wanted, and O'Keeffe replied that she wanted to paint full time for a year. Stieglitz equally promised to secure her freedom, and guaranteed at least $1,000 for the coming year (borrowed from one of his gallery supporters). As he so often helped the artists of his circle, he now took O'Keeffe under his wing, even as his ardour for her far superseded any prior attachments. He wrote to Strand solemnly that he had committed to take on the young woman as his 'responsibility'.[5]

The sexual attraction between the two built to a crackling intensity once they were reunited for the first time in a year, stoked by the long, slow prelude in letters and shared passion for art. But there remained other restraints apart from O'Keeffe's health. The artist's youth (she was 23 years younger than Stieglitz) and Stieglitz's marriage had made their love affair seem unthinkable at the beginning. His 25-year marriage had long faltered, and he avoided scenes at his unhappy home. He had established evenings out at the theatre or concerts with his circle of artist and writer friends, and created an artistic and intellectual world from 291, now shuttered.

O'Keeffe had been prescribed bed rest at first, but within days she jotted a note provocatively before Stieglitz arrived: 'The hot setting sun so brilliant – And lying here – wanting you with such an all [over] ache . . . A volcano is nothing to it . . . Still I some way feel I can be quiet when you come.' She ends with another kind of ultimate surrender: 'Trust – Why do you know – the trust I have in you is the finest thing I've ever known – It's absolute.'[6]

His response as he read her letter under a lamppost, 'the street so quiet – not a soul – No stars – just the light & I', reveals that he knew he must stay away. 'I could have run to you within a minute

. . . But I looked at the sky & at the silent street & hope the Woman Little Girl would fall asleep.' Writing incantatory phrases to her that intertwined O'Keeffe's youth, innocence and sexual being, Stieglitz regarded his beloved through the polish of an ideal lens: 'Tonight I see white snow mountain peaks looking into dark boundless skies . . . like the one human soul I've found – A Woman – A Little Girl – a Child – All Innocence – And Purity Unheard of '.[7]

By her own account aged 90, O'Keeffe painted in the nude due to the attic heat. With his perfect memory for dates and events, Stieglitz mulled over their first days: 'And don't I remember June 15 – six days after you arrived & I touched a spot & you jumped & I sat on a chair & felt like a murderer.'[8] After taking Kitty to summer camp in New Hampshire, Stieglitz brought O'Keeffe to his own home at 1111 Madison Avenue, where his wife Emmy returned unexpectedly to find her husband photographing O'Keeffe. The artist was quickly dispatched, and Emmy uttered her ultimatum. Stieglitz refused to give up the young artist as his wife demanded, and he was 'out of 1111 – in one hour and fifty minutes'. Back at 59th Street, Stieglitz arranged a blanket to be drawn through the centre of the room, and the two lived side by side, creating their art in the cramped rooms.[9] Stieglitz's photographs of that hot summer have become legendary, and O'Keeffe's early abstractions fed her new experimentation in oils.

Energized by the presence of 'You Wonder of all Wonders – You Glorious Bit of all that's Human', Stieglitz pivoted to a new creative trajectory, and left behind his former melancholy generated by closing 291 and the war. He regained the stamina for long days of darkroom work, always seeking the perfect print of each of his photographs, though he now had to resort to palladium prints, rich in red-brown tones, due to the prohibitive cost of platinum.[10] To a colleague from 291 days, he wrote of the creative fervour of his first year with O'Keeffe:

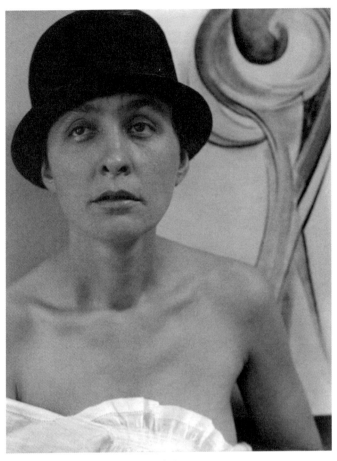

Alfred Stieglitz, *Georgia O'Keeffe*, 1918, palladium print.

At last I am at last photographing again . . . It is straight . . .
No sentimentalism. Not old nor new. – It is so sharp you can
see the [pores] on a face – & yet it is abstract . . . It is a series
of about 100 pictures of one person – head & ears – toes –
hands – torsos. – It is the doing of something I had in mind
for very many years.[11]

O'Keeffe renewed his aesthetic purpose, and the photographer began a composite photographic portrait of her, a deeply passionate chronicle of their love, thickened with the artistic tropes of muse, child, sphinx, Madonna, Venus, creative spirit, dancer – all facets of Woman. Their collaborative erotic playfulness led to the best new photographic work Stieglitz had created in a decade. He had begun the portrait as he photographed her hands in 1917, the same images that Arthur Macmahon had seen in the developing tray, when she arrived from Texas in her black schoolmarm's dress with its prim starched collar.

Now Stieglitz discovered abstracted studies of the body in her form: taut tendons in the neck, elegant hands held against the light filtering through a window, the sensuality of breasts, torso, belly and pubic area. O'Keeffe was a willing subject: she was in love, and collaborated with his photographic project in all ways. Her erotic charge and compliance, linked to their intimacy, more than fulfilled Stieglitz's dream of discovering the woman artist, his Eternal Feminine. And he linked her body to her own images, her creative product; in one of his portraits, her images issue from her mouth and head. She respected his art: 'His idea of a portrait was not just one picture. His dream was to start with a child at birth and photograph that child in all of its activities as it grew . . . it would be a photographic diary.'[12]

Although his nineteenth-century Symbolist-influenced ideas could not encompass O'Keeffe's entire life, Stieglitz saw her as both child and woman, and poured all the fantasy and desire he had felt for every woman onto her person. The idea of *pars pro toto*, the part to represent the whole, fed his delight in parsing his beloved as he recreated 'Woman'.[13]

The summer heat rolled on. O'Keeffe remembered 'at a certain time of day the light was best for photographing', and the northern skylight kept a steady light entering the room.[14] She remembered that she stood uncomfortably on the radiator, hardly the pedestal

Alfred Stieglitz, *Georgia O'Keeffe*, 1918, palladium print.

of Pygmalion's sculpture. Stieglitz arranged her dance-like postures before the window, and cropped her body to the expressive torso in an S-curve evoking ancient marmoreal goddesses become human. The photographing went on obsessively, and O'Keeffe recalled that the exposures were often long, as many as three or four minutes, leading to 'much fuss' if she twitched or moved. Images of ecstasy, repose and exhaustion alternated with close-up compositions devoted to the elements of the body of the 'Woman'. Stieglitz later described the portrait portfolio as '8 hands, 3 feet, 3 hands and breasts, 3 torsos, 2 "Interpretations"'.[15]

In August 'we went to the country to his mother's house – she met us at the porch steps', O'Keeffe remembered.[16] The Stieglitz family gathered each summer at Lake George, and as the eldest son of seven children Alfred Stieglitz relaxed in the serenity of the lake, offset by the constant noisy gathering of relatives at the family home, Oaklawn. To O'Keeffe the 'house was shocking . . . so very full of all kinds of things collected by a traveling family'. For her Stieglitz came from another world, the gallery: '291 – the simplest, barest of rooms – not even a chair'.[17] The old house overlooked the shoreline of natural beauty that was Lake George, titled the Queen of Lakes in the Adirondacks Mountains of upper New York State. Made welcome by Hedwig Stieglitz, O'Keeffe joined the family while the mother provided a safe haven, delighted to see her son transformed from the 'morose ghost' he had been.[18] There the love affair continued, and reached a fever pitch.

O'Keeffe had taken the mother's place, and now Stieglitz's daughter Kitty felt abandoned and furious. Separated for only three days while he tried to placate his daughter at camp, Stieglitz ardently wrote to O'Keeffe early in the morning of 9 August. It was at Lake George that 'Virginity Day' came at last. Stieglitz recalled the ferocious storm: 'you gave me your virginity. During thunder & lightning . . . I still see your face . . . and see you on the floor afterwards naked with a bandage on – a wounded bird. So lovely.'[19] Stieglitz always remembered the date, 9 August 1918, and referenced it almost every August as 'a sacred story'. To O'Keeffe he declared: 'your virginity was in my trust. Is today.'[20]

They remained at the lake throughout September, and there O'Keeffe experienced the 'volatile madhouse of a family' that delighted the irrepressibly loquacious Stieglitz. His apt aphorism says it all: 'Everything is relative, except relatives and they are absolute.'[21] O'Keeffe found them absolutely difficult, and resisted their argumentative confrontations over the dinner table. Soon it was assumed she would oversee the cooking, and she planted a garden. The family, especially Stieglitz's younger, diva sister Selma, found O'Keeffe's manner off-putting (and the feeling was mutual) because the artist dared to prepare her own salad with fresh greens and refused to stay at table to eat heavier fare. Prosaic details captured Stieglitz's adoring camera eye: her hands peeling apples, reaching for a bunch of grapes, her quizzical frown over an ear of shucked corn. This last records her appalled reaction to the family of twenty gathered at the summer table, eating corn.[22]

Rowing and hiking up Prospect Mountain became escapist pleasures for the lovers, and the lake allowed for nude bathing near the Oaklawn property. The photographing continued. Elegant in an oversize cardigan as the autumn weather cooled, O'Keeffe posed yet again with her hands against rough tree bark and seated on the bare earth working on a watercolour, the grace of her long fingers visible. The lengthening of summer distilled into a productive, creative autumn that became a yearly cycle. Over the next several years, O'Keeffe painted her first oil abstractions of autumnal colours and Adirondack hillsides at Lake George, including the strange glowing white forms in the oils of 1918, *Series 1, No. 10*, which evoke the human back, and another her knees, as she rowed across the lake. Another painting of swirling red and green forms suggests Stieglitz's habitual cape with red lining in the dense forest above the lake.[23]

Back in New York for the autumn season, but without a gallery, Stieglitz boasted to Strand: 'Visitors galore all coming to see our work.'[24] O'Keeffe experienced Stieglitz's unique magnetism for drawing a crowd with quiet tolerance at first, sitting silently, rarely objecting to the onslaught of interpretations of her new work. Those who 'streamed to our apartment' became her introduction to New York intellectuals and writers drawn to Stieglitz, and plunged her into the 'maelstrom of talk'.[25] Both in the nightly gatherings where the Stieglitz writers and artists had dinner together, and at Lake George with his family, O'Keeffe sat by as Stieglitz expounded on her art.[26] The lively brew of intellectual discussion became the artist's graduate education.

Stieglitz made his new work available alongside O'Keeffe's abstract ventures in watercolour and oils. Fellow artist Arthur Dove, celebrated for his earliest abstractions at 291, starting from 1910, became an important friend to O'Keeffe. On seeing the first year's work together, Dove observed that the photographer and young painter united to possess 'the same abstract force'.[27] O'Keeffe began to employ grey shadings in her abstractions, evocative of photographic tonal scale, and gave Dove one such work.[28] And Stieglitz emphasized to Paul Strand: '114 East 59th quite a centre. Seeing Georgia's work. And mine . . . Great strides forward [Leo] Stein very much impressed'.[29] Stein, the brother of Gertrude, was among the first Americans to buy significant Cézanne and Matisse paintings, and brought his culture from the Paris studios to the critics and artists frequenting Stieglitz's pop-up gallery. Stieglitz proudly sought the opportunity to exhibit his first photographs of O'Keeffe when a small show took place uptown on 110th Street, in March 1919.[30] This is an early indication that O'Keeffe knew he planned on taking their private attic documents to show with his other portrait work, but she refused to pose in the nude after that year.[31]

O'Keeffe took a great risk in her intimacy with the married Stieglitz, but the risks of their new union balanced what she later recalled as the 'nerve' required in pursuing her art. Searching for a way to explain the 'new colors' she found within herself as she explored innovative abstraction in watercolour, O'Keeffe wrote to Stieglitz: 'what you have of mine [is] a whole woman spread out.'[32] Stieglitz had written to her in Canyon with a forceful, unembarrassed assertion: 'You have met virtually no one – are working entirely from within – womb & brains – & all that goes with both.'[33] Such ideas current in bohemian, liberal Greenwich Village, explored by sexologists such as Havelock Ellis, had been Stieglitz's frequent reading matter and obsession since 1912.[34] To the artist Stanton Macdonald-Wright, Stieglitz wrote of the O'Keeffe who combined 'the Great Woman-Child' with artistic freedom: 'Woman is beginning – the interesting thing is *she has actually begun*.'[35] He extrapolated: 'Woman feels the World differently than Man feels it. And one of the chief generating forces crystallizing into art is undoubtedly elemental feeling . . . The Woman receives the World through her Womb. That is the seat of her deepest feeling. Mind comes second.'[36]

Given her focused absorption in new painting ideas and the excitement of Stieglitz's presence, the quiet O'Keeffe had no means to contradict him. But her points of origin diverged sharply: she continued to explore motifs evolving from her Texas watercolours, and memories of the sky and plains. Music also remained a point of inspiration. Spiralling forms, the arcs of ribbons of coloured tones far bolder than most contemporary palettes, and her juxtaposition of angled geometric shapes against a field of colour defined the experiments. *Music, Pink and Blue No. 2* (1918) is but one example of O'Keeffe's new oils painted in New York, and these have been interpreted as exercises in musical synaesthesia, her bright colour echoing the flow of rhythm and sound waves. But to Stieglitz there was no question – the arching colours represented her inner sensation, the site of creation, in both senses. Before O'Keeffe's paintings gained a New York viewing, Stieglitz put three of her new works on view in the Pennsylvania Academy of the Fine Arts compilation of 300 contemporary works in 1921. One of these was *Music, Pink and Blue No. 2*, against which he photographed the artist Arthur Carles.[37] In this same year, Paul Rosenfeld began to write of her 'ecstatic climaxes'. Stieglitz's endless extolling of O'Keeffe based on Freudian interpretations echoed far beyond the

59th Street enclave, and O'Keeffe's paintings were not as yet fully on view to an eager public.

Apart from the Freudian theories and the sexologist Ellis's interpretations reaching America, two other innovators of this time, Isadora Duncan and D. H. Lawrence, created work that celebrated the vital, ecstatic and sensuous forces in nature. These two, along with the often-cited poetry of Walt Whitman, ran parallel to Stieglitz's converging (over-determined) definition of 'Woman'.

Duncan represented the renaissance in dance, as she envisioned the future: 'She shall dance the freedom of woman', so that 'the natural language of that soul will have become the movement of the body.' Duncan's dancer expresses a union of the corporeal and the sacred: '[to] realize the mission of woman's body and the holiness of all its parts'. O'Keeffe owned Floyd Dell's book *Women as World Builders*, which quoted these very excerpts from Duncan's book *The Dance*, profiling Isadora Duncan in one chapter. Her dance troupe performed in New York in the very month that Stieglitz and O'Keeffe were reunited, June 1918. Indeed, one of Stieglitz's disciples, Abraham Walkowitz, drew obsessively from Duncan's dance movements, making thousands of watercolours and drawings over a twenty-year period, beginning in 1906.[38] O'Keeffe and Stieglitz both absorbed Duncan's credo for the coming generation, and as radical artists in the post-war period, they shared the vision of the 'dancer of the future, the free spirit [would be] . . . the highest intelligence in the freest body'.[39]

The other great prophet for an acknowledgement of vital sexuality came in D. H. Lawrence's writing of the 1910s and early 1920s. Both Paul Rosenfeld and Paul Strand absorbed his powerful literary influence, seeking to understand how men and women had become polarized, and how liberation of the creative force might escape Victorian strictures. Rosenfeld gave his Stieglitz and O'Keeffe a book of Lawrence poems, *Look! We Have Come*

Through, at the beginning of their affair, inscribing their copy: 'To whom this book belongs'.[40]

Years later, O'Keeffe looked back on the days when she was free, when 'she was surrounded by people who didn't care'.[41] Had O'Keeffe planned to yoke her artistic ambition to the famous Stieglitz, or had she been scripted for the passive Galatea of Pygmalion's craft? Or was she herself becoming a Faustina? She talked little, preferred quiet, loved immersion in nature through long walks up Prospect Mountain at Lake George. At the same time, she gained artistic opportunities in the city in the midst of a bustling art crowd who gathered round her brilliant lover, Stieglitz, led as always by his voluble interpretations. At the height of her passion, she had ceded to him her trust.

Reinvigorated in his art and life, Stieglitz decided to exhibit a comprehensive retrospective of his photographic work early in 1921, in borrowed galleries at the Anderson Galleries run by his friend, also a publisher, Mitchell Kennerley. Writing his manifesto as a catalogue statement for the exhibition, the renewed Stieglitz proclaimed: 'I was born in Hoboken. I am an American. The Search for Truth is my Obsession.'[42] His fascination with O'Keeffe's Midwestern rootedness helped him to absorb a pioneer American immigration history that balanced his own heritage. From the 146 photographs on view in the galleries, 45 were recent images, presented in a section called 'A Woman', from 1918 to 1920.[43]

The photography made clear to all that Miss O'Keeffe, the unnamed woman artist, appeared as the subject on full view. Stieglitz had metamorphosed her into the Eternal Woman, as he described eagerly to a fellow photographer: 'Clean cut sharp heartfelt mentally digested bits of universality in the shape of Woman'.[44] The storm of critical interpretation that broke over O'Keeffe's embryonic career had its roots in these photographs. Her work became indelibly stamped with the interpretation that Stieglitz made unforgettable.[45] O'Keeffe was known to all now, and stricken by the public display and resulting press. The artist became 'what is known as a newspaper personality' as the critic Henry McBride described it. He quipped: 'Mona Lisa got only one portrait of herself. O'Keeffe got a hundred. It put her at once on the map. Everyone knew the name.'[46]

O'Keeffe's immediate reaction at the first viewing in 1921 is not recorded, but it is well known that the critical writings, which quickly flowed from both Paul Rosenfeld and Marsden Hartley, brought her to 'fury'.[47] Rosenfeld, Stieglitz's young friend and a music critic, wrote of her Plasticine sculpture, retitled *Inspiration*, as photographed against the sky: 'A tiny phallic statuette weeps, is bowed over in weeping, while behind, like watered silk, there waves the sunlight of creation.'[48] This had been the small sculpture that she crafted in the month after her mother's death, a mourning figure. As an example of Stieglitz's displacement, he photographed her where the phallic statue once stood in the gallery, in front of *Special No. 12* (see page 81). O'Keeffe herself became an erotic foil to her own drawing.

O'Keeffe soon had to acquire a first layer of self-protective armour, since her first comprehensive gallery opening, slated for two years hence, generated outsized expectations. McBride reported on the residual effect of the photographs: 'People did stop you on the street . . . and people did dispute about them.'[49] Predictably, the Anderson Galleries filled with the merely curious: Stieglitz himself conceded that the public was perhaps not ready to receive his images. Just as Stieglitz had lined up critics quickly to review his triumphant return to photography, so he stirred the publicity to O'Keeffe's continued advantage in anticipation of her exhibition of 1923.

Opinions quickly formed about O'Keeffe's art before the oil was dried, indeed before she sent the new work out of her studio. The Freudian and sexual interpretations of her work that followed became inescapable fodder for critics and paralleled the fascination with the 'New Woman' of the 1920s, a subject of both fear and desire. The writing of Stieglitz acolytes followed. First the artist Marsden Hartley published *Adventures in the Arts* in 1921, a book of essays dedicated to Alfred Stieglitz, with a chapter on women artists, including O'Keeffe. His overwrought phrases on O'Keeffe limned a personal, painful image as he compared the artist to Teresa of Ávila, the Spanish saint of Gian Lorenzo Bernini's famous sculpture, pierced by an arrow. Hartley classified O'Keeffe's pictures 'as living and shameless private documents as exist'. While he seemed to possess some understanding of her early peripatetic beginnings, he encoded her past in dreadful terms: 'Georgia O'Keeffe has had her feet scorched in the laval effusiveness of terrible experience.'[50]

Rosenfeld also wrote of O'Keeffe in purple prose that had its origin in his music criticism, and he loved the outsize metaphor. Writing in *The Dial* late in 1921, he traced the arc of American art to the artists of the Stieglitz circle, Marin, Hartley, Dove and now O'Keeffe. The text to image comparison is telling. Rosenfeld's article, written while O'Keeffe's paintings – three works among 300 – had briefly been in the PAFA 1921 exhibition, stated: 'Her art is gloriously female. Her great painful and ecstatic climaxes make us at last to know something the man has always wanted to know.'[51]

Given such a sexualized interpretation of her abstractions, the viewer might have been distracted from the actual fact of the painting. At the centre of *The Black Spot*, illustrated in the article, there is no 'spot' but rather a black rectangle – its suggestive title devised after the fact. O'Keeffe's inventive back-and-forth rhythm enlivens the two-dimensional space surrounding the rectangular black form. The shape soars up and forward to float before the curving coloured swells of delicately tinged pink, blue and yellow forms.[52] O'Keeffe's desire to 'paint as I wanted' had backfired in the face of the now infamous photographs. If she had the good fortune to be grouped with emerging modernists, she paid for the

MARGUERITE ZORACH
The "better half" of that ménage known as "The Zorachs", she first attracted attention by her modernist tapestries and hooked rugs executed in coloured wools. Her drawings, and paintings in water-colour and oil, mostly done in Provincetown and the Yosemite, are a happy blending of abstract design and poetic realism

ILONKA KARASZ
A native of Hungary, and influenced by the modern Arts and Crafts movement that had originated in Germany, she first won recognition in America for her textile designs and decorative work. In her more recent paintings in oil she reveals, in addition to a delightful sense of form and colour, a romantic and spiritual imagination

GEORGIA O'KEEFE
Her history epitomizes the modern artist's struggle out of the mediocrity imposed by conventional art schools, to the new freedom of expression inspired by such men as Stieglitz. Her work was undistinguished until she abandoned academic realism and discovered her own feminine self. Her more recent paintings seem to be a revelation of the very essence of woman as Life Giver

LYDIA GIBSON
One of that interesting group developed by "The Masses," she has recently attracted considerable notice by her sympathetic drawings and paintings done in the South Sea Islands

FLORENCE CANE
Studied under the academic and "strongarm" masters without much satisfaction. After an idle interim she returned to art, and finally achieved self-expression under modern influences

EYRE DE LANUX
One of the most successful of the younger portraitists, she has worked for the most part in pastel. Her work is possessed of great delicacy and charm

The Female of the Species Achieves a New Deadliness
Women Painters of America Whose Work Exhibits Distinctiveness of Style and Marked Individuality

Photograph of O'Keeffe (top) by Alfred Stieglitz, *Vanity Fair*, July 1922.

exposure once again in Rosenfeld's discovery of her inner being: 'the pure, now flaming, now icy colours of this painter, reveal the woman polarizing herself, accepting fully the nature long denied, spiritualizing her sex'.[53]

At the same time that Rosenfeld equated O'Keeffe's abstract forms with her sexuality, he also opposed her feminine expression to the maleness and 'profound virility' of Arthur Dove.[54] In an article for *Vanity Fair* in October 1922, a different Stieglitz photograph defines O'Keeffe. Here she stands against the landscape at Lake George, wearing a black cape wrapped around her body and sporting a black hat, head proudly held up. She had adopted the black cape that was also Stieglitz's signature coat, now her protective gear. To prepare audiences for the winter exhibition, Rosenfeld dwelled again on her art as 'arrestingly female'. He discovered there an embodied nature, its encompassing spirit, 'the mysterious brooding power of woman's being'. Even O'Keeffe's realist still-lifes could not escape, seen as 'gaping tulips or wicked, regardful alligator-pears' by Rosenfeld's sexualized anthropomorphism.[55]

It was not only Hartley or Rosenfeld who made O'Keeffe cringe with fury at descriptions that made her seem 'a strange creature'. The issue of *Vanity Fair* for July 1922 summarized the achievements of six emerging women artists with the headline: 'The Female of the Species Achieves a New Deadliness'. The page featured O'Keeffe's portrait at the top of the page, in front of *Special No. 21*, her Palo Duro Canyon work. While the copy clearly emphasizes the barometer of rising societal anxiety, the descriptions of the women's work and emergence are factual and impressive. O'Keeffe's artistic work, however, is explicitly tied to 'new freedom of expression inspired by such men as Stieglitz', and her art said to be 'the very essence of woman as Life Giver'.[56]

Had it not been for the deleterious effect that redounded into the criticism and interpretation of O'Keeffe's future work, the aesthetically and sexually charged photographs that Stieglitz created might be known only as nudes of compelling immediacy from a century past, portraits of his muse. Stieglitz's interpretation defined the modernist female nude. But as much as his creative images of O'Keeffe belong to the history of art in photography, these also forced her art and its interpretation into the public arena. What was remarkable was her response, especially after her first showing of her art in 1923. O'Keeffe's emergent artistic project heightened her sensitivity and determination to make her voice heard, to remain true to her inner compass, a lifelong project – yet in 1924 she would abandon the abstractions. In 1920 the U.S. Constitution gave women the right to vote, and the struggle for universal suffrage had been won. Georgia O'Keeffe, a woman of independent resilience, exhibited her new paintings amid competing anxieties about abstract art, gender and the shifting societal balance.

5

New York: 'The Nimbus of Lustre'

In January 1923 *Alfred Stieglitz Presents One Hundred Pictures by Georgia O'Keeffe, American* unveiled O'Keeffe as an artist, again at the Anderson Galleries.[1] With this lengthy title Stieglitz emphatically announced her origins as American to the New York art world, a self-evident declaration that distinguished O'Keeffe among the other artists of the Stieglitz circle as the one who remained 'innocent' of European sources, in sharp contrast to all who had studied in Paris. The artist most surely could claim her heritage 'of the American earth', even as Stieglitz saw her through the lens of his own Jewish, German-educated background. Her innovative work done in Texas created a basis for further abstraction, as did the new material she energetically generated during her first five years with Stieglitz.[2] Certainly she had developed new pathways based on her nature meditations and the rhythms of music, but O'Keeffe also built upon the modernist, innovative techniques around her in the Stieglitz circle, and principally those of the photographers. In a pre-exhibition article, giving her the opportunity to introduce herself and her artistic affinities, she stated: 'I have looked with great interest through rafts of photographs done before the war.'[3] Her high rate of production was exemplified by 55 works completed at Lake George the previous summer. This first comprehensive solo show drew large crowds, more than 500 visitors per day. Many well remembered the buzz from the Stieglitz 'Woman' revelations of 1921. More than twenty of the paintings and works on paper sold.[4]

This cheered Stieglitz enormously, and mitigated O'Keeffe's nervousness about exhibiting the work to a hostile or perplexed audience. It all led to her predictable collapse – she diagnosed herself with the grippe (a cold) and spent a week in bed.[5]

For the exhibition brochure, Stieglitz followed his *Camera Work* practice of reprinting already published material. He ignored, however, his lover's distress over Hartley's enflamed writing, and published the very essay from *Adventures in the Arts* that so upset her ('I wanted to lose the one for the Hartley book when I had the only copy', she wrote to a friend).[6] Opposite Hartley's contribution, O'Keeffe now gained a second chance to write her own words, and prosaically framed her story:

> I grew up pretty much as every else grows up and one day seven years ago found myself saying to myself – I can't live where I want to – I can't go where I want to – I can't do what I want to – I can't even say what I want to – School and things that painters have taught me even keep me from painting as I want to. I decided I was a very stupid fool not to at least paint as I wanted to – So these paintings and drawings happened and many others that are not here. – I found that I could say things with color and shapes that I couldn't say in any other way – things that I had no words for.[7]

Her plain-spoken voice also communicated a startling turn of free expression to those who saw the work as generated from the body, not the mind. The prism memory of Stieglitz's photographs most certainly added a provocative layer to public perception, and from there the critical interpretations of O'Keeffe flowed. Stieglitz's hand clearly shaped the selection of images among the brilliant hues of her Texas watercolours. The high mark of the many letters and her reflections on the night sky, such as *Light Coming on the Plains* and *Starlight Night*, were chosen. Stieglitz had reacted to her *Nudes* viscerally upon first receiving the roll of watercolours: 'several chilled me as music often does',[8] and selected six from the series of ten nude watercolours. These had been experiments, abstracted swathes of colour, made with her own body as model before her Canyon bedroom mirror.

O'Keeffe and Stieglitz found their creative time at Lake George squeezed by multiple pressures. By 1922 Stieglitz's mother Hedwig was dying, having suffered a stroke, and her eldest son reacted badly to her final illness. He developed a heart arrhythmia that summer.[9] Hoping to avoid a potentially fraught family gathering at the lake, anxious for the winter show, O'Keeffe escaped to York Beach, Maine, to paint, stopping in Boston. Stieglitz wrote to reassure O'Keeffe, 'still my Little Girl', even as she was on the way.[10] The Boston Museum of Fine Arts represented an inspiring high point for the artist, as she explored the non-Western holdings – a legacy of her professor Dow – especially Chinese and Egyptian sculpture. She delighted in the sixth-century *Guanyin, Bodhisattva of Compassion*, cut from an 8-foot-high limestone, with slender profile, still touched with traces of paint.[11] That the Asian art had been curated by Ernest Fenollosa, with whom her teacher Dow had once worked, surely prompted her attention. On a second day, she picked out for special mention to Stieglitz the world-famous double portrait of the Egyptian king Menkaure and his queen striding forward, and wrote to him of a painting she admired: 'The El Greco man was a little like you too – very tender – something about the eyes.'[12]

A third long letter details the pleasures of being allowed to handle jade sculptures in the museum collection. Guided by the curator, probably Ananda Coomaraswamy, Stieglitz's friend and frequent correspondent, to look at the jade as symbols of earth and heaven, she let go in a revelatory stream of consciousness that highlighted her mystical side: '[a] sense of oneself lost in the wholeness of nature'. She paralleled William Blake's examination of the grain of sand, as she began with the sand that first shaped jade:

To have created in these little pieces of rock a thing so simple and so satisfying – comprehensive – that one does not ask what it is – a some thing in your hand that gives one the coldness of rock – the smooth warmness of fine flesh – the consciousness of centuries of wind and water and sun and earth.[13]

Once in York Beach, O'Keeffe's view looked directly towards the rising sun, above the glistening beach and across the ocean's horizon. She mused: 'if I didn't feel that you love me – the thing that's *me – myself* if I didn't feel it very surely – I wouldn't have come'. The reason for her worry (Stieglitz assured her: 'I did not love you only as an Idea') returned after dancing one night with the family, and O'Keeffe reminded him: 'I have so many selves.' Softening her letter with an inviting description of her puffy down cover and warm bed, she provocatively added: 'Fluffy is doing nicely.'[14]

Her state of excitement recalled the Canyon period where she had often remarked on the parallels between the wide land and the ocean; now the terms were reversed, and Stieglitz noted her return to a state of wonder, 'like Canyon'. She chose simple materials for working in pastels, and made them in a borrowed room. Once again, she watched the storms: 'wonderful lightning – then the setting sun suddenly breaking through – blazing on all the madness', or she went hiking on the rocks, 'walking up the wilder coast' on the cliffs near Ogunquit.[15] Her passion for fixing the natural energy before her in pastel was frustrating, what she called 'some foolishnesses', and she admitted: 'I am beginning to feel that I might be interested in painting.'[16] Despite her self-scrutiny, the spectacle of *Lightning at Sea* in two large pastel versions, a red zigzag slicing down the centre of a darkened blue-black ocean and sky, distilled her most dynamic abstraction from nature.[17]

The good food and rest at the Schauffer boarding house, but above all her enjoyment and wonder before nature, awakened her physical longing for Stieglitz, and the importance of their powerful sexual connection. Writing about her work, she turned to fill a letter with desire: 'wanting to be spread wide apart – waiting for you – to die with the sense of you – the pleasure of you – the sensuousness of you touching the sensuousness of me – All my body'.[18]

Stieglitz eventually joined her for the last days of her retreat in Maine, and the two journeyed back to Lake George by mid-May. Not only did the 1923 exhibition divulge the emotional, sensual expression of Woman, according to most of the published critics, but Stieglitz's and O'Keeffe's mutual creative exchange became evident. O'Keeffe's work based on music, and Stieglitz's sequence of experiments of 1922, skyward abstractions of clouds above Lake George,[19] demonstrate their closeness at this time.

O'Keeffe had opened herself to nature's sensation, and the critics tried to make sense of it all. The critical avalanche became so intense in response to her 1923 exhibition that she stopped making abstractions almost completely in 1924. Two major threads of criticism emerge in the writings of Henry McBride, a writer gifted in his sense of humour and capacity to write intelligibly on the arcane or mysterious quality of new art, and that of Helen Appleton Read, who had studied at the Art Students League just after O'Keeffe. The curiosity of O'Keeffe's scandalous images and their association in public with Freudian theory led the critics to discuss theories about free association and the release of sexual desires. Though Read approached O'Keeffe with some background and sympathy, she initially wrote as the men did, contending that the new paintings were 'a clear case of Freudian suppressed desires in paint'.[20]

As critic for the *Brooklyn Eagle*, Read headlined her review as O'Keeffe's 'Emotional Escape'. She introduced Stieglitz with his own words; he already bore the reputation of being a mesmerist in the gallery, wrapping critics in his 'impalpable net'. In this way he promoted O'Keeffe: 'Women can only create babies, say the scientists, but I say they can produce art, and Georgia O'Keeffe is the proof of it.' Read questioned whether the public 'would "get" these emotional abstractions' without the sponsorship of Stieglitz and the interpretation of Hartley. The paintings might reveal more than the artist intended, Read allowed, but she highlighted the 'expression of a powerful personality . . . [unconnected] to any of the "isms"'.[21]

For some critics, women's right to vote meant that women artists gained an alarming access to speaking out. Henry McBride's headline, published in the *New York Herald*, telegraphed his slant: 'Free without Aid of Freud, She Now Says Anything She Wants to Say'. McBride cast the bohemian mood of New York, the 'Freudian recommendations preached upon this side of the Atlantic', as arriving early in the Stieglitz circle. McBride's memorable phrases, free of Hartley's bleak drama, ribbed the artist and her public humorously: 'Georgia O'Keeffe is what they will probably be calling in a few years a B. F. [Before Freud] since all her inhibitions seem to have been removed.'[22] O'Keeffe recalled that hers were called the 'fur coat' shows, and McBride vowed to keep an eye on the audience reaction, the many women who flocked to her work: O'Keeffe is 'prayed to by all the super-respectable women of the country for receipts that would keep them from the madhouse'. While he grappled with the abstraction, McBride did not seek deeper analysis, but concluded generously: '[We] have peace in the present collection . . . there is a good deal of clear, precise, unworried painting.'[23]

Curiously, the hygienic image of O'Keeffe's technique jousted with the scrutiny for anatomical symbols that rose in the sexist cacophony. One of the critics in 1923 found evidence of 'the customary duties of woman', saying that her paintings looked 'swept clean'.[24] Nonetheless, the critical voices more often discerned the body in her art, just as Paul Rosenfeld had done before her work reached the public; now another critic described her Maine pastels of the ocean as 'the breastlike contours of cloud and the black cleaving of lake shore'.[25]

When summer arrived, in June 1923, just as both Stieglitz and O'Keeffe started for the lake to recuperate from the art season and the weight of two consecutive shows, tragedy befell Kitty Stieglitz, the only daughter of Alfred and Emmy. Stieglitz's newly married daughter Kitty gave birth to her first child in the early summer, but by mid-June came the news that her delivery of a son had resulted in severe postpartum depression. The crisis reverberated through the family, still recovering from the matriarch Hedwig's death the previous November. Stieglitz particularly grieved, due to the unresolved anger his daughter carried towards him about O'Keeffe, and his inability to repair his family. Not only did Kitty require hospitalization, but the bright chemistry student and graduate of Smith College, just before her 25th birthday, deteriorated so severely that she had to remain institutionalized, diagnosed with dementia praecox, now known as schizophrenia. Kitty's death-in-life illness provoked further waves of intense remorse for Stieglitz. Indeed, his presence set off her fits of rage, and eventually her mental capacity was reduced to that of a child. Though Stieglitz rarely saw his daughter after her institutionalization, Stearns, Kitty's husband who brought up his son, Milton Jr, visited the gallery, if infrequently.[26] For Stieglitz, Kitty's illness put to an end completely any thought of having a child with O'Keeffe. He came to refer to his family, dramatically, as cursed.[27] There are several indications that O'Keeffe wanted children; she had said as much in letters when watching children play or teaching the primary classes while in Canyon. In the beginning, Stieglitz had provoked her future dreams, addressing her 'Dearest Child': 'Can anything bring you peace on earth unless its home & a child?'[28]

O'Keeffe retreated from Lake George in early September to escape the family pressure cooker, after an onslaught of guests, including Paul Strand and his wife of one year, Rebecca Salsbury Strand. Their new friend 'Beck' stayed on to assuage Stieglitz's melancholy, while O'Keeffe considered the residue of her 'first show's overemphasis of abstract puzzles' from her Maine retreat.

She concluded, writing to the novelist Sherwood Anderson, that her 'work would be very much on the ground'.[29] Her restorative time near the sea evaporated when she returned to autumnal motifs of the lake in early October, only to discover that the ailing Stieglitz had rallied with a series of photographs of Beck Strand, her classic nude torso barely submerged in the cold water of the lake. For O'Keeffe, these images not only represented an unwelcome reminder of Stieglitz's flirtations but derived from those that had been her own defining moment, and scandal.

Stieglitz 'presented' her once again in 1924, as the headline of his exhibition stated. For the first time, he paired his own recent photographs with 51 of her paintings. For O'Keeffe, this represented half the number of the prior debut exhibition, still a remarkable rate of production for a single year. Now she exhibited only three abstractions in 1924, and began to explore flowers, an aesthetic approach that expanded between abstracted forms and realism. As she had explained: 'Nothing is less real than realism. Details are confusing. It is only by selection, by elimination, by emphasis that we get at the real meaning of things.'[30]

The energetic *Brooklyn Eagle* critic Helen Appleton Read found Stieglitz's photographs 'perfect as ever', but stopped her review in midstream to state in a separate single sentence paragraph: 'This is O'Keefe's [*sic*] show.' She highlighted O'Keeffe's distinctive voice: 'Pictures . . . allowed to speak for themselves'. Seven paintings of the calla lily dominated one wall, a hothouse plant that became a signature image, defining O'Keeffe as the Lady of the Lilies by the end of the decade. Read further opposed the 1923 criticism that 'caused a public fed on Freudian catchwords to view these abstractions with suspicion'. She lifted up O'Keeffe's flowers as a shield of virtue: 'probably no one has painted them so simply and with an equal appreciation of them as pure form . . . her flair for painting white so that it remains white yet suggests all colors, make them an especially sympathetic subject'.[31]

Read wrote two reviews of the 1924 exhibition, and the second of these clearly followed a talk with O'Keeffe herself. She steered clear of the Freudian shoals, and highlighted 'the only American woman painter who paints like herself, who reflects no teaching or influence'. She also pointed to O'Keeffe's artistic freedom from Europe and her 'innocence'. Given Kitty's tragedy, the melancholy encircling the lake and O'Keeffe's resulting blues from the previous summer, the artist gave Read an uncharacteristically sunny gloss for the last lines of the April review: 'Wise men say it isn't art! But what of it, if it is children and love in paint? There it is, color, form, rhythm. What matter if its origin be esthetic or emotional?'[32]

Henry McBride, the sympathetic but frank critic of the *New York Herald*, drily commented on the 1924 exhibition: 'Miss O'Keeffe did not, as I advised her last year, get herself to a nunnery.' He wonders at O'Keeffe's new paintings of the calla lily, a flower he states that the 'botanists assure us is not a lily at all', where he finds that O'Keeffe is 'finding the secrets of the universe'. He praises a 'yellow that sounds Miss O'Keeffe's new note . . . a flaming arrangement of yellows, very spirited and pure'.[33]

The divorce decree that dissolved the marriage of Emmeline Obermeyer Stieglitz and Alfred Stieglitz came through at last in September 1924. Though O'Keeffe strongly resisted marriage ('I had lived with Stieglitz for seven years prior to that, taking all the scandal', she recalled), the two were married in a civil ceremony at the end of the year. The bride did not repeat the familiar troth to 'honour and obey'.[34] The ceremony with a Justice of the Peace took place at the home of John Marin, in Cliffside, New Jersey, on 11 December 1924, just before the couple at last moved into their first studio apartment, free from the in-laws at last. O'Keeffe retained her maiden name, and all who knew her henceforth learned to expect a censure if she were called 'Mrs Stieglitz'.

Stieglitz bent to the clarion call of the advertising world, opening his next ambitious venture in March 1925, again at the Anderson

Galleries. The comprehensive exhibition, a twenty-year anniversary celebration of the founding of 291, was bombastically titled *Alfred Stieglitz Presents Seven Americans: 159 Paintings, Photographs & Things, recent and never before publicly shown, by Arthur G. Dove, Marsden Hartley, John Marin, Charles Demuth, Paul Strand, Georgia O'Keeffe, Alfred Stieglitz*. Although the exhibition placed O'Keeffe into a direct comparison with her more seasoned male colleagues, there was a newcomer added: the Pennsylvania artist Charles Demuth, a friend of Hartley's, soon came to ally with O'Keeffe.

Demuth stacked the opening room of *Seven Americans* with poster portraits to introduce the core artists of the Stieglitz circle, symbolic imagery of each artist painted on panels in signboard fashion. O'Keeffe's portrait featured her name spelt out in the shape of a Latin cross, alongside a *Sansevieria* (snake plant) in a red pot. The letters 'FEE' created the arm of the cross (evoking word play on the commerce of art, in addition to the Spanish word *fe*, 'faith'). Rays of light from the O'Keeffe cross seared the tip of a blade in the plant sitting amid gourds and a fallen apple.

The 1925 exhibition became an important turning point as a broader circle of the New York literary and cultural world encountered O'Keeffe's art. As the only woman, she recalled: 'The men did more for me than the women, to help me. They didn't understand me . . . but they helped me.'[35] Although Marin's *Broadway at Night* held pride of place in the 1925 summary of Stieglitz's *Seven Americans* on the front wall, O'Keeffe did not gain any such desired spot, nor did she exhibit her first painting of the new skyscrapers of Manhattan. Just two years earlier she had admitted to Henry McBride: 'I don't mind if Marin comes first because he is a man – in a different class.'[36] But by 1925 she felt frustrated by the reproof 'you can't paint New York; you're well-launched on the flowers.'[37]

Her first effort, *New York with Moon*, is not properly speaking a skyscraper painting, but rather a sky enclosed by tall buildings.

She related that it began with a 'sky shape . . . near buildings . . . going up'.[38] O'Keeffe observed radically new urban interpretations all around her. It is more than evident that she stared up at the orphaned moon amid Manhattan canyons to retrieve another moon – perhaps the 'pink moon – nearly full – [that] grew out of the grey over the green sea' in Maine, or the one shedding lavender light over the prairie in Texas.[39] The street lamp casts a stronger white orb outweighing the distant moonlight. In November 1925 Stieglitz and O'Keeffe moved into an apartment on the 28th floor of the Shelton Hotel, and her vista enlarged to overlook the city's grid. When the melancholy *New York with Moon* sold quickly in the next year, 'No one ever objected to my painting New York after that.'[40] Today the series of O'Keeffe's more than 30 skyscraper paintings are judged among the most expressive modernist interpretations of the vertical city from the 1920s.

Following her early declaration 'I prefer to live in a room as bare as possible',[41] O'Keeffe and Stieglitz found that their long months at Lake George for creative work paired well with the services of a first-class residence hotel. The Shelton, first planned for bachelor apartments, had no kitchen in the rooms, but provided a cafeteria and gym for the tenants. The view, unobstructed by curtains, faced north, with eastern and southern views from the sitting room. Frances O'Brien (1904–1990), a young portrait artist studying at the League, met O'Keeffe and Stieglitz in the gallery in 1926 or thereabouts, and found an immediate welcome. O'Brien became O'Keeffe's protégé and long-time friend, and Stieglitz photographed her in 1926 in disarmingly semi-nude wrappings as she emerged from a swim in the lake.[42] The young artist wrote a profile piece for *The Nation* that indicates she watched O'Keeffe painting in 1927, a rare privilege. O'Brien described O'Keeffe's technique in tandem with the stream-lined environment: '[her] glass palette [was] virginal . . . very large, very clean, each separate color in its surface remote from the next.'[43] Two years later, another visitor described O'Keeffe's thirtieth-floor

Georgia O'Keeffe, *Grey Tree, Lake George*, 1925, oil on canvas.

apartment (they had moved to the penthouse) as 'as bleak as the North Pole . . . a cloister or the reception room of an orphanage, so austere was it with its cold gray walls, and its white covers . . . the only spot of color . . . a red flower on the easel'.[44] These spaces would be O'Keeffe's only New York studio for the next ten years.

The series of skyscraper paintings and views of the East River that followed, as O'Keeffe shifted her attention to the towers and canyons of New York, culminated in *Radiator Building – Night, New York* (1927), an encoded portrait of Stieglitz's dynamic aura emanating from lower Manhattan. She paired the new modernist black-and-gold-topped Art Deco building on West 40th Street, lit by floodlights at night, with a red neon light beaming 'Alfred Stieglitz' from the distance of lower Fifth Avenue. She rendered a blue-green brightness in stylized steam clouds and the syncopated rhythm of the window pattern, conveying the magic of the nocturnal New York scene. At the same time, *Radiator Building* presents her only emblematic portrait of Stieglitz, associated with his black cape and his lifelong energy, 'radiating' support to the cause of American art and nurturing his artists. O'Keeffe drew upon Demuth's abstract poster-portraits, as well as the earlier mechanomorphs of Francis Picabia, when she created the *Radiator Building*, a true evocation of Stieglitz's spirit and his full-throated advocacy for modern art and artists.[45]

O'Keeffe's evolving adjustment to life as a liberated role model in full view of an active press – whether depicted as sex-obsessed or housewife 'spotless' – depended on having a thick skin, since her art increasingly became both mirror and magnet for the changing gender roles of American women. Living high above the city became an odd everyday retreat where, as Stieglitz remarked, 'We feel as if we were out at midocean – All is so quiet except the wind.'[46] In this haven within the city, they cultivated new friends in the Shelton Hotel cafeteria: Claude Bragdon, a theosophical thinker and architect, as well as the aristocrat Lady Dorothy Brett. Her friend D. H. Lawrence, with whom Stieglitz began to correspond in 1923, became Stieglitz's new enthusiasm.

Building upon the critical advance brought by *Seven Americans*, Stieglitz committed to his second gallery, the Intimate Gallery in Room 303 (often simply called 'The Room') at 489 Park Avenue at the corner of 59th Street. He opened the gallery officially in late December 1925 with a showing of new work by John Marin, followed in early January by the art of Arthur Dove, who had his first solo show of recent collages and abstractions after a decade's absence. Stieglitz devoted The Room over the next four years to monographic exhibitions drawn from his Seven Americans, the 'six plus x'. He left the last position open for himself, or often, Charles Demuth.

The new literary magazine the *New Yorker* arrived on the cultural scene at the same moment, and trumpeted news of O'Keeffe's exhibition, which opened in February 1926 at The Room. Her first exhibition there led with nine skyscraper paintings: 'For if ever there were a raging, blazing soul mounting to the skies it is that of Georgia O'Keeffe . . . One O'Keeffe hung in the Grand Central Station would even halt the home-going commuters.'[47]

Murdock Pemberton, the *New Yorker* art critic who used the pen name 'Froid', joined the critic Edmund Wilson (who found 'the fierce white line strikes like an electric spark') in using metaphors of light and energy for O'Keeffe's work. Rather than following the tired clichés of sexuality, Froid also discovered in O'Keeffe 'the Emersonian creed of equity in all things can see here the magnificent leveling of nature'.[48] This interpretation of O'Keeffe's vision of unity set a new direction, an intellectual vein of American expression later explored by the art historian Barbara Novak and the critic Barbara Rose.[49] Pemberton, despite some false starts, initiated the turn in O'Keeffe's mid-decade reorientation. The artist explored new forms in her tree imagery, as in *Grey Tree, Lake George*, incorporating elements of Cézanne's flattening of the picture plane. Nonetheless, her curvy, whimsical tree, encircling the greens of the forest pines, remains uniquely her own. Soon she loaned the work to the Société Anonyme exhibition in Brooklyn in 1926, privileging the work as one of her most adventuresome compositions.[50]

From the first exhibitions in 1926, Stieglitz's friend Herbert J. Seligmann began to record his daily 'conversations' with the gallery visitors. To be sure, he praised his artists, but Stieglitz dominated: 'The Room could not exist without the work of Marin and O'Keeffe, and one or two others. But Marin's nor O'Keeffe's work would have existed without Stieglitz. . . . was not their work also an expression of Stieglitz?'[51]

The 'romantic and lucky marriage' that McBride described as part of her good fortune had become restrictive. O'Keeffe took off for two brief trips to Washington, DC, in the winter of 1926, on the invitation of Anita Pollitzer, to speak at the National Woman's Party annual conference. Pollitzer's life work had shifted from art to activism, and she assumed the role of vice-president of the feminist organization. From 1923 the NWP worked diligently to continue the work of women's enfranchisement, and to make the Equal Rights Amendment part of the U.S. Constitution. Pollitzer, her close friend and energetic spirit, kept O'Keeffe abreast of developments and engaged, and her time away was greeted with infectious relief.[52]

From 1927, O'Keeffe also travelled several times to Merion, Pennsylvania, to see the famous collection of Dr Albert Barnes. Recent discoveries in the archives have revealed over twenty letters written by O'Keeffe to Barnes, with his typed responses, dating from 1927–49. These overturn the prevalent view that she did not like looking at art and remained innocent of French art. Therefore, O'Keeffe's later self-mythologizing – both the resistance to the art that she had been taught, and the idea that she relied upon no sources – must be judged in light of her much deeper exposure to great works of French post-Impressionism and masterpieces by Cézanne, Matisse and Picasso than has been known.

O'Keeffe dated her gradual withdrawal from Stieglitz to 1926, as she became increasingly exhausted by the threat of a new love interest in Stieglitz's life. This was Mrs Dorothy Norman (1905–1997), a wealthy woman brought up in Philadelphia, married at a young age, and yearning for intellectual challenge and cultural fulfilment. Norman's gracious, adoring manner imbued Stieglitz at the age of 62 with a new sense of vigour and prophetic wisdom, and her youthful ardour soon became an indispensable aid to The Room.

There she began to organize and document the gallery's business records. O'Keeffe continued to seek brief summer respites at York Beach, and felt increasingly unwelcome in The Room.

In January 1927 O'Keeffe was honoured with a small exhibition of fifteen works at the Brooklyn Museum, her first solo museum show. The *New York Times* critic of the period remembered: 'With regard to Miss O'Keeffe the year 1927 wears a nimbus of special lustre. It was then that she painted some of her most beautiful abstractions.'[53] The powerful, brooding and altar-like *Black Iris* (then titled *Dark Iris, No. III*) was highlighted by McBride as one of his favourite works, drawing him towards 'abysses of blackness'.[54] Other works from the nimbus created by O'Keeffe in this remarkable year were the six views of the Shelton, more than a dozen big paintings of roses, one with the calla at its centre, and dark purple petunias. In strong contrast, *The Old Maple, Lake George*, a ghost portrait with knots and hollows anthropomorphically evident in the tree bark, like eyes or mouths that spoke of mortal resilience, paralleled Stieglitz's own photographic portraits of the trees at Lake George. Stieglitz himself acknowledged the symbolism of his photograph *The Dying Chestnut Tree – My Teacher* (1927), a decade-long study of an iconic tree at the lake: 'A cry of the Human Soul – unheard – alone'.[55]

One of the most monumental callas, *L. K. – White Calla and Roses* (1926), vied for attention with the commanding *Black Iris* and the rest. McBride described the callas as being a yard (3 feet) wide, but this flower extended to 4 feet in width. The calla lily, rendered with absorbing technical mastery and lush botanical forms, also encodes a retort to O'Keeffe's many years of suffering the critics' interpretations – it is sticking out its (phallic) tongue! And the initials L. K. suggest one critic in particular, Louis Kalonyme, whose fulsome prose regarding O'Keeffe's last show appeared in 1926, rhapsodizing on 'woman as an elementary being, closer to the earth than man, suffering pain with passionate ecstasy'.[56]

In sharp contrast to Kalonyme's words, wrapped within the Stieglitzian 'impalpable net', E. A. Jewell of the *New York Times* called O'Keeffe 'a mystic in paint'.[57] He named the chief joys of that year: 'those exquisite small studies of shells and flowers . . . so small in compass and so vast in spiritual content'.[58] He did not interpret her paintings as revelations of sex. By the late 1920s the critics themselves consciously wanted to 'turn off the emotional faucet', as O'Keeffe noted in relief to McBride. Even 'Froid', the *New Yorker*'s Pemberton, observed that the tide had turned so that the urge to release all repressions had become shorthand for yet another intellectual elite fashion.

Life itself presented a terrifying health crisis late in 1927 for O'Keeffe. She was diagnosed with breast tumours, and her doctor performed two operations, the first in August and another in December for what were benign cysts.[59] When Dr Berg advised a third procedure, the artist resisted due to the debilitating recovery period, and decided to seek 'her own cure'. From later letters, it is apparent that Stieglitz was kept in the dark as O'Keeffe divulged her problems only to her sister.[60] The puzzling painting *Black*

Georgia O'Keeffe, *L. K. – White Calla and Roses*, 1926, oil on canvas.

Abstraction, a black spherical field overlaid with an undulating downward curve, represents O'Keeffe losing consciousness under ether, fading into blackness as her arm dropped and the light above her faded to a tiny dot.[61]

Her annual showing in January 1928 followed closely on the ten-day hospitalization with her latest profusion of blooms and an extraordinary number of visitors in the tiny Intimate Gallery. The *New Yorker* noted: 'O'Keeffe has folded up her maple leaves and petunias after a record attendance of eleven thousand.'[62] But in the wake of this success, the tense mood of the gallery, where Dorothy Norman now held sway, drove her away. As O'Keeffe later wrote to Stieglitz, his affection for her 'when I felt very close to you' had waned so much that 'it [her spirit] seemed only to meet cold – cold.'[63]

During her fourth trip to York Beach away from the family chaos at the lake, she wrote to Stieglitz of a terrifying ocean with spray, 'like the manes of wild white horses'. The sea mist over an isolated beach brought her to speak openly of her dependence:

I want to put out my hand to you for reassurance – maybe because I have gone farther into the unknown with you than with anyone else – Going into it alone terrifies me – I would want to go with you – even tho I know I must go alone – I at least want to feel your love with me . . . [64]

O'Keeffe then left the lake a second time that summer, and travelled in July to visit her younger sister Catherine and brother Alexis, as well as Aunt Ollie, who had sponsored a critical year of study in in 1914–15 at Teachers College. The trip back to Wisconsin brought her together with her family for the first time in twelve years. A letter written from the train expressed her anxiety over leaving Stieglitz: 'I have wept a handkerchief wet over this.'[65] Georgia painted barns with Catherine that summer, as she framed their solid rectangular solemnity, saying 'the barn is a very healthy part of me . . . it is my childhood.'[66] On returning to New York, she praised and continued to support Catherine's fledgling efforts: 'The purity of the thing you do makes me so very conscious of the fact that I live in the market place – and I feel the market place marks me quite sorely.'[67]

In April 1928 Stieglitz had announced in a letter to *Art News* that he had sold a group of O'Keeffe calla lilies for $25,000 to a collector in France, thus securing her a new type of press notoriety.[68] This was actually a deal brokered with his old friend Mitchell Kennerley, who operated the Anderson Galleries, then hoping to woo a wealthy General Motors heiress to be his bride, by showering her with O'Keeffe callas.[69]

The decade drew to a close in 1929 with O'Keeffe's seventh annual exhibition. The sinuous burgundy shoreline facing a darkened sea, *Wave – Night*, captured critical attention, and audiences now admired her as mystical far more often, as the erotic, emotional interpretations of 1923 and 1924 receded. Pemberton joked about those who rushed to the 'altar of St Georgia', and McBride pledged to set a new barometer, to listen to many who said that 'she is occult.'[70]

The exhibition ended on 17 March 1929, and O'Keeffe already began preparations to leave for a first painting campaign in New Mexico. Paul Strand's new photography was on view, as the closing show for The Room, and the Intimate Gallery.[71] Stieglitz faced an uncertain future, as he had done in the finale at 291 Fifth Avenue in 1917. Then, however, O'Keeffe had been the expression of the spirit of 291. Now she had become a determined, accomplished artist, and a woman who longed for the vast sky of the West. Stieglitz, at 65 years old, had no gallery for the autumn. O'Keeffe left on 27 April with her friend Beck Strand for the painting season in Taos, New Mexico. Both Strands had urged her adventure based on their revelations of artistic possibility in the West: 'Georgia too would do extraordinary things.'[72]

6

New Mexico: 'I Feel Like Bursting'

Wearied by the see-saw of her relationship with Stieglitz, and
by the vagaries of the art critics who told her (and the art world)
what she had painted each year for seven seasons, O'Keeffe sought
to re-focus her identity and her career. She had felt a profound
attachment to the Southwest from her Texas days. About a summer
break in Colorado and New Mexico with her sister Claudia in 1917,
she said afterwards: 'I was always on my way back.' In late April
1929 she set out for a two-month painting season, but spring
turned to summer and she remained in New Mexico until August.
Stieglitz blamed McBride, 'who steered you Southwestward'.[1]

O'Keeffe and Rebecca Salsbury Strand, known as Beck, made
perfect companions for such an undertaking, and decided to travel
together since each had her reasons to seek artistic adventure in New
Mexico. Beck had literally grown up with the Wild West, though
she was born in London in 1898. Her birth linked Western identity
to the wider world because her father had created and managed
Buffalo Bill's Wild West Show, which performed at Queen Victoria's
Diamond Jubilee. Beck grew up travelling in the rough and tumble
of this world-famous spectacle.[2]

On the way to Santa Fe, O'Keeffe and Beck stopped briefly in
Chicago to visit Georgia's brother Alexis and his new infant daughter,
Barbara June. O'Keeffe did not send effusive congratulations to
Alexis; rather, she painted a cloud-shimmering abstraction titled
Celebration, meant to symbolize the birth for her favourite brother.[3]

After the train arrived at the Lamy station, O'Keeffe and Beck Strand settled into O'Keeffe's favourite hotel in Santa Fe, the historic La Fonda on the square, and on their first day visited the Palace of the Governors to look at Native American pottery. Stieglitz had written ahead, and O'Keeffe found three letters already waiting. She wrote to him: 'Oh I'm so glad I came that I feel like bursting', adding: 'I would like to kiss you.'[4] Within a few days, the two women encountered Mabel Dodge Sterne Luhan at the annual corn dance ceremony of San Felipe. Though Mabel invited everyone to Taos, she had not expected their arrival.[5] This wealthy, colourful figure had first settled in New Mexico in 1917 with her artist husband Maurice Sterne, only to divorce him and marry the Taos Pueblo Indian Tony Lujan. She built a large pink adobe complex called Los Gallos outside Taos.

Mabel Luhan went to New Mexico with the idea that Indian culture would change her life, or that she might change it. Of her many guests, the most important was D. H. Lawrence; she wrote and cajoled Lawrence and his wife, Frieda, to New Mexico, where they arrived in 1923 from Ceylon via Australia on his first voyage away from Europe.[6] She naturally extended her hospitality to Los Gallos, the cultural gathering spot that brought together an extraordinary range of artists, writers and musicians. In 1929, when O'Keeffe first came to Taos, she met Ansel Adams there, who made the photographs that spring for his debut portfolio book, *Taos Pueblo* (published 1930), with text by Mary Austin. To O'Keeffe, Mabel volunteered La Casa Rosita, where Frieda and D. H. Lawrence had previously summered. O'Keeffe wrote: 'there was nothing to do but follow', and the motifs for new work confirmed the rightness of it all.[7]

The artist's reaction to the clear atmosphere of the high desert plateau brought on an ecstatic rush she felt to be singular, a connection to the land that was just hers. At the age of 89 she still remembered her sense of possessing the wide-open country:

'as soon as I got to New Mexico, that land was mine . . . that was my country . . . the air was different – the stars were different the wind was different.'[8]

An early founder of the Taos school, Ernest Blumenschein (1874–1960), felt just such a summons to paint; O'Keeffe's feelings, if unique to her retreat from New York, had been shared by earlier artists there, who had also seen the possibilities of the vast skies and landscape. Blumenschein wrote in 1898: 'No artist had ever recorded the New Mexico I was now seeing. No writer had ever written down the smell of this air or the feel of that morning's sky. I was receiving . . . the first great unforgettable inspiration of my life.'[9]

What made the paintings and photographs of the Stieglitz circle artists different? Marsden Hartley arrived in New Mexico in 1918, just one year after Mabel Luhan established her new home in Taos. As the later travellers to the West would do, he resisted the painting of the resident Taos Society of Artists, of which Blumenschein was one of the talented founders, finding their work old-fashioned, folkloric and too regionalist. Hartley created Cézannesque watercolours of New Mexico landscapes in 1918–19, and admired the Indian ceremonial dances. He wrote the essay 'Red Men Ceremonials' while there, and later painted dark, expressive clouds over the mountains, which he considered a failure. Writing to Beck Strand, he quipped: 'Taos (another spelling of Chaos as far as I am concerned)'.[10]

Like Hartley and Strand in 1926, O'Keeffe brought her modernist eye with her, and at the same time her vision expanded in the context of the vast landscape. Her contemplative focus on the layering of Native American and Hispanic cultures within the desert and mountains of northern New Mexico ignored the Anglo artists in the region. All the forces in her life at the time, the weariness of the city, her marriage and the pressures of yearly exhibitions, brought her to consider how best to embody the deeper motifs of land and culture she observed around her. As one critic noted,

O'Keeffe 'got' the Southwest, because she knew best how to capture 'the living deadness' that the land expressed.[11] It might be argued that her fierce determination, what she later called her 'relentlessness', focused her in a time of readjustment and isolation in her relationship with Stieglitz.

She also built upon the tools and techniques she imported to the Southwest: magnification influenced by photography; her means of unfurling motifs to the full width of the canvas (as in *Black Cross, New Mexico*); her increased use of larger canvas sizes that accommodated forceful shapes; and her tendency to immerse herself in the rhythm and realism of painted nature. And when she exhibited the pictures in New York the following winter, McBride found the new work astonishing, reporting: 'O'Keeffe got religion.'[12]

O'Keeffe's own memory of her second sight of northern New Mexico and her multitude of letters on the landscape recall her state of wonder. Mabel generously offered her a studio across green fields behind the adobe villa. In her painting *After a Walk Back of Mabel's* O'Keeffe transformed the rocks along the path into two monoliths of red and black stone, backlit by strong shafts of blue and red.

She described the studio interior as 'grand . . . so big and still . . . the natural place for me . . . nobody comes to see me – [with] white walls – the floor and woodwork dust gray like the dirt outdoors'. With its monochrome seclusion, it suited her taste exactly as had her austere space at the Shelton. The landscape, however, became O'Keeffe's first studio because she was a sun worshipper, and often painted semi-nude outdoors in the mornings: 'I take off my waist and just cook in the sun as I work', she wrote to Stieglitz.[13] She remembered well into her ninth decade the isolated space between Mabel's house and the field: 'I could always run across that field and slip even beyond that, beyond the bushes where no one ever went . . . I could run across the field and meet the world, whichever I wanted, because the world comes to Mabel's house.'[14]

Georgia O'Keeffe, *Untitled* (*Cross*), 1929, graphite on paper.

The artist had a direct view through the north window to the Holy Mountain, also known as Taos Mountain, the massive contour rising up behind the crosses of her paintings. Several of these works came from the Penitente cemetery near the *morada*, abutting the Holy Mountain, referenced by Lawrence: preparatory drawings for the *Grey Cross with Blue* and the resulting paintings exemplify her many crosses of that summer. Her solitary forms also reveal an odd ebullience, an anthropomorphic spirit of exaltation or solemn power, most evident in the drawing in pencil. In McBride's review, these were identified with special names, one as St Francis of Assisi for its tones of blue, another as 'the Parsifal!' for the largest *Black Cross* (actually painted near Cameron, Arizona), another indication of the individual expressive power that each cross possesses.

The Penitente sect, intertwining native ritual with Spanish Catholicism, originated in the early eighteenth century. They still exist as a religious group in New Mexico, where they meet in specially designed windowless buildings, called *moradas*. Their rites of worship include self-flagellation and re-enactments of the Stations of the Cross, processing with the cross on Good Friday. Their crosses were symbols of the Mystery ceremonies, and drew O'Keeffe's attention. Her enlarged Penitente crosses, hovering over the landscape or swaying sculpturally, became dominant motifs against the mountains and sky.

To McBride in the gallery, O'Keeffe commented: 'If you don't get the crosses, you just don't get that country.'[15] This sent his thought spinning, and he extrapolated her terse comment into his interpretation of the intractable skein between death and beauty in his essay 'O'Keeffe in Taos'. For O'Keeffe, educated by nuns at the Sacred Heart, the crosses expressed the 'thin dark veil of the Catholic church spread over the New Mexico countryside'.[16]

O'Keeffe's Southwestern quest has often been seen in parallel to the literature of Willa Cather (1873–1947), the novelist of the American plains who had stopped at Mabel's Los Gallos some years earlier while researching her books on the Southwest; she knew Mabel's fourth husband, Tony Lujan. Cather published *The Professor's House* (1925) based on her travel to Mesa Verde, and then gained acclaim for *Death Comes for the Archbishop* (1927), a novel that details the historical settlement of the New Mexico territory led by French priests, and the attempts to interrupt the traditions of Native American culture. Their rebellion takes place on the high mesa of Acoma pueblo, during 'The Mass at Acoma'.

O'Keeffe climbed up to Acoma in June: '[the] finest thing up there is a church–very high large white room . . . a gay somber altar . . . the most beautiful room I ever saw excepting 291', she wrote to Stieglitz.[17] The affinities between Cather and O'Keeffe, though they were a generation apart, extended to admiration for Tony Lujan. He served as Cather's inspiration for the character Eusebio in *Death Comes for the Archbishop*, who 'accepted chance and weather as the country did . . . He talked little, ate little, slept anywhere, preserved a countenance open and warm.'[18] O'Keeffe found Lujan a 'noble, quiet presence', and he became her primary conduit into Native culture.

Tony formed a friendship with O'Keeffe based on his need for a scribe to write and interpret letters to and from Mabel, since he could not read; the artist needed someone who could drive, and paid him for the help.[19] Then he taught O'Keeffe to drive. Beck Strand detailed all O'Keeffe's first swerves and side scrapes in letters to Paul, as well as other escapades; but O'Keeffe bought her own car, a black Ford sedan, for $678.[20] She waited weeks to tell Stieglitz, finally confessing that it was the 'worst thing she had done' while away. Beck and Georgia named the car 'Hello'.

On a first foray up to the Taos Pueblo, Tony took Beck and Georgia 'up the river past the most beautiful grove of cottonwoods . . . just a tangle of silver'.[21] From this first visit to the pueblo, she began the painting called *Gray Trees*. Impatient with her first

Morada at Abiquiu, winter 2013.

efforts, she wrote to Stieglitz: 'It isn't really of this country . . . and it isn't exciting.'[22]

Drawing upon what Beck called her 'working fever', O'Keeffe relied on her abstract vocabulary to render the indigenous architecture of the *Rancho de Taos Church*, a sculptural form that also drew Ansel Adams's camera eye in 1929. The site lies 4 miles south

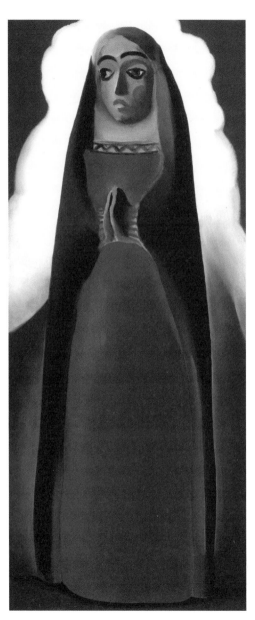

Georgia O'Keeffe,
The Wooden Virgin,
1929, oil on canvas.

of Taos itself, in a smaller village. She started to draw from 'the back of an old church . . . the queerest shape you ever saw and has no windows'.[23] Then the artist rendered its uneven surfaces, re-plastered each year by the hands of the *enjarradoras*, women who mixed and applied the plaster, thickened with bits of golden straw, a form both ancient and modern, made of its place, materials and process. The technique used to preserve the adobe structure seemed to call forth O'Keeffe's empathic reaction to the quality of surface and line. These paintings are smaller than the crosses or the enlarged rocks of *After a Walk Back of Mabel's*, visible in Stieglitz's gallery photograph of O'Keeffe (see page 131). Three oils and a drawing of the church's apse and buttresses against a grey-blue sky were completed by late May. The *Ranchos Church, New Mexico* (see page 14) followed the next summer, with its sky enlivened by dramatic blue-grey clouds; O'Keeffe worked assiduously in a disciplined routine that 'began before eight again this morning' and ended at five in the afternoon. She added a smaller painting to the series, the right buttress shaped in profile. She placed it on her studio wall, just 'a piece of it for color'. O'Keeffe recognized that she had captured the spirit of place, because, when comparing it to *Gray Trees*, she could see that the former 'didn't seem to belong at all and this one does'.[24] This right buttress painting, imbibed from the photographic detail that one might use as the expression of the whole, in fact mirrored the synecdochic method of Stieglitz's photographs of her.

In American art, the affinity for the so-called primitive (tribal or indigenous art) at the root of modernism took a different turn from the European model of colonialist appropriation of African and Oceanic arts, employed by artists such as Picasso, Matisse and Brancusi to strip away old conventions and artistic habits of figuration. Instead, for Anglo-Americans the contact with Native American arts in the Southwest seemed to confirm and deepen the desideratum of a uniquely American artistic culture. Given Stieglitz's devotion to the artists of the American earth after 1925, and his rejection of 'that damned French flavor', he found that his artists' search for the spiritual element in nature represented a core element of American-ness. But he never advocated that his artists should travel to the desert Southwest, particularly O'Keeffe. Now Southwestern motifs had certainly seized the attention of the Stieglitz circle. In search of America, extolled as 'plowmen' and workers of the American earth, pursuing soil and spirit, O'Keeffe joined those who had gone before her. John Marin, also wanting to see the Southwest, soon became the latest art pilgrim to Taos in May 1929. Paul Strand returned to photograph new motifs signalled by O'Keeffe's paintings in 1930, a practice that continued for three summers. He followed her lead in photographing the Ranchos de Taos church in 1930, after her initial efforts, and the Penitente cemetery. The California-born Ansel Adams, who arrived in Taos in May 1929, concurrently with O'Keeffe, would make his debut at Stieglitz's last gallery, An American Place, in 1936.

O'Keeffe found no reason to paint the picturesque folklore or the Native American rituals now attended by masses of tourists arriving in Harvey tour buses. Her technically svelte management of rich colour allowed her to summarize a colourful fiesta of new sights into abstraction, as the painting *At the Rodeo* demonstrates.[25] In July Tony escorted Beck and O'Keeffe to the rodeo in Las Vegas, and on the night they arrived they followed a group of Indians who danced for ready money to a nearby hotel. She witnessed an extraordinary spectacle of young Native Americans, 'two of them practically naked' once they shed their blankets, wearing hand-crafted 'feathers and blankets and bells' and little else. Tony and a friend 'stalked in . . . their handsomest blankets – Tony a burning red . . . the other man in the same red and black blue', and they began singing.[26] She witnessed a staple of Western culture, first the

Native American dancing, and then the rodeo the next day, with its bronco riders and bareback stunts. Taking all the sense impressions together, she swirled ribbons of red, dark blue and green out of yellow into a centripetal frame moving from the perimeter to the centre of the canvas. *At the Rodeo* emits a kaleidoscopic swirl of lighter hues in the centre eye, very like colour reflections around the iris – one unforgettable American Fourth of July.

On the same 4 July in the east at Lake George, where cold prevailed, Stieglitz wrote gloomily that he had had no letter from O'Keeffe: 'morning gray & winterlike . . . fourth morning forty degrees! Iceland's relation'.[27] She had been to Mesa Verde in Colorado for a week's touring before the July holiday, and on the way back she and Beck, with Tony as driver, had got lost in a wooded area driving through Navajo lands. Though she meant to assuage Stieglitz's hard feelings about the missing letters, she spared no detail, writing with a reckless energy of the driving through a 'most pitiless desert . . . with a blinding sort of white hot wind'. They encountered a flock of sheep in the night, where the car's headlights created a glare in their eyes, 'like a moving mass of phosphorus'. And nothing to eat for breakfast but 'oranges and whiskey' while lost.[28] The abstemious Stieglitz experienced these wild tales as fearful evidence that she would never return from her beloved country.

At Lake George, there was no lively gathering of friends to distract him, and he continued to receive most of O'Keeffe's energized news in a state of dismal reassessment of his art, his career and his life at the age of 65. The Room (or Intimate Gallery) closed permanently in late June, after only four years of Stieglitz's increasing focus on the Seven Americans. Forced to clean out his stock, his own negatives and masses of paperwork from the gallery, Stieglitz began to set bonfires that summer.[29]

In a second letter, obsessing over his collection, he suggests a division of all of his best prints between the Metropolitan Museum in New York and the Museum of Fine Arts in Boston. Of O'Keeffe's things, however, he wrote: 'I consider but very few "mine" . . . the "blue and white drawing" [*Blue Lines X*, 1916] . . . That I wish cremated with me.' For the first time, O'Keeffe saw the consequences of her work, and Stieglitz's legacy, endangered.[30]

While camping in the mountains of New Mexico, O'Keeffe received the recognition of her first *New Yorker* profile, 'Abstraction – Flowers', published in early July. Stieglitz earlier described the set of interviews that he had given in her stead in May to the '*New Yorker* man', the art critic Pemberton.[31] Uncharacteristically, Stieglitz did not remember significant dates, nor relate certain significant achievements of O'Keeffe's early career. The first paragraph of the article describes her early charcoals as flower abstractions, sent to Pollitzer from Amarillo, Texas. Thus both place and image were confused with the actual period in South Carolina, the autumn of 1915, when O'Keeffe created charcoal landscapes. Stieglitz re-crafted his discovery tale of O'Keeffe's work with foreboding, when he recalled a warning delivered with the roll of drawings from the artist: 'She said particularly not to show these around . . .', young Pollitzer related, and then: 'she said to throw them away when I'd done with them'.[32] The 'gloomy afternoon in November [*sic*]' and exaggerated, destructive impulse characterized Stieglitz's own sense of self that summer.

Miguel Covarrubias designed the Art Deco-style graphic of an elongated, angled, black-and-white O'Keeffe holding a tubular calla lily to lead the article. The *New Yorker* reported the $25,000 sale of five callas, but said the owner wished to remain anonymous. In fact, the entire story was a false ploy. Here the Lady of the Lilies icon was created, and O'Keeffe would garner new press and more interviews. In writing to Stieglitz she mentions only that 'Mabel sent me the *New Yorker* clipping', indicating her detached reaction to the profile.[33]

On 30 June 1929 O'Keeffe found fifteen of Stieglitz's letters waiting for her in Taos, and he wrote on the following day that he had written 40 letters, 'all forty going into the fire'.[34] By 6 July his pace had not slackened, and rising at 5.30 a.m. he wrote more than 25 pages to her (only the first of two letters written that day!). The long letter begins with an intimate description of an erotic dream in which O'Keeffe came to him in their bathroom, both naked, opening herself to him, but there was a thwarted climax. At the end, he exclaimed: 'I & mine are accursed.'[35] He revealed the equation of *Black Iris* (1926, Metropolitan Museum) to her body, and its centrality for him. During this disturbing, manic period, Stieglitz threatened to take poison to bed with him, and then anguished about his 'mind [that] has been sick', in contrast to her clarity and health, and 'Your gay time in Taos'.[36] Whether she found six or fifteen letters piled up after her trips away, O'Keeffe read them all; often she wrote back immediately, sending a night letter, or overslept, since 'your letters put me in such a daze'.[37]

Her letters gave daily accounts of her adventures, posted from 'any crazy little place' when she travelled to Mesa Verde, in late June, or on briefer camping trips. But O'Keeffe assured the increasingly frantic Stieglitz: 'I have not missed writing for more than a day',[38] by which she tried to smooth over their erratic arrival. The lack of a letter sent him further into self-pity: 'Do you know this is the first time in thirty-seven years I have not had a woman near me to care a bit for me?'[39] To the July onslaught, O'Keeffe replied with one of her clearest declarations of purpose and new sense of energy: 'Now listen Boy – I am all right.' And she continued to explain her renewed spirit: 'when it was always checked in moving toward you – I realized it would die if it could not move toward something.' Finally, she urged Stieglitz not to hug all his misery to himself, and concluded, 'I could not feel the stars touch the center of me as they do out there on the hills at night . . . '.[40]

In mid-July Paul Strand and a friend, the American theatre director Harold Clurman, stopped by at Lake George only to become inadvertent witnesses to Stieglitz's near-breakdown.

Standing over their beds talking on and on, after an evening of lamentations, with 'enough detail in his rambling . . . for a full-scale biography', Stieglitz suddenly broke down.[41] Strand sent O'Keeffe a telegram telling her: 'Your letter this morning telling him you loved him actually saved him.'[42]

Stieglitz, recovering his mystical attachment to her, wrote to O'Keeffe echoing her long-ago wish for him, when she had written from Canyon of the 'space out there which is between earth and sky'. That breathing space of creativity now hovered over the profile of the Adirondack hills surrounding Lake George. His uncanny recall of past events poetically infused his feelings as he described his new photographs conceived in pain and desperation: 'Kitty's illness – your not being completely happy! My vision of forces'. Two of these, called the *Equivalents*, he framed and sent to her:

> In former years I tried to find an equivalent for that trembling something where the hills and the sky meet, the thing you had painted and I have tried to photograph. In place of the hills and the sky, I can see only you and me. I am trying to see this trembling line, that breathing something which is pure spirit between two people. A relationship that is holy. As I see the relationship of the hill and the sky as holy.[43]

O'Keeffe's fusion of nature and the abstract was resolved at the end of her remarkable first summer in Taos in *The Lawrence Tree*, created at the end of July. D. H. Lawrence eventually spent three important years in Taos, due to Mabel's insistent campaign, from 1923 until September 1925. Luhan ultimately gave him 160 acres of ranchland on Mount Lobo, north of Taos, in return for the original manuscript of *Sons and Lovers*, but he had abandoned Rananim, his utopian colony, several years before the time of O'Keeffe's transformative summer.[44]

In 1923 Stieglitz had become intrigued by reading *Studies in Classic American Literature*, and launched a correspondence with Lawrence. Though they never met, the author sent Stieglitz and O'Keeffe a first edition of his most controversial novel, *Lady Chatterley's Lover*, in 1928; O'Keeffe remarked that she enjoyed it. Stieglitz wrote to O'Keeffe: 'There is certainly a deep relationship between his writing & my photographs & feeling about life. – And between your work & his too.'[45]

It was at Kiowa Ranch (Lawrence's Rananim) that O'Keeffe fell under the spell of the towering pine that marked the site of Lawrence's creative work and spirit. O'Keeffe and her friends wanted to visit Dorothy Brett, the British amateur artist, who was living at Kiowa in a tiny cabin on stilts. Brett, partially deaf, carried an ear trumpet she called 'Toby' and wore cowgirl gear; she was one of the few remaining devotees to the simple life of Lawrence's ideal, and pursued writing and painting. O'Keeffe's group rode up Mount Lobo, 20 miles north of Taos, on horseback 'in the rain with good crashes of thunder and lightning – Nobody minded'. They first 'slept up there by the big pine tree' under a sky that turned from stormy to a clear night with its star-studded canopy, so intensely vivid in the high desert air. Though O'Keeffe next bunked in Lawrence's cabin, she spent glorious days outdoors in complete freedom, sunbathing in the nude, all of which she mischievously detailed to Stieglitz: 'Dearest – I wish you could be sitting here beside me under a huge green pine tree on the side of the hill – in my red coat – nothing under it – waiting to continue the sun bath that was interrupted by a cloud . . . a sort of feeling that no one will ever come here – that I can sit forever.'[46] By extension, her work exemplified an admiration for Lawrence's botanical analogies, his bold embrace of nature and its corollary vital sexual expression. Underneath the towering pine, looking up into the starry sky, O'Keeffe gathered sensations of her first night there, and of Lawrence's prose. The artist depicted an upward view to the dark red tree trunk overhead, branching out into an arterial system that shelters the viewer.

Her process of inventing the motif began with the sky, but the next day progressed meditatively, so that she 'went out to that pine tree . . . I just sat and looked at the green in front of me for hours it seemed.'[47] Though she had to leave, on horseback again in the rain, she returned to the high pine in order to finish the painting. Just as she had first seen it, lying on the old weathered bench under the tree to see the sky, so she painted it, insisting in a letter that her painting be installed so that the tree branched downwards. The resulting work, first titled *Pine Tree with Stars at Brett's, N. M.*, defines the commemorative sense of place.[48] Soon after Lawrence's death from tuberculosis in March 1930, during the run of her winter exhibition at An American Place, she changed the title to *D. H. Lawrence's Tree*, memorializing him as the 'guardian spirit' of place. Her wilful disorientation of the view enhanced a painting that, she admitted, 'sort of knocks my own head off'.[49]

O'Keeffe prolonged her sojourn for one last trip in early August, for which she attempted to convince Stieglitz there was an 'absolute' necessity; she dreaded arriving back at Lake George in high season because of the 'absolute relatives'. His outsized grief and turbulence seemed to dissipate, though in part his terrors were mitigated by summer correspondence with the attentive Dorothy Norman. O'Keeffe did not escape Stieglitz's criticism as he wrote to 'My Grand Canyon Madness'. She succumbed to a sudden invitation – 'ten days to the Grand Canyon and Navajo country' – from friends in Alcalde (south of Taos on the Rio Grande), Henwar Rodakiewicz and his wealthy Bostonian wife, Marie Garland. They owned a Rolls-Royce and had use of a Packard, and she assured him: 'I am your child and your wife truly this morning' as she prepared to drive cross-country and 'greet the sky'.[50] The energy of her summer – learning to drive the reliable

Alfred Stieglitz, *Georgia O'Keeffe*, 1930, gelatin silver print.

Ford, horseback riding, and now this last – only fed Stieglitz's anxious anticipation. This became the finale of O'Keeffe's New Mexico adventure: the well-heeled drivers could head straight west, off-road, where there were no fences. With sunburned noses, they pushed on to see the Painted Desert, and into Colorado.

At the end of the career-changing summer, O'Keeffe telegraphed Stieglitz about her return. On the same day, he wrote: 'This letter

. . . will be the last you'll get from me . . . I fly to New York & back for a lark.' He had consented to fly from Albany down the Hudson, the aeroplane ride a gift from Norman.[51] Surviving this, Stieglitz was met by his friend Louis Kalonyme at the airport with the news that O'Keeffe had wired: 'Yes Yes Yes' – she was on the way home. His excited telegram to her, still en route, rivals the denouement of a Hollywood movie. Once he landed at Flushing Bay airport (New York), 'a man came rushing breathlessly calling Stieglitz', who handed over 'your wire . . . Can you imagine my state . . . '. He then took a waiting speedboat up the East River to 42nd Street, so that he could catch the next train from Grand Central. He arrived in time to greet her at the Albany train station, and she fell into his safe embrace, in the green Adirondacks for the end of summer 1929. Both were joyous and renewed and, even better, Stieglitz admired her new work.

The reports to friends on their life at the lake, and new work in harmony, indicate a season of success in autumn 1929. O'Keeffe's return from New Mexico brought an important trio of achievements: the opening of Stieglitz's new gallery venture, An American Place, on 15 December 1929, with a Marin show at 509 Madison Avenue; and O'Keeffe's representation by five paintings in *Nineteen Living Americans*, the second exhibition of the new Museum of Modern Art, which opened on 13 December 1929. Finally, O'Keeffe's important New Mexico paintings were prepared for her first American Place exhibition to be installed by February 1930. The success of the summer's work and her robust health set a pattern that O'Keeffe followed in subsequent summers.

After the richly deserved autumn respite at Lake George, however, with the chance to paint autumn foliage and the excitement of a new gallery, underwritten with support from Dorothy Norman's husband and the Strands, January 1930 arrived with depressing news. O'Keeffe's favourite younger brother, Alexis, succumbed to a sudden heart attack on 7 January, exacerbated by his war injuries in France more than a decade earlier. Alexis's new baby girl had been O'Keeffe's focus the summer before when she and Beck were on their way to New Mexico, and now another was on the way. O'Keeffe wrote a peculiar condolence note to his widow, Betty, admitting that her letter 'makes me cry every time I read it'. But she mused: 'I was sorry to see Alexis marry . . . I thought it would create trouble for you . . . I cannot even say to myself that the things that have hurt me most have been worth most to me.'[52]

Though tactless in her words, O'Keeffe's meditations on death in the landscape became a homage to Alexis at her first American Place exhibition. The painting *After a Walk Back of Mabel's* (1929), with its stones made large like looming tomb monoliths, were captured in Stieglitz's photograph of O'Keeffe. O'Keeffe's summer painting became Stieglitz's new presentation of her 'faraway' self. There the black-garbed artist, wearing a white scarf that falls into a cross pattern, was highlighted as an ascetic, a nun returned from the desert. The abstract burst of billowing forms in *Celebration*, for Alexis, also went on view in the new gallery; it now eerily recalled the gas attacks on soldiers in the trenches, distilling fresh emotion that she could not express in words.

7

The Great Depression:
New York and Lake George

The new Museum of Modern Art, backed by the Rockefellers
and other wealthy philanthropists, opened in rented spaces on
57th Street, New York, on 7 November 1929. The museum held its
inaugural exhibition, *Cézanne, Gauguin, Seurat, Van Gogh*, attracting
more than 75,000 visitors, only days after Wall Street plunged
steeply on Black Thursday, 24 October 1929. Against the odds in the
chilling economy, the fledgling museum next debuted *Paintings by
Nineteen Living Americans*. The place, and indeed the origins, of
American artists in the new museum became a topic of debate, as
did the selection of which nineteen artists represented American
art. As the only woman chosen for inclusion, O'Keeffe represented
all women artists, and her turn to realist subjects in the 1920s
now became linked to her American profile. O'Keeffe's five works
included her flowers, but also one of her most abstractly conceived
nature paintings, *Grey Tree, Lake George* (1925). The choice bridged
her worlds and showed an interest in the integrated spatial planes
of French modernism. Edward Hopper's quiet, melancholy
American landscapes reached a broad public, and marked the
tenor of the changing times. In short, the critical consensus
established a canonical history for modernism at the museum,
giving less weight to the American painters, and thus began an
institutional history with allegiance to the French post-Impressionist
generation that defined MOMA despite the first early effort to
showcase American art.[1]

Stieglitz, who railed against the wealthy Rockefellers erecting such a monument, and ignoring emerging artists, next gained a larger, modern platform for his Americans one month later: An American Place had its first exhibition in December 1929. In early February 1930, exactly one month after Alexis's death, *Georgia O'Keeffe: 27 New Paintings, New Mexico, New York, Lake George, Etc.* went on view. Stieglitz's new rooms, chosen by Norman and the Strands in a new skyscraper at 53rd Street and Madison Avenue, gave *Seven Americans* a white cube space. When he and O'Keeffe first toured the new premises they were pleased with the simplicity of the 'clean . . . unadorned plaster walls, scored cement floors, and heavy frosted-glass doors', establishing an early prototype for today's pristine white galleries.[2]

O'Keeffe faced a precarious future, steeped in residual memories of her own family's financial collapse just fifteen years earlier. She now sought to gain some control over her ability to sell and place her art, always Stieglitz's bailiwick. Her friendship with Dr Albert Barnes resulted in an impromptu summons to join a weekend party in Merion, while her friend from Taos, Lady Dorothy Brett, was his guest in March 1930. Barnes wrote to her: 'Invitation includes bed, board and booze . . . Come on – to hell with everything else!' Brett chimed in with a reminder of the 'wonderful music'.[3] Soon after her weekend trip, Barnes attended O'Keeffe's winter show at An American Place, full of the recent summer's Southwestern imagery, on view through late March. The collector had just wintered in New Mexico, and bought two of O'Keeffe's works from Stieglitz's gallery. But he still managed to make the transaction independently of the dealer, giving a cheque to O'Keeffe for $2,400 (spending far more than he normally budgeted for American artists, or for works by women artists).

In the American Place installation in 1930, the painting from O'Keeffe's time under the high pine, *Pine Tree with Stars at Brett's, N. M.*, recalled her absorption in the literary and spiritual legacy of the recently deceased D. H. Lawrence. This did not suit the Barnes aesthetic, centred on the French modernist styles of Renoir, Cézanne and Matisse, whereas Duncan Phillips, who had purchased Renoir's great *Luncheon of the Boating Party* for his Washington collection, bought the larger version of her *Ranchos de Taos* painting from the exhibition.[4] Instead, Barnes chose two smaller paintings, *Indian Woman* and a still-life, based on his own particular criteria for his formally balanced walls. The vertical work that he called the '*Indian Woman*' (which was most likely *Wooden Virgin*, 1929, visible in the photographs of the 1930 hanging) could be placed 'alongside . . . [his] bright Rousseau'.[5] He then imagined O'Keeffe's still-life to be placed 'over' his rose-toned Picasso, *Girl with a Goat* (Gosol).[6] Barnes concluded hopefully: 'You'll have as fair a show as any artist ever had and the odds are in your favor.' He added a cautionary phrase: 'they will survive or die on what they have in themselves.'[7]

Enthusiastic at first about his new O'Keeffe paintings, Barnes wired Stieglitz in late March, with his usual broad sense of humour: 'Pictures received and although hanged hours ago are still living=ACBarnes'.[8] But by December Barnes had changed his mind. He wrote to Stieglitz, gently stating that he did not wish to 'cast a shadow on her sunshine', meaning that he had difficult news to communicate to O'Keeffe, whom he valued as a friend. His full typed letter to the artist, enclosed in Stieglitz's letter, informed her that the paintings were no longer on the walls.[9] O'Keeffe saw both letters at once, as Stieglitz felt no need to protect her. It was a stunning blow, given the economic free fall continuing in 1930, and Barnes requested the full refund of $2,400 on the two paintings. Barnes's payment had provided much-needed income, and O'Keeffe was forced to write to him about their precarious financial situation – others had not paid their bills. All in all, the fee, returned to Barnes in early January, hit O'Keeffe's income and hopes for some independence at a critical moment.

O'Keeffe's reply to Barnes, spliced at four seams in its original draft with pencilled edits, is a masterpiece of her tact in business dealings. She insisted on her own rights, because he paid her directly. But she failed to persuade the indomitable Dr Barnes to sell his works elsewhere, as was his right. At the height of the drama, Barnes's gloves were off and he let Stieglitz know his real thoughts: 'during the past eight or ten years the American critics have been saying that O'Keeffe's paintings owe their appeal to the revelations of her intimate sexual life.' He admonished Stieglitz with gusto about how best to show proper concern for O'Keeffe: 'If the critics keep on repeating that kind of stuff, you as her husband would be justified in killing the ignorant sons-of-bitches.'[10]

In the springtime, before the year-long high and low of dealing with Barnes, O'Keeffe began to observe the first unfurling buds of the stalky flowers of May at Lake George. She had to face the difficulty of leaving Stieglitz yet again. Now she knew both the sacrifice and importance for her art, the benefit to her own well-being, if she could keep the vital connection in painting New Mexico.

O'Keeffe anticipated Stieglitz's potential misery when she was away travelling, and began a series of paintings at Lake George, *Jack-in-the-Pulpit*. With a burst of energetic investigation, she evolved six variations on a theme of increasing abstraction, the images becoming erotic love notes to Stieglitz, visual reminders that he should not forget all that they had shared. Critics have seen Stieglitz's cape in the unfurling of the purple hood over the jack, and ultimately the abstracting impulse isolated the provocative jack (nos v and vi). Arthur Dove wrote in defence of O'Keeffe's paintings against new, if familiar, attacks of her sexualization of motifs: 'The bursting of a phallic symbol into white light may be the thing we all need.'[11]

O'Keeffe chose to paint 'poor artificial flowers' on her return to Taos in 1930, and again in 1931. Where there were few flowers except cactus blossoms and the nocturnal jimson weed, the calico flowers spoke of the decorative Hispanic culture and the adornment of gravestones and cemeteries. The summer of 1930 also yielded her first paintings of the green cottonwood trees of the Rio Grande riverbank, backed with sculptural renderings of the pink, blue and black mountains – *Out Back of Marie's*, paintings done at Marie Garland's house in the Rio Grande Canyon, south of Taos. This summer, seeking distance from Mabel's salon, though still using her white studio, O'Keeffe took the opportunity to drive her Ford to the Chama River valley, exploring as far as Abiquiu, a remote Penitente village atop the mesa, far to the west: 'I drove almost daily out from Alcalde toward a place called Abiquiu – painting and painting. I think I never had a better time painting – and never worked more steadily and never loved the country more.'[12]

O'Keeffe's winter exhibition at An American Place in 1931 presented 33 paintings, including the series of the *Jacks*, two startling black and blue abstractions with vectors of white, and her recent

Georgia O'Keeffe, *White Calico Flower*, 1931, oil on canvas.

New Mexico images of architecture and the landscape. The foremost poet of the day, awarded the Pulitzer Prize for Poetry in 1923, Edna St Vincent Millay (1892–1950), recorded her admiring reaction to the exhibition. Millay, an ardent voice for the freedom of modern women, wrote that the paintings made her feel 'pretty vulnerable' as she and Eugen Boissevain slowly toured the gallery, but there she felt snubbed by O'Keeffe. This awkward moment was partly covered by Millay's gracious praise for the works: 'I was so happy that day I last saw you – even though you were very cold to me, or hurt me, rather & I had to go back to the One White Cloud for comfort & the apple-blossoms & the shaft of light & the one with the pond or some small body of water.'[13] Seeking a reprieve in O'Keeffe's art, Millay continued: 'I had been at your pictures for one hour & they always remove at least one layer of my skin, so that . . . when I saw you, & wanted to run, [but] my husband made me speak to you.'[14] Millay ended by inviting O'Keeffe to visit her at Steepletop, their mountain home in Austerlitz, New York, near the Hudson River Valley.

O'Keeffe responded with a stunning letter of apology, filling a page with her characteristic calligraphic pen strokes. She did not reply to the invitation to visit in a direct way, but explained away her behaviour: 'My dear Edna St Vincent Millay! I did not mean to be cold – I was surprised to see you.' She described a hummingbird that once flew into her large white studio in New Mexico and became trapped, and how she tried to capture it four times. She summed it up: 'It is that I am at this moment willing to let you be what you are to me – it is beautiful and pure and very intensely alive.' Millay responded with delight: 'Your letter made me happier than I can tell you', but there is no documented exchange between them after this.[15]

O'Keeffe mounted a second exhibition at An American Place that winter. There the bleached bones and skulls appeared on view for the first time; she had shipped a barrel of bones back to Lake George to prolong her summer painting. The most famous of these, *Cow's Skull:*

Red, White, and Blue, came about when O'Keeffe set out to play a little joke on 'the men' who opined about the Great American Novel, and the Great American Thing. She decided to make her skull all-American with a blue background, and added red vertical stripes down the sides. The remainder of her oft-quoted tale delivers a rejoinder to those unnamed men: 'Cézanne was so much in the air that I think the Great American Painting didn't even seem a possible dream.'[16] Where else had she seen the greatest collection of Cézannes in America, if not at the Barnes Foundation? Her immersion in the great collection had yielded no place for her paintings. *Cow's Skull*

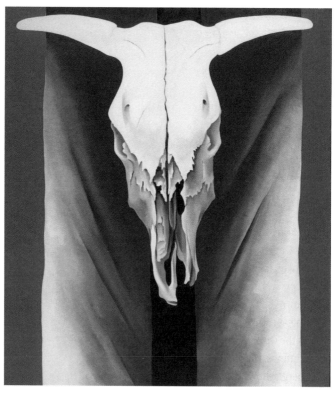

Georgia O'Keeffe, *Cow's Skull: Red, White, and Blue*, 1931, oil on canvas.

created a powerful image for her celebration of 'the Great American Thing'. It may also encode her private rebuke to Barnes and 'the men' for her rude dismissal from his collection in 1930.

During the 1932 season, what must have felt like the ultimate humiliation for O'Keeffe cascaded down upon her splintered marital relationship. Stieglitz put together a 40-year retrospective of his own photography with 127 images, which immediately followed her 1931–2 show.[17] Casting a backward look over his production brought inevitable comparisons, especially when the public knew Stieglitz's photographs of O'Keeffe well. He now juxtaposed the most powerful of his earlier work with images of the 26-year-old Dorothy Norman (seven years younger than his daughter Kitty) in semi-nude poses in bed. It was all a cruel blow. After 1919 O'Keeffe had stopped posing nude for Stieglitz, except for the 1931 series of her slender, elegant form, framed as a tensely elongated torso, from the breasts to the knees. During the summer of 1931, Stieglitz and Norman had escaped briefly to Boston, Stieglitz writing to O'Keeffe to delay her early return from New Mexico on the pretext of visiting Kitty's husband Milton and the grandchild.[18] During their tryst, the renowned photographer captured Norman in a flowery meadow in the nude.[19] With the exhibition Stieglitz announced a late-career resurgence, showing intimate images of Norman. If Pygmalion had sculpted his Galatea to life, now he could destroy her as well, or create a new one.

The Depression stirred up O'Keeffe's sense of despair about buyers who failed to pay accounts, the sharp reversal at the Barnes collection and Stieglitz's open infidelity. The artist slowly began to shut down bit by bit. Her flat affect can be read into the grey void opening at the centre of the painting *Green Grey Abstraction* of 1931. This is the work of which she wrote: 'I remember hesitating to show the paintings, they looked so real to me.' When the owner, Jane Weinberg, who saw her work as embodying the seed of creative force, asked about the meaning of the painting, O'Keeffe 'froze and said only "It's all there."'[20] Once, the high-up floors of the Shelton had provided her with expansive views of the city streets, yielding the innovative skyscraper series in the late 1920s, but now the dramatic vista held a crippling sense of avenues blocked. Seeking any chance to save their sinking finances, O'Keeffe now hoped to find commercial commissions. Once in 1926, as a team, Stieglitz and O'Keeffe had entertained a proposal from the pioneer advertising man Edward Bernays. Both an early 'Mad Man' and a nephew of Sigmund Freud, Bernays was known as the 'Father of Public Relations' in New York advertising, and used skilful psychology to sell artistic designs. O'Keeffe therefore agreed to design abstract patterns for silk scarves to be sold in elite retail markets.[21]

Now on her own in 1932, O'Keeffe sought mural commissions. The mania over mural production after the highly praised Diego Rivera exhibition at the Museum of Modern Art in 1932 had resulted in Rivera's commission for a mural at the Fifth Avenue entrance to Rockefeller Center. To foster new opportunities for artists, a mural exhibition at the Museum of Modern Art was hastily proposed: *Murals by American Painters and Photographers*.[22] O'Keeffe prepared a 7-foot canvas, *Manhattan*, that drew heavily on Stieglitz's recent views of the rising buildings of Rockefeller Center, documented in photographs taken from the American Place windows. The Depression-era-inspired mural project did not inspire O'Keeffe's self-generated imagery, and she contributed to the work with a sketch for a triptych. Critics expressed the general distaste for the MOMA's 'saddest event of this none too cheerful winter'. One questioned O'Keeffe's compositional movement of skyscrapers, curiously scattered with 'a few adroit pink-and-blue roses for color'.[23]

Despite her poor reception at the MOMA exhibition, in June 1932 O'Keeffe received an invitation to paint a wall mural from Donald Deskey, project manager for the new Radio City Music Hall. She signed the contract for the ceiling painting of the women's

O'KEEFFE

Georgia O'Keeffe, painter. Born in Sun Prairie, Wisconsin, 1887. Studied in the Chicago Art Institute under John Vanderpoel; later at the Art Students' League, New York, under Cox, Chase, and Mora. Yearly one-man exhibitions at Alfred Stieglitz' Gallery. Represented in the permanent collection of the Brooklyn Museum, The Barnes Foundation, the Whitney Museum of American Art, and the Phillips Memorial Gallery, Washington.

Large panel (illustrated at right)
   based on central section of Study

Study for three-part composition (below)
   Manhattan

Medium: Oil on canvas.

Page from the catalogue of the exhibition 'Murals by American Painters and Photographers' at the Museum of Modern Art, New York, 1932, showing O'Keeffe's *Manhattan*, 1932, oil on canvas.

powder room on the second floor at Radio City for $1,500 in 1932, without Stieglitz's approval or involvement. The stock market had lost almost 90 per cent of its value in the past three years. She was now willing to accept the prominent commission for much less than the value of the paintings returned by Barnes, or the prices set by Stieglitz for her work.

The first O'Keeffe purchased by the Whitney Museum of American Art, through the acumen of Juliana Force, who did not want to deal directly with Stieglitz, came from her *Skunk Cabbage* series (1927), snapped up for $450 on the secondary market. The Whitney, with its new museum about to open its doors on Eighth Street, New York, and supported by the enthusiasm and financial heft of Gertrude Vanderbilt Whitney for an American art, next purchased two other works, *Single Lily with Red* and *The Mountain, N. M.*, both from 1930, for the permanent collection in February 1932. This time Force agreed to higher prices negotiated by Stieglitz.[24]

The Radio City Music Hall commission, however, appeared to be a way forward, a fulfilment of O'Keeffe's desire 'to paint it big', a means of making public art and reaching for a broader audience beyond An American Place.[25] The women's powder-room mural, by Stieglitz's standard, appeared to be beneath her reputation. He opposed the 'prostituting' mural adamantly, and added that the $1,500 price for the commission would not cover her basic costs. Since this was to be the largest painting she had ever undertaken, O'Keeffe planned a pattern of white blossoms spreading across the ceiling and down the walls. Her green and white motifs would complement decorative Art Deco spaces in the stylish mirrored lounge. She took no time for a summer respite in New Mexico, and argued with Stieglitz endlessly about the project. Friends that summer at Lake George found the 'violent storms' between O'Keeffe and Stieglitz shocking, but she held her position, unmoved.[26]

Then came delays that prevented her starting the painting, with a fixed deadline for the gala opening of Radio City Music Hall in mid-December 1932. It all brought on the spectre of failure played out in the public realm. O'Keeffe could not even get into the 'mad house' at Radio City, where she planned to start on 1 September, nor begin work until mid-October. When at last she began to prepare the surface, the dampness of the wall plastering caused the canvas surface to peel away, and the artist abruptly walked off the job. Stieglitz took over and marched into Deskey's office, telling him that O'Keeffe was 'a child not responsible for her actions' and had suffered a nervous breakdown.[27] O'Keeffe soon escaped to her sister Anita's spacious Park Avenue apartment and waited until the end of the year, avoiding Stieglitz. Their marriage had come to breaking point. Looking back three decades after Stieglitz's death, she summed it up: 'I seldom argued with him . . . He was the sort of person who could be destroyed completely if you disagreed with him . . . Of course, you do your best to destroy each other without knowing it.'[28]

January came, and Stieglitz opened an exhibition with 23 of her paintings from 1926–32, *Some Old & Some New*, including the dominant *Cross with Red Heart*, 7 feet high, painted the previous summer on the Gaspé Peninsula. O'Keeffe's condition did not improve. Her symptoms were an irregular heartbeat, bouts of crying and piercing headaches. Her Canadian cross, and the delicate *Bleeding Heart*, a pastel of two pendant blossoms, can be seen as signalling messages of despair overtly.[29] Here too Stieglitz chose to re-exhibit the dominant *Black Iris* (1926), the painting he identified with her, a touchstone for their erotic life together. This augmented two other strong black images, including *The Wave*, her last from the Maine coast in 1928, and *Black Abstraction*, her painted sensation of going under ether. Stieglitz consciously drummed up sympathy for her condition with a focus on her white paintings, including six of her recent *Barn* painings. He wrote to her frequently, though his appearance at Anita's apartment provoked O'Keeffe's symptoms, and the Youngs intervened to limit his visits.

For an entire year, O'Keeffe stopped painting. The voice of her usually lively, imagistic and evocative letters went silent, and she reported listlessly in early November: 'My only regret is for the way I feel that I disturb you.'[30] She checked herself into Doctors Hospital on 1 February 1933, a private hospital for the well-to-do in search of retreat and recuperation. Dr Edwin Jenks admitted her with the condition named as 'psychoneurosis'.[31] Stieglitz remarked to her in January 1933: 'He understands you & me better psychically than Lee.'[32] The bleak views from the windows at Doctors Hospital convey O'Keeffe's depression, captured in the photographs of her friend Marjorie Content.[33] Outside those sky-less windows, with dank lightwells strung with laundry, there was little to dispel a looming sense of worldwide disaster. Adolf Hitler was appointed Chancellor of Germany that January, and the banking crisis in the United States caused President Franklin Roosevelt to close the banks in February, and to take the country off the gold standard.

While in hospital, O'Keeffe received a caring, concerned note from Frida Kahlo, written from Detroit where the artist had been hospitalized in 1932 due to a miscarriage, while Rivera completed his Ford-commissioned murals at the Detroit Institute of Art. Kahlo remembered O'Keeffe's eyes and beautiful hands, and rhapsodically urged Georgia to allow Stieglitz to take good care of her, having no idea of the true situation.[34] The two would remain friends until 1950, when O'Keeffe twice visited Kahlo at the Casa Azul on a trip to Mexico.

At this lowest ebb of her life and career, two of her younger sisters exhibited their work in the Delphic Gallery on East 57th Street, apparently unaware of any repercussions for their artist sister. Catherine had received Georgia's encouragement on the visit to Wisconsin in 1928 and through her letters. The younger sister, trained as a nurse, had painted for only five years. In contrast, Ida had trained as an artist and teacher, following her older sister's example, and studied at Teachers College after becoming a nurse. In Catherine's solo show, opened on 27 February 1933, she used her married name 'Klenert', but exhibited work in the style of her famous sister, the magnified blooms associated with O'Keeffe. In self-defence, Catherine later said: 'I lived out here in a little small town. I had a morning glory in that exhibit, I never knew Georgia painted the morning glory. She never wrote to me for four years after that.'[35] The wrath of her older sister came down upon the intrepid Catherine, who had left home at the age of eighteen; they ultimately reconciled and often travelled together in their later years. Ida, exhibiting in July with works representing the two grandmothers, used her middle name, also their mother's name, 'Ida Ten Eyck'.[36] The opening review of Catherine Klenert's exhibition that March, while polite, said it all in the final line: 'Georgia Reigns Supreme.'[37]

Nonetheless, O'Keeffe's harsh fury against a once-beloved younger sister and her sense of betrayal destroyed Catherine's ambitions in painting. Stieglitz drummed up sympathy for his wife, holding back little in gallery talks, or in writing to Dr Barnes: 'She is very ill in the hospital.' Barnes responded in surprisingly warm terms: 'Give her my love and earnest wishes for a quick recovery.'[38] Henry McBride praised her 1932 *Barn* series painted in Canada, and picked out *Cross by the Sea*, a watercolour shown in 1933, for his short list of 27 'Favorites' from a lifetime of art criticism.[39]

O'Keeffe drew closer to Marjorie Content, a friend who was known for her accomplished Southwestern photography and images of Navajo and Apache tribal members. Content tried to leave a bad marriage, while O'Keeffe remained at Doctors Hospital, contemplating the end of hers. They decided to travel together to Bermuda for O'Keeffe's first restorative trip. Leaving in late March 1933, the pair stayed at the luxurious resort home of O'Keeffe's Alcalde friend, Marie Garland. On her return, O'Keeffe finally tolerated a few weeks of the summer with Stieglitz at Lake George. Her nerves required that there be no visitors. To Dove at midsummer, comparing Georgia to Kitty's condition, Stieglitz wrote: 'I feel like a murderer.'[40]

After almost a year, the artist's letters to Stieglitz remained brief and intermittent, and still she did not resume painting: 'Frankie [Prosser, the housekeeper's son] even made efforts to encourage me to paint . . . Everything sits here waiting for me and I no good [*sic*] – nothing in me.'[41]

A friend in their circle, the African American novelist Jean Toomer, had also suffered a terrible loss. His wife and O'Keeffe's friend Margery Latimer, a poet and writer from Wisconsin, died in childbirth after only one year of marriage, with the baby daughter surviving. Toomer's fame came from his ground-breaking work *Cane* (1923), known as the first African American novel, one that showed the harsh realities of racial segregation, Jim Crow policies and the lynching tragedies of the South. After *Cane*'s sudden ascent to fame, Toomer abandoned his bi-racial heritage and leading position in the Harlem Renaissance and became a follower of G. I. Gurdjieff. Stieglitz photographed him, read his recent work and sent supportive letters about his new direction in writing after the early success. In 1928 O'Keeffe, visiting Wisconsin where Toomer then lived with his first wife, reported caustically to Stieglitz: 'It seems that in Chicago they do not know that he has negro blood.' By the winter of 1933, the itinerant author, seeking a place to write, was invited to Lake George.[42]

Toomer had also become involved in the project marking Stieglitz's seventieth year, the forthcoming book *America and Alfred Stieglitz*, edited and compiled by Dorothy Norman. Two inscriptions on the frontispiece from the Book of Isaiah and the Gospel of St John set the tone, honouring Stieglitz as prophet. O'Keeffe remained conspicuously absent from the book, to which 26 of Stieglitz's artists, writers and disciples sent their encomia. Toomer arrived at Lake George at the beginning of December.

Stieglitz visited O'Keeffe on weekends at the lake; only at the end of December was he amazed to see O'Keeffe not with an

Studio photograph of Jean Toomer, 1932.

'uncertain smile' but with 'life in her eyes'.[43] It was not that he ended his affair with Norman. Rather, in her own slow recovery she found someone who understood, and grappled with parallel patterns of loss and grief. Toomer's presence, his philosophical bent and his gentle sense of humour in the quiet winter sanctuary began to set her aright once again. The Toomer–O'Keeffe letters, suggestive of an intimacy that tempted both, date from the beginning of January 1934. They demonstrate O'Keeffe's ability to come closer to Toomer while apart, as in her first letters with Stieglitz.

Alone together in the Lake George farmhouse, Toomer continued working on writing projects while O'Keeffe ignored her painting, all under the watchful eye of Margaret Prosser, who managed the household. After his departure on New Year's Day, O'Keeffe wrote to him from the lake of having slept for ten hours, 'feeling very good as tho there is nothing the matter with me any more'.[44] More importantly, she told him a few days later: 'I started to paint on Wednesday – it will undoubtedly take quite a period of fumbling before I start on a new path – but Im [sic] started.'[45]

O'Keeffe's score of letters and postcards record her progress in healing despite a January freeze when her car spun round on icy roads. Toomer had provided the catalyst that allowed her to rejoin her greatest love, painting. Toomer's notes for his novella *York Beach* – which O'Keeffe read just after his departure – written from the same site where O'Keeffe sought respite in the 1920s, draws upon a page of notes titled 'Aloneness' that details his thoughts on loneliness and solitude.[46] As she took her first steps back into working, she responded, highlighting her understanding and the improbable connection between them: 'I miss you . . . even tho I miss you I am glad to be alone. I like the feeling that you are very busy . . . and that you wear the red scarf.'[47]

Back in New York to choose the paintings during the bitterly cold winter, O'Keeffe dreaded the return of her former symptoms as she mounted a new exhibition with no new work. She confided to Toomer that she had chosen a painting for him in the display (*Pink and Red Trees*, 1925), one that long pre-dated their December interlude of snowbound winter quiet. Disarming in her candour, she related her ambiguous feelings: 'I waked this morning with a dream about you just disappearing . . . I was neither surprised nor hurt that you were gone.' She concluded: 'If the last year or two or three have taught me anything it is that my plot of earth must be tended with absurd care – By myself first – and if second by someone else it must be with absolute trust.'[48] Toomer responded by urging her to protect herself further from 'the result of these shocks' and to 'let them flow in you and flow from you without fear'.[49]

The retrospective of works culled from the years of O'Keeffe's meteoric rise, *44 Selected Paintings, 1915–1927*, opened on 29 January 1934 at An American Place. The exhibition attracted 'nearly 9,000 people', and Stieglitz wrote to Ansel Adams that it had been 'a very grand one'.[50] No surprise then that O'Keeffe remarked to Toomer in the string of revelatory letters of that winter: 'Maybe the quality that we have in common is *relentlessness*.'[51]

Leaving New York for the sun and further recuperation, she wrote letters to both Toomer and Stieglitz, from on-board the *Queen of Bermuda*, on 5 March. Toomer hoped to see O'Keeffe on his return to New York in late March; he wrote to her plaintively: 'Your faculty for disappearing and blotting yourself out is quite perfected.'[52]

By the time she considered a return to New York in April, her first painting had been purchased by the Metropolitan Museum of Art; this represented a generous interpretation of summer blossoms from Taos, *Black Hollyhock and Blue Larkspur* (1930).[53] O'Keeffe was one of three women artists acquired by the museum in that year of the continuing Depression, an acquisition for a contemporary collection that failed to flourish there until the post-Second World War period. Then O'Keeffe's eventual gift of the most significant portion of the Stieglitz Collection was donated to the museum in 1949.

The artist remained in Bermuda until early May, while Toomer visited the gallery in early April to see 'his' painting, writing: 'Something deep and rich came to me from the storm pictures and the abstract in between them. An amazing whole'. But rather than languishing for the return of O'Keeffe, Toomer had in fact met her good friend, Marjorie Content. Valiantly, he tried to recapture his and O'Keeffe's special feeling: 'But don't you miss . . . this wold [*sic*] man, namely, Uncle Toomer? . . . My eye, one of them, is on the southwest for a month or so during the summer . . . perhaps some frozen thing in me too should be melted.' In fact, Toomer had recognized that her trajectory led away, and teased her: 'lest one of the bright stars, seeing you, be convinced that you weren't meant for this dark planet anyway, and really completely spirit you to its far regions'.[54]

The last of their exchanges came after a brief reunion in New York, where O'Keeffe stopped for only a day, and then wrote to Toomer: 'I remember vividly that you seemed startlingly beautiful to look at – and . . . my feeling of relief and pleasure in the quality of your mind – your way of thinking.' She ended by giving the new couple a generous blessing: 'I like it very much that you and Margery [*sic*] have started what I feel you have – I like it for both of you because I feel deeply fond of both of you.'[55] Toomer responded with relief: 'you splendid great woman'; and in fact, he and Marjorie Content were married in September 1934 in the Southwest, with O'Keeffe as a witness. She had travelled there with Marjorie as her companion, while her friend awaited the final decree of her divorce.

O'Keeffe's period of 'whiteness' – as Stieglitz's icon of purity – had ended in the 1930s with the unsettling fear of economic disaster and divorce. Out of it all, the pair established a new balance where Stieglitz continued to see and collaborate with Norman (both vowed they would never divorce their partners), while O'Keeffe gained her separate space for painting in her wide world of the Southwest. The regenerative relationship with Toomer, an African American man who rejected his own bi-racial heritage to embrace a search for spiritual wholeness, had opened her to a new sense of healing and to the resumption of her art. Toomer's poetic worry that 'a star [might] completely spirit you to its far regions' proved prescient later that summer as she discovered Ghost Ranch. O'Keeffe sent back a postcard to Toomer, while driving on to New Mexico through Iowa. Joking about her recent trials, she referred to the aptly named Lamb Hospital depicted on the front of the card, 'Maybe we belong here – We don't know but are going on.'[56]

8

Ghost Ranch

Georgia O'Keeffe discovered Ghost Ranch in early August, sleuthing her way there when she spotted a truck marked 'GR' near the Rio Grande crossing. She followed the driver to what would become her place, her centre in the world. Three critical years had passed since she had made the first paintings nearby, for example, her vigorously shaped image, *The Mountain, New Mexico* (1931), one of her first paintings acquired for the new Whitney Museum of American Art.

The affinity she felt for the windswept plains and wide skies of Texas and New Mexico found its culmination in the Piedra Lumbre, the Valley of the Shining Stone. This prehistoric exclamation of red hills and rock formations, erosions from an ancient tropical sea dating back millennia, erupts suddenly 20 miles north of the mesa of Abiquiu village along the winding Chama River, whose name means 'wrestling' river. The Mesozoic Era striations visible in the cliffs at Ghost Ranch, also the site of the astonishing discovery of the *Coelophysis* ('little dinosaurs'), the great-great-grandmothers of *Tyrannosaurus rex*, by Dr Edwin Colbert in 1947, just two years after the war, date from 200 million years ago.[1]

Imposing red rocks indicating the changing geologic rhythms en route to the ranch, looming up along the road like the prows of ocean liners, claimed the painter's spirit as she followed the unpaved roadway along the Chama River. At the Piedra Lumbre, distinctive cliffs of red, yellow and salmon-pink rock surround the desert plateau. The cliff face serves as a welcoming backdrop to the low adobe houses of Ghost Ranch, at that time a dude ranch, about a mile back from the post at the road. O'Keeffe's immersion in the stark, isolated landscape distanced her further from her attachment to Toomer, and set her divided life of months away from Stieglitz into a new zone. She reminded everyone that she lived far from the nearest telephone – she and Stieglitz continued to send letters to one another on a daily basis, but there was no longer the tumult and barrage of midnight telegrams. At Ghost Ranch she began by tilling her own plot of earth insistently, the end of a remarkable year of healing.

O'Keeffe's time painting at Ghost Ranch, named Ranchos de los Brujos (literally 'Ranch of Witches') in the nineteenth century, situated her in the midst of the badlands, the remarkable desert epicentre of the earth's ancient outcroppings. The name of the ranch and terrain evoked the lore of dangerous spirits who caused people to disappear, the tales of the criminal Archuleta brothers, cattle rustlers who first lived there and stole from nearby herds in the early nineteenth century. The brothers, true desperadoes, killed some who came calling or dared to seek revenge for their stolen cattle. The ranch's ownership was rumoured to have hinged on a bet in a poker game.

The Pedernal dominates the horizon to the south and is visible everywhere, from all points on the ranch and even from a distance of 50 miles on a clear day. O'Keeffe said that she knew the mountain was 'hers' and 'God had said so', 'if only she painted it often enough'.[2] The mountain is also sacred to the Navajo people, whose tribal lands lie just to the north of Ghost Ranch and centre on the Pedernal, where the creation myth of a being wrapped in light, 'Changing Woman', first emerged.

O'Keeffe's bones parallel other resolute images of the American enduring spirit during the Dust Bowl drought and the Depression years. 'A bone-lover like O'Keeffe could not have come to New Mexico at a better time', one chronicler of Ghost Ranch observed.

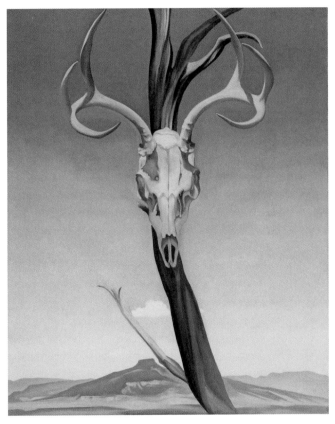

Georgia O'Keeffe, *Deer's Skull with Pedernal*, 1936, oil on canvas.

'In the mid-1930s . . . drought claimed countless wild and domestic animal lives . . . bones – bleached to a gleaming white, or still covered with tendons and bloodied fur – were as easy to find as the ravens who fed upon them.'[3] As her attachment to the desert's living emptiness grew, the artist began to paint bones.

With the first skulls she picked up near Taos, whether painted against blue cloth or Indian blankets, she whimsically chose to stick a calico flower in the horse skull's eye socket. The calico flowers led

her to comment later: 'the rose in the eye looked pretty fine.'[4]
Horse's Skull with Pink Rose (1931), illustrated in colour, celebrated
her desert lifestyle in a *Life* magazine article, though a subsequent
page with photos of Stieglitz, and a tiny O'Keeffe atop her penthouse
terrace against the East River, bore the title 'Alfred Stieglitz Made
O'Keeffe Famous'.[5]

In her third summer at Ghost Ranch, O'Keeffe began painting
skulls with antlers and started to float them above the landscape.
Two paintings of the same 'very delicate little deer's skull' that
O'Keeffe associated with the memory of an abandoned house
present very different moods. The flower tribute of *Summer Days*
(1936, Whitney Museum) transports the viewer up to celebratory
clouds, whereas the sombre, monumental impact of *Deer's Skull
with Pedernal* offers a stark grounding.[6] Anchored to the tree
whose lower branch parallels the immutable profile of the Pedernal
on the distant horizon, *Deer's Skull* evokes a sacrifice that draws
upon the spirit of the Cross at Golgotha. The artist's rendering
of bright sunlight, sculpting shadow across the turning antlers,
ennobles the tragic image. Both paintings, each in its way, convey
a sense of memento mori. The tender gesture of red Indian paint-
brush and yellow sunflowers, visible in *Summer Days*, adds the
memory of the many brilliant floral watercolours by O'Keeffe's
friend the painter Charles Demuth, who died the previous year.

However explicitly the bones may seem to meditate on the great
themes of death and transcendence, O'Keeffe denied that they were
about death, and she did not want to be called a Surrealist. Henry
McBride, noting the recent turn toward skulls, wrote 'Mourning
Becomes Georgia' as the leitmotif for her annual exhibition in 1932.
But she claimed no affinity with Surrealism, though she contributed
Cow's Skull: Red, White, and Blue (1931) to the Museum of Modern
Art's first comprehensive exhibition of Surrealist and Dada art in
1936.[7] She resisted that label, and all others. While certain of the
skull motifs suggest the disjunction of dreams, the images rest more

Pan-Yo-Pin (Tomás Vigil, Tesuque Pueblo), *Deer Dancer, c.* 1925–30, watercolour.

firmly in her awareness of a growing Native American watercolour tradition, sparked by anthopological interest and exhibitions documenting Native American ritual.[8]

Gathering together the force of nature and culture in the landscape, O'Keeffe's work lifted the antlers to a place of suspended time and meditation. Her third variation in the bones series began in the 1940s, with trial and error. O'Keeffe began to pick up neglected pelvis bones from the Ghost Ranch patio, and looked through the hip sockets into the deep blue sky. Just as she showed a visitor, she found new designs there, even painting the mice-chewed edges of the pelvis bone.[9]

This unsparing confrontation changed quickly into the sculptural surfaces that turned, or danced against, the blue sky above. O'Keeffe explained: 'it never occurs to me that the bones have anything to do with death . . . they were quite lively.'[10] Daniel Catton Rich, curator at the Art Institute of Chicago, pushed further, and described the bones as symbols of 'concrete immortality' that 'outlast death itself'.[11]

O'Keeffe could not foresee the future, but her instincts for painting the bones left by the ravages of severe drought proved more prescient than she could have imagined. A decade later, in 1947, a remarkable dinosaur trove – the greatest find of early dinosaurs in the continental United States – was uncovered, bringing new visitors and general excitement to Ghost Ranch in the post-war period. O'Keeffe could not escape the importance of bones in her world.

The palaeontologist Dr Edwin 'Ned' Colbert, curator of fossil reptiles at the Museum of Natural History in New York, stopped at Ghost Ranch for a brief rest on the way to a planned summer's fossil expedition at the Petrified Forest in Arizona. One morning after breakfast he took a stroll with museum colleagues into the nearby hills above the ranch compound. There his associate uncovered the first tiny claw, a sign that led to the source of millennia-old buried bones, an enormous quantity of the articulated skeletons of the earliest Triassic dinosaurs, the 200-million-year-old *Coelophysis*. Colbert marvelled at the yield hidden in the Chinle formation – the brilliant red sandstone cliffs that lined so many of O'Keeffe's paintings. The grey gypsum rock, a softer, constantly eroding formation that partially covered the bones, is also the last layer of the Cretaceous-period formation of the top coating 'skyline' at Ghost Ranch. The geological vertical display of prehistoric epochs is revealed everywhere on the Ranch, and O'Keeffe also painted a 'portrait' of the layered cliff face that pushes up to a thin edge of sky in *Cliffs Beyond Abiquiu – Dry Waterfall* (1943).

The *Coelophysis* bones, of prehistoric antiquity compared to O'Keeffe's skulls, made Colbert's national reputation, and became his life's work. O'Keeffe, of course, wanted to visit this amazing field of discovery, about 3 miles from her house, as soon as possible. She gained permission from the scientists, and on 29 July 1947 visited the newly staked out site.[12] A tent, then a wooden frame, was erected over the excavation site where the brittle bones were immediately treated for conservation as they emerged from the earth. Colbert also observed the colours that 'almost defy belief', the same that O'Keeffe herself painted and credited as 'all the colors of the painter's palette', out there in the desert. Her behaviour was aloof, but it was logical that O'Keeffe and Colbert would become friends, though she never painted the *Coelophysis* bones. Colbert also avoided discussing art with her, and observed that 'she erected a psychological shield around herself' in order to maintain her privacy. He recalled that 'she was full of questions about geology, about the colored rocks that surrounded her, and about specimens that she had picked up during the course of her walks.'[13]

Dr Colbert recorded O'Keeffe's next visit to the site with a photograph of the artist and her friends. She returned, and brought a group of four 'jolly nuns . . . from Abiquiu, and two from Ohio', their long skirts folded into a jeep.[14] When the *Life* photographers arrived in August to document the site for a feature article, the copy trumpeted 'one of the most important dinosaur finds in the history of paleontology'.[15]

O'Keeffe, often implacable in her demands, began to rent Pack's house in the summer season of 1937 but still relied on the ranch's services of water, the kitchen garden and the cowhands. Now that O'Keeffe's windows faced squarely onto the majestic Cerro Pedernal to the southwest, her visual world became a panoramic palette of desert vista, while to the northeast were the purples, pinks and yellows of the high Jurassic-period cliffs.

The California-born photographer Ansel Adams came to the ranch in 1937, just a year after his debut exhibition at An American Place. Stieglitz had suffered his most debilitating heart attack earlier that year, and after a lifetime photographing people, his world and the sky above, the tireless, innovative photographer was forced to lay down his heavy camera equipment at last.

As Adams documented O'Keeffe's bone obsession for a national profile in *Life* that appeared in February 1938, he captured a rare, wide smile as she showed off the prize of a massive bleached vertebral column, with ribcage still attached, while in the other hand she grasped the horn of a fur-covered steer's head.[16] This image circulated to document her rough-and-ready Western life, and O'Keeffe's exploration of landscape and bones became exemplary of the national devotion to homeland during the years of the rise of fascism, an affirmation as the wartime horrors soon mounted in the same news-weekly pages.

She called her place in New Mexico the 'Faraway' and Stieglitz often wrote to her as 'my Faraway One'. In 1937 she painted a magnificent, almost impossibly complex deer antler rack in *From the Faraway, Nearby*, one of her best-loved images of the magnificent bones. Her patio at the Ghost Ranch house was littered with many skulls and bones, many of which were gifts to her from the cowboys who worked there. Towering antlers marked O'Keeffe's space as she later installed a sculptural elk rack in the *zaguan*, or passageway, to her Abiquiu house.

She prepared her own annual exhibition statement for An American Place in 1939, a rare opportunity to tell her story. She effectively wrote to deflect the prevalent interpretations of those who saw her as obsessed with death, and McBride so enjoyed her new poetic voice that he quoted her words in his review:

I have wanted to paint the desert and I haven't known how. So I brought home my bleached bones as symbols of the desert . . . The bones seem to cut sharply to the center of something that is keenly alive on the desert even tho' it is vast and empty and untouchable – and knows no kindness with all its beauty.[17]

While on the trail of new motifs in the Southwest, O'Keeffe used her Ford car as a mobile studio; the seats could be turned around, and served as easels for the largest canvases. In Ansel Adams's photo of O'Keeffe painting *Gerald's Tree*, the artist is at work in the back seat of her car. He excelled in capturing her unconventional methods of work, whether carrying her desert bones, sketching above the rocky formation of Canyon de Chelly or not working, as in Yosemite.

O'Keeffe's output of landscape paintings increased dramatically at the ranch, because the solitary artist hiked so often in the wide-open spaces of desert and canyon, seeking new motifs and views. In one of her daily letters to Stieglitz, she sketched her pattern: 'I was up early – painted all day – out in the car from 7 to 11 . . . just some red hills'.[18] The lower red hills of the Chinle formation fill many canvases of this period. She often obliterated the sky (as in *Gerald's Tree*), filling the background with the pink and red Jurassic rock, and the viewer cannot miss the point of ancient geology often paired with palaeontology.

The Cerro Pedernal is the knife-edged flat-topped mountain O'Keeffe made famous in her many paintings, rising high above the desert plateau. Turning towards the south, she began to paint the *cerillo* or 'knife' profile of the Pedernal, a mountain that the artist could hardly have failed to equate with the great Mont Sainte-Victoire so famously rendered in multiple canvases by Paul Cézanne, especially given her many visits to the Barnes Foundation.[19] O'Keeffe at times would paint the mountain as emphatic centring presence on the horizon, as it buttresses the dead tree in *Deer's Skull*. The large pastel *Pedernal* (1945) centres an uncanny abstracted altar of mountain, bone, sky: a perfectly symmetrical pink arc of the pelvis bone cups the sky beyond Pedernal, a peaceful centre in the horrific last year of war.[20]

The many examples recall O'Keeffe's love of Asian art from her earliest years. She owned a nineteenth-century edition of Katsushika Hokusai's *Thirty-six Views of Mount Fuji*.[21] The Japanese artist, self-styled as 'The Old Man Mad with Painting', explored the great mountain, both large and small, in strength or in sly glimpses. O'Keeffe never presented her Pedernal paintings as a series, to be sure, but her daily view absorbed its abiding presence. The mountain, whether inconspicuously small or central to the pictorial field, appeared as signature, symbol, witness.

Trips from the 'Faraway' to other remarkable places became possible in the late 1930s. O'Keeffe's friendship in New York with David McAlpin began at a New York dinner party given in her honour in 1928, and continued for more than twenty years. Later, according to McAlpin's account, she introduced him to Ansel Adams in 1933, and the two men became lifelong friends.[22] To O'Keeffe, McAlpin 'was a treasure' because 'the Art world was just a foreign country to him' (even if her statement overlooks his critical role in founding the Department of Photography at the Museum of Modern Art).[23] McAlpin and Adams planned trips in the summers of 1937 and 1938 that included O'Keeffe, and their first outdoor trip covered ancient sites in Colorado and Arizona.

Yosemite in 1938 was their next destination, and O'Keeffe, McAlpin and his Rockefeller cousins Godfrey and wife Helen joined the team, primed for roughing it. Adams reported their set-up for outdoor camping: 'We leave tomorrow morning for the high mountains, about fourteen mules, guide, packer, cook, much food, warm bedding, photographic equipment and great expectations in general.'[24] O'Keeffe prepared for a scenic vista quite different from the prehistoric formations of Ghost Ranch. As Adams remarked: 'there is no human element in the High

Sierra.'[25] He need not have worried: she understood the raw power of place, but Yosemite was a sheer beauty apart, and Adams's photography defined that place. It was not hers, and she did not bring along her sketching pad. If disappointed, Adams put the best face on her reaction: 'Her work remained centered in her beloved New Mexico and this was a true vacation, a change in visual experience.'[26] He wrote to Stieglitz about O'Keeffe's excited reactions on entering Yosemite at dusk, 'a very favorable hour': 'she was practically raving.'[27] Adams made individual portraits of the five travellers, and they all considered her 'a good sport'.[28] For hers, O'Keeffe sat in profile with her back straight against a massive tree trunk. Adams prepared three copies of the handmade book for his friends; it featured 48 of his world-class photographs, hand-mounted on 42 pages and laced together with brown cord. His interpretations of the austere beauty that O'Keeffe found so compelling became a scrapbook first for friends, now for posterity.

In sharp contrast to the Ghost Ranch bones, O'Keeffe took on a new commission to travel to Hawaii in the winter of 1939, and accepted a contract to paint two works of plants for Dole Pineapple Company. She would not regret it, as she wrote to Adams: 'I often think of that trip at Yosemite as one of the best things I have done – But Hawaii was another.'[29]

O'Keeffe had become exhausted with her duties at Lake George in the summer of 1938, after Stieglitz's second heart attack and continuing illness, but she did not leave him to travel west until September. Her role as principal breadwinner was becoming explicit to them both. She considered the commission for an all-expense-paid trip to Hawaii, and in fact the work created there marked a brief return to flowers, with twenty new paintings in her 1940 exhibition.

Her long voyage out to Hawaii began by train to San Francisco, across the country in late January 1939, and then by ship to Honolulu on 8 February. The celebrated artist was greeted and adorned with red, coral, pink and white flower leis.[30] She soon toured the Dole plantation, and was spellbound while driving past the 'sharp and silvery leaves of the [pineapple fields] stretching for miles off to the beautiful irregular mountains . . . I was astonished.'[31] But Dole sent a 'manhandled' pineapple to her hotel, creating a misunderstanding since O'Keeffe stubbornly hoped to work near the fields and observe the workers' process. She took a detour to Maui in early March, staying near the Ka'eleku Sugar Plantation, a paradise for painting with its lava rock beaches. O'Keeffe's sojourn on Maui was enhanced by receiving the solicitous attention of her hosts, the Jennings, both father and daughter, who arranged expeditions along the coast and up to the Haleakala volcano. There they rose before 4 o'clock to see the sun rise from the volcano crater, above Wailuku on the far shore of the island. To Stieglitz she confessed: 'I sit up nights talking with Mr Jennings when I might be writing but he is interesting.'[32] With his daughter, Patricia, O'Keeffe's pleasures centred on a shared love of perfect black stones chosen from the river bed, called Pele's tears after the volcano goddess. The child hid hers on a rocky ledge in the grotto, and cautioned Georgia that the fiery spirit would take revenge if her stones were ever removed.

The artist left the Hawaiian Islands in April with twenty new works, but without completing a pineapple painting. This resistance to the commissioned pineapple became a point of contention with the Dole Pineapple Company on her return to New York, since O'Keeffe insisted that, contractually, she had a free choice of plant subjects, and offered a painting of the papaya tree (their rival). The Ayer advertising company eventually, within 36 hours, shipped a pineapple plant in bud to O'Keeffe's New York apartment.[33] She completed the composition, recalling her first glimpse in the field: 'When it is little and you look down into it as I did into the corn when I painted it – it is very handsome.'[34] In the end, the work she exhibited the following year pleased the critics enormously. Works

Georgia O'Keeffe, *Jimson Weed*, 1936, oil on linen.

with titles such as *Silver Cup of Ginger* and *Belladonna* refer to herbal properties of the flowers as well, and seem to exude health.

Forced to leave Stieglitz once again or to choose the Southwest, O'Keeffe continued to seek a balance after 1940. Her nerves vanished and her appetite returned in the Southwest, while in New York her painting sales were more than plentiful. The commission of a mural titled *Jimson Weed* in 1936, for Elizabeth Arden's Sports Salon on Fifth Avenue, negotiated between Arden and Stieglitz, is a case in point. Another painting followed for Arden herself, the commission for a *White Camellia* two years later.[35] *Jimson Weed*, also known as loco weed, or the noxious datura flower, had its own distinctive appeal. To O'Keeffe's eye, a profusion of the white flower became a signature motif of the late 1930s, as she literally counted 125 blooms one night, all in her sagebrush-covered patio.

O'Keeffe, eschewing make-up while doing business with Arden, the cosmetics queen, had become reliant on Stieglitz's insistence on securing high prices as the Depression wore on. The artist, concerned both for her own future and for Stieglitz as his health declined, purchased the Ranchos de los Burros house for $3,000 in 1940. Stieglitz, indifferent to possessions and always circling back to his inherited family home at Lake George, had never owned a home of his own in the midst of their busy art lives. He replied to her after she wrote about the purchase of the Ghost Ranch house: 'You have finally achieved a dream of yours – may be your chief dream.'[36] Once it was hers, she painted summer and autumn views of the dominant Pedernal opposite the southern exposure of her house, titling a new work *My Front Yard*.[37] The inconsequential place of humankind in the high desert remains encoded in her people-less vista. She was in her element: 'Sometimes I think I'm half-mad with love for this place.'[38]

As the terror of the Nazis invading Eastern European countries, the surrender of France and the nightly Blitz over Britain continued, another theatre of war burst over the United States from Japan, with the bombing of the U.S. naval fleet at Pearl Harbor on 7 December 1941. O'Keeffe's fantasy of a return to her beautiful Hawaii evaporated. Even before the attack, she wrote to the child Patricia who had charmed her in in Hawaii: 'we seem so aware of the war here that the States seem the best place to be.'[39] War brought back harsh memories, too sharp for words – the cost of her brother's life and the young students she lost to the war effort in 1917–18. O'Keeffe was at heart a pacifist. As her paintings shifted from skulls and mountains to pelvis bones against the blue, she seemed intent on seizing the eternal solitude of the desert.

Back in New York, she made sure that Stieglitz had more comfortable quarters than their Sutton Place penthouse near the East River, too cold for him and too many blocks away from his gallery. In October 1942, when Stieglitz was 80 years old, the pair moved for the last time to live at 59 East 54th Street, one block away from An American Place. Once Stieglitz had resettled, O'Keeffe continued to make the summer pilgrimage to her western home, but hardly indulged in creature comforts. The house had no running water and had a hand-cranked generator, and the nearest post box was a mile away.[40]

The Art Institute of Chicago retrospective of 61 paintings and drawings, her first in a civic museum, opened in 1943, arranged by the curator Dan Rich. The exhibition generated a new height of publicity for O'Keeffe. She also received her second honorary doctorate of letters from the University of Wisconsin, the first having been awarded by the College of William and Mary in 1938, where Francis, her eldest brother, had attended college decades earlier. O'Keeffe and Stieglitz arranged a choice exhibition of eight paintings to be sent to Virginia in 1938, since Abby Aldrich Rockefeller had donated her O'Keeffe painting, *White Magnolia*, to the College, her alma mater.[41] All three honours taken together reflected her growing fame in the state of her birth, Wisconsin, the state of her girlhood education, Virginia, and finally in Chicago, the city of her first art training in Vanderpoel's anatomy class in 1906, where she had studied as a young woman in the School of the Art Institute, and now returned to be celebrated, four decades later.

For the Chicago exhibition, Stieglitz requested an unusual part of the deal, that the Art Institute purchase one O'Keeffe painting. Without a quibble, Dan Rich chose *Black Cross, New Mexico* from the summer of 1929, when she first had met Rich at Mabel's house in Taos. The *Chicago Tribune* accompanied its review with a double-page spread of colour images, and praised not only her artistic achievements (the museum's press release called her 'the most famous woman painter in the world') but the financial heights she had reached, reporting that one work sold for $10,000 [*sic*].[42]

Rich had great admiration for O'Keeffe, and accommodated her involvement in the installation, allowing the gallery's pale violet walls to be changed to a clean white. He gave her work its first scholarly catalogue essay, detailing her 'great contribution to the development of a native art in this country'.[43] And as so often occurred with her annual openings, she worked herself to exhaustion. Stieglitz reported: 'had she known that she'd have a breakdown after the exhibition she would have gone right ahead.'[44] O'Keeffe missed the opening celebration, downed by the common cold.

O'Keeffe's success in Chicago and time in the Midwest allowed time to meet with fellow Wisconsinite Frank Lloyd Wright. Out of her admiration for his architecture she created an abstraction from her new work that followed her retrospective, *Pelvis with Shadows and the Moon*.[45]

Among the new works of 1943, *Pelvis with Pedernal* and *Pelvis with the Distance* created a spirited mood even lighter than the antlers. O'Keeffe seized new energy, generated more variations on the *Pelvis* series and showed these new bones in her American Place exhibition of 1944. Rich, astonished by the new production, published an article about the nineteen new paintings that appeared in New York after her Art Institute exhibition, writing: 'She is like no one else – a highly original and intuitive mind.'[46] Others praised the 1944 exhibition at An American Place as 'O'Keeffe's Best'. Her 'handling of *matière*' and emphasis on the 'huge pelvis bones of these animals bleached and desiccated into a remarkable texture' delighted another critic, who became lost in 'deep, dazzling blue sky . . . an infinity of space', though later critics found the pelvis symbolic of her state of childlessness, continuing to project sexual interpretations onto bones. In this period, the *Black Place* paintings continued, inspired by hills of lava-like formation. The black and grey rock '[was] not a black landscape at all, but a subtle play with pink and white layering that define the solidity of massive forms', wrote the critic

Margaret Breuning, who asserted that the *Black Place* works alone established O'Keeffe's 'distinction as an artist'.[47]

O'Keeffe's 1944 catalogue statement 'About painting desert bones' describes her work's origin and deeply held pacifism, all in her spare and succinct prose:

> For years in the country the pelvis bones lay about the house indoors and out seen and not seen as such things can be – seen in many different ways. I do not remember picking up the first one but I remember from when I first noticed them always knowing I would one day be painting them. I was the sort of child who ate around the raisin on the cookie and ate around the hole in the doughnut saving either the raisin or the hole for the last and best. So probably – not having changed much – when I started painting the pelvis bones I was most interested in the holes in the bones – what I saw through them

Georgia O'Keeffe, *Pelvis with the Distance*, 1943, oil on canvas.

– particularly the blue from holding them up in the sun against the sky as one is apt to do when one seems to have more sky than Earth in one's world – They were most wonderful against the Blue – that Blue that will always be there as it is now after all man's destruction is finished.[48]

O'Keeffe found the more distant, remote Black Place near Nageezi, about 150 miles straight into the west on the road towards the ancient site of Chaco Canyon, with the assistance of Orville Cox in 1935. She recalled first seeing the Black Place 'driving past into the Navajo country . . . It became one of my favorite places to work.' To the artist, the Black Place first looked like 'like a mile of elephants – grey hills all about the same size with almost white sand at their feet . . . with surfaces evenly cracked so walking and climbing are easy'. Getting there and surviving the harsh weather conditions, by sweeping away snow from the campsite or roasting venison wrapped in bacon, presented real challenges.[49] This became the duty of her trusted friend Maria Chabot, who tended to O'Keeffe's camping and tough insistence on braving both summer heat and bitter cold. The low mountains of the Black Place shelter the site believed to be home to the Anasazi, the most ancient peoples of the Pueblo tribes. O'Keeffe gave an interview there, nearing her ninetieth year as she sat atop the remote, rough rock surfaces of the Black Place, and responded to the inevitable question: 'Have you climbed over these peaks?' The years fell away as the artist replied: 'Certainly! (and laughing) Wouldn't you? wouldn't you climb if you were here?'[50]

The dark truth of the early 1940s overshadowing northern New Mexico was that the atom bomb was being developed at a site 62 miles from Ghost Ranch to the southwest, across the Jemez Mountains at Los Alamos. The brilliant nuclear physicist Robert Oppenheimer chose the site for its remote location and difficulty of access, 200 miles from any United States national border. The requirements set down by the Department of Defense for the highly secret Manhattan Project led Oppenheimer to the spot he knew well. He had attended the Los Alamos Ranch School when as a boy he had been sent to this remote place, and had often traversed the single road that led up to the high Pajarito Plateau. Government Defense agents quickly closed the school, and rumours abounded. O'Keeffe's house, 3 miles distant from the Ghost Ranch conference centre, enabled her to remain remote from the German and Italian atomic scientists who were given security passes for weekends, if she chose. But the Packs, still the owners of the dude ranch, now had security clearance, and the word buzzed that secret government operations were involved.[51]

The year 1943 became a difficult one for rationing, both for petrol needed to obtain materials and the scarcity of food. The ranch offered little prospect for growing fruit or vegetables. It all convinced O'Keeffe that she needed a property with irrigation rights going forward. On 16 July 1945 the first bomb detonated at 'Trinity Site', an area now part of the White Sands Missile Range in Southern New Mexico, and the world soon knew the enormity of all that had been invented in the remote desert. As the Second World War ended in devastation over Hiroshima and Nagasaki, the atomic era began.

O'Keeffe was approached by James Johnson Sweeney of the Museum of Modern Art in New York to consider a solo exhibition there, the first to be devoted there to a woman artist. O'Keeffe became intractable, and she refused all dates except the spring of 1946 (the trouble arose from the museum's plans to open an exhibition of the works of Marc Chagall, many of which were difficult to ship from Europe in the post-war chaos). She opposed the museum's plan to shift the schedules, and her stubborn insistence – however self-centred – in retrospect appears prescient in light of Stieglitz's continuing decline. Sweeney, however, never produced a catalogue for the exhibition. Stieglitz would not have seen her greatest New York triumph without her famous relentlessness. The elderly photographer aged 82, debilitated by heart disease over a decade's decline, visited her exhibition in mid-May on the day before the opening, but he was not well enough to attend the evening celebration.

O'Keeffe wrote to Chabot: 'Alfred was very pleased – really pleased to a few tears – it was very sweet – no one there but James [Sweeney] and Alfred and myself – after that I felt it was all right.'[52] O'Keeffe made the cover of the *Saturday Review of Literature* that summer with a woodcut portrait created by O'Brien, and numerous accolades from the popular media, including the *New Yorker* and *Time* magazine.

Stieglitz lived into July, when the superlative review written by James Thrall Soby in the *Saturday Review* was read to him. Soby wrote memorable phrases that define O'Keeffe's important contribution to American art. Stieglitz asked to hear the words again in his final days: 'Hers is a world of exceptional intensity: bones and flowers, hills and the city, sometimes abstract and vigorous, sometimes warm and fugitive. She created this world; it was not there before; and there is nothing like it anywhere.'[53]

Stieglitz's end came slowly while experiencing increasing chest pain and minor strokes. When notified that he had collapsed in their apartment and was immediately hospitalized in a coma, O'Keeffe – already in New Mexico – rushed directly to the airport in Albuquerque without returning home to pack. She stayed at Doctors Hospital where Stieglitz lay under an oxygen tent; she alternated with Dorothy Norman in the bedside vigil.[54] He died on 13 July, at the midpoint of her summer retrospective. Over the weekend after his death, O'Keeffe became fixated on securing a simple pine coffin, and then found it had a pink lining. This she tore out and replaced by sewing in a plain linen cloth.

Though the announcement went out that 'no funeral service is planned', a small group of friends, including a visibly distraught

Dorothy Norman, gathered at the funeral home on upper Madison Avenue. Not a word was spoken at the funeral rites. Edward Steichen, long estranged from Stieglitz, appeared and placed an evergreen branch on the casket. Stieglitz's great-niece remembered that O'Keeffe, 'with a majesty I shall never forget, eluded the hands of sympathizers and entered the limousine that would carry her behind the hearse'.[55] At the end of July O'Keeffe travelled one last time to Lake George with her close friends, Stieglitz's niece Elizabeth Davidson and David McAlpin, to scatter her husband's ashes in the earth by a great tree at the lakeside, writing: 'I put him where he could hear the Lake.'[56]

9

Sky Above Clouds

In the first days after Stieglitz's ashes were scattered, O'Keeffe retreated in grief to the shelter of her sister Anita Young's luxurious cottage, Fairholme, in Newport, Rhode Island, which was furnished with Louis xv furniture and a superb selection of her canvases. She sensed the weight of 'one man's warm living ideas', and felt keenly the crisis over the issues they had tangled over many times – what would become of Stieglitz's estate of more than 850 works of art, their correspondence and An American Place?

The third act of O'Keeffe's life now began. Her Museum of Modern Art retrospective continued, and opened one pathway for her future reputation. The other rested on Stieglitz's legacy, and her intertwined reputation in getting it right. At this point in her career the critics identified her as the nation's most famous woman artist, though Clement Greenberg famously dismissed her work as both 'hygienic' and 'scatological'. His agenda turned modernist taste towards Abstract Expressionism, and explicitly buried the recent past, even revising his view on John Marin as 'one of America's greatest painters'.[1]

One news weekly titled the review of O'Keeffe's signal achievement 'Austere Stripper', and her friend McBride reminded the public of the youthful scandal of Stieglitz's photographs. In summary, he praised her capacity for hard, sustained work (he counted 29 exhibitions in twenty-plus years): 'Practically anybody can participate in a sensation and be known for a day, but not everybody can keep it up. Miss O'Keeffe can and has.'[2]

To her new dealer, Edith Gregor Halpert of the Downtown Gallery, O'Keeffe granted few opportunities for exhibitions, and Halpert never made the long trip to New Mexico. After the artist closed An American Place in 1950 with an exhibition of 33 of her latest paintings, she stayed out of the limelight contentedly. However, she suggested a rare thematic show of works in pastel in 1952, organized by Halpert. Once again her mystic nature struck the critics. In 1955 she wrote: 'My first [show] at "291" was 40 years ago . . . I hope to work the next 40 years and have no show.'[3]

The motifs of her painting centred on her home in Abiquiu, completed in October 1948: the patio door, the sky and hills of the landscape compelled her vision. Now, almost three decades after her death, the mystery of the black patio door that compelled her to buy a crumbling adobe ruin in late 1945 on the Abiquiu mesa, a struggle she characterized as wresting the property from the Catholic Church, is revealed. The door that became an obsessive motif in her painting from the late 1940s, a heavy wooden double door in the centre of the adobe wall, opens onto her creative world. In fact, her paintings were stored behind that brooding presence, in a room called the *salita*.[4] From the simple wooden oblong, she began to derive much-simplified horizontal compositions of sky, wall and earth, beginning with the *Patio Door* series in 1948, continuing to explore new colour combinations: green with tan, red-orange and yellow, pink against white. By the mid-1950s she was painting the black door alone, looking at an angle down the wall in bright snow or sun. Seeing the form obliquely, she torqued the door with a twist of paint. The doorway suggested a place of no return, an implacable black floating rectangle that could move forwards or backwards. Its mystery gave the feeling that one might pass through that strange black portal into the unknown. In fact, O'Keeffe kept many of her best works in that hidden space, far from New York.

Back in New York, she maintained the apartment at 59 East 54th Street until the Stieglitz estate was settled in 1949. Stieglitz had no longer exhibited his work after 1935, except on rare occasions, and the public's memory of his artist innovation had quickly waned.[5] O'Keeffe's final gift to Stieglitz and to the cities

Georgia O'Keeffe, *Patio with Black Door*, 1955, oil on canvas.

Abiquiu house, *salita* interior with *Sky Above Clouds*, 1967, photographer unknown.

that nourished their art and ambitions became, in effect, her greatest installation piece. She explained in a late-life interview: 'I wanted to disperse the Stieglitz collection because I knew no single museum was going to take all of it. We had terrible fights about this.'[6]

This led to an even-handed distribution of the art collection across numerous institutions, as she explained in a *New York Times* article in 1949: 'the three largest groups of the Collection have gone to the Metropolitan Museum of Art, the Art Institute of Chicago, and to Fisk University, Nashville, because I think it is a good thing to do at this time and that it would please Stieglitz.'[7] The most significant set of the Stieglitz photographs, the best prints of each subject photographed during his long career – more than 1,320 examples – were donated to the National Gallery of Art in Washington, DC. The Fisk University selection of 101 works of art, today shared with Crystal Bridges Museum in Arkansas in a two-year rotation, continues as the single best distillation of the Stieglitz Collection, both in the spirit of Stieglitz's galleries and the range of artists exhibited. O'Keeffe included *Radiator Building – Night, New York* (1927) for Fisk, as the most dramatic of her modernist skyscraper paintings, radiating in red neon Stieglitz's place and fervent advocacy for American modernist expression. Finally, O'Keeffe chose images that branded the collection, including Florine Stettheimer's sly codes for the artists around the wiry figure of Stieglitz in his gallery, and the photographer's own self-mythologizing, his Rembrandtesque *Self-portrait* (1907).

O'Keeffe's philanthropic gift of the Alfred Stieglitz Collection to Fisk University, an African American university chartered in 1866, remains an astonishing choice. Alfred Stieglitz never exhibited black artists, and there is no indication that he ever considered such a gift. But O'Keeffe responded to the mood of a changing country: African American soldiers had been integrated with the troops for the first time during the Second World War. Moreover, as a young teacher O'Keeffe keenly felt the need to educate students without means; she knew well that Fisk students suffered from cultural discrimination under the continuing Jim Crow segregation of the South, telling an interviewer: '[if] the exhibition had been at a white institution, the blacks could not come and see them.'[8] If Dr Barnes, or her fond memories of Jean Toomer, presented inspiration for the Fisk gift, the novelist and photographer Carl Van Vechten was its catalyst. An old friend of both O'Keeffe and Stieglitz, Van Vechten compiled a photographic series of the most prominent African American jazz musicians, writers and artists from 1932 until his death in 1964. He introduced the artist to his close friend Charles S. Johnson, the brilliant sociologist, activist, professor and author of *The Negro in American Civilization* (1930), recently appointed president of Fisk, who opened the Fisk doors to advocacy of post-war cultural integration on campus.[9] Soon O'Keeffe and Johnson met in New York to go over the terms of her gift. Subsequently she spent ten days in Nashville in 1949, repainting and overseeing the installation prior to the opening ceremonies in October.

Just a year later, the O'Keeffe family experienced yet another tragedy after the artist's nephew was drafted into the Korean War in 1950. John Robert O'Keeffe ('Bobbie' as O'Keeffe spelled it), the son of her brother, Alexis, died in Korea in September 1951. Catherine Klenert, Georgia's younger sister, tersely recalled the double tragedy of the deaths of father and son: 'Alexis came home on a cot [from the First World War], and he was married, and his son was killed over in Korea.'[10] Alexis's death in the winter of 1930 meant that he never knew his son, who was born in March 1930 and was then killed in action in North Korea on 17 September 1951.

Notified of Bobby's death, O'Keeffe's response was distant and terse. In fact, she had been quite concerned about the boy's education and speech therapy, and sent money for his remedial therapy; she asked her sister Claudia in Los Angeles to send updates on Bobby's progress, and as a teenager Bobby had visited Ghost Ranch the week in July when Stieglitz died. Finally allowing in some feeling, she mused: 'Yes – it seems very strange that Bobbie has gone.'[11]

In 1952 and 1953 O'Keeffe created fierce, disturbing images. She wrote to Edith Halpert: 'I have a small piece of an Antelope head (14 inches high – 32 inches wide) that I like very much – I have a cedar stump painted red . . . when I finished . . . discovered that I had two monsters.' She continued, either ruminating over the recent events or simply brooding: 'I don't really expect any one to be very interested in what I'm doing now.'[12] One such work was the defiantly sun-struck *Red Tree, Yellow Sky* (1952); the other monster was the *Antelope with Pedernal*, a grisly image of a skull with its prong-horn antlers overlapping the white orb of the moon, which originated in a series of eight drawings.[13]

In New Mexico, O'Keeffe distilled the Native American culture around her, observing the spirit world of the antelope and deer. Based on annual cycles of tribal ritual and deterioration of the wall paintings in native kivas, there ensued an early twentieth-century revival of watercolours by Native American tribal artists. Theirs is a tradition of simplified design, pure colour against the background with no perspectival space, because when animal spirits are summoned, in the snake or deer dances, offerings to the ancestors, earth and sky cannot be recorded on site, only from memory. *The Above World Universe* by the Zia artist Velino Shije Herrera (Ma-Pe-Wi, 1902–1973) is a depiction of the afterlife in this tradition. Antelope or deer leap among the eagles, sun and trees, with abstract symbols derived from Pueblo pottery. These motifs evoked the sacred lands that mark the hallowed site of Anasazi (ancestors). The clean lines and symmetrical composition by Ma-Pe-Wi possess affinities with O'Keeffe's increasingly spare, reductive vision. Her antelope spirit became subsumed in her own 'Above World' meditations in an expanded field.

Soon O'Keeffe began to examine the clouds above, as she began to travel by aeroplane. In 1950 O'Keeffe began the travels that dominated the next two decades. First she drove to Mexico with friends and the photographer Eliot Porter, and stayed in Mexico City with Miguel Covarrubias and his wife. There she visited her friend Frida Kahlo twice at the Casa Azul in Coyoacán, just a few years before Kahlo's death in 1954.[14] Travel plans dominated her painting routine after the Mexico trip by car, and she took to the air. At the age of 66, in 1953, O'Keeffe travelled to Europe for the first time. She finally saw Paris, though she much preferred Chartres Cathedral. The artist found it to be of greater interest than museums, and stayed for a second day to see the stained glass windows in the

Velino Shije Herrera (Ma-Pe-Wi, Zia Pueblo), *Above World Universe*, *c*. 1925, watercolour.

morning light. Her friend Mary Callery, the Picasso collector and the sculptor of O'Keeffe's portrait bust, could have introduced her to Picasso, but O'Keeffe declined. It was Spain that truly compelled her interest, however, and she travelled there again in 1954. She took in the glories of the Prado where she discovered a deep affinity for Spanish painting, particularly Goya.[15]

O'Keeffe enjoyed inclusion in an exhibition at the Metropolitan Museum of Art in 1958, *Fourteen American Masters from Colonial Times to the Present Day*, a choice list including Mary Cassatt.[16] There in the gallery dedicated to her work, the painting *Ladder to the Moon* (1958) appeared, her most Surrealist work to date. The painting, a magical realist motif, marked the end of what O'Keeffe called a two-year period during which she characterized herself as a 'loafer'. In 1956 the artist travelled to Machu Pichu and through the Peruvian landscape, and for once completed a few watercolours while on holiday. In the early spring of 1958 she had rushed to aid her sister Anita upon the sudden death of her husband, Robert

Georgia O'Keeffe at Friday Mosque, Isfahan, Iran, 1959, photographer unknown.

Young. As director of the New York Central Railroad, Young had been accused of fraud, and committed suicide in the billiard room of their Palm Beach mansion. 'Being in Florida was difficult – Oh the whole trip was hard', she wrote to Claudia, while confiding to another friend: 'one of the saddest times of my life'.[17] Despite the tragedy, O'Keeffe hid her recent troubles: 'I hate the times when I don't work.'[18]

O'Keeffe had just passed her seventieth birthday when Daniel Catton Rich, who had recently left Chicago to become director of Worcester Art Museum in 1958, wrote to encourage her to consider another retrospective. Rich had visited her in Abiquiu in 1957, and knew about her health and her cessation of painting (always a bad sign for the artist). Moreover, he understood where she stored the goods: 'I have a strong feeling you have kept the best of your last few years in Abiquiu.'[19] Though Rich knew she would seize the chance, O'Keeffe deflected the notion, saying that instead she might travel to Japan for the chrysanthemum festival: 'I don't really enjoy having a show you know!! It has always been one of the necessary evils of my life.'[20] And indeed, she joined a round-the-world tour in 1959, travelling from Hawaii to Asia, through the Middle East and on to Iran. A striking image from Isfahan locates O'Keeffe in front of the Shaykh Lotfollah Mosque (or Friday Mosque), the famous early seventeenth-century blue-tiled Safavid sanctuary with its delicate honeycombed vault (*iwan*), wearing a white head covering. The white (or black) head covering became part of her desert attire when at home in later years.

O'Keeffe eventually agreed to Rich's plan, and her third retrospective opened at the Worcester Art Museum in autumn 1960, far from the major urban centres where she had once exhibited. In planning an overview with focus on the recent work, Rich responded to her late style, commenting: 'I like its severity.' The press, meanwhile, bemoaned the lack of huge flower paintings, and reported on one example 'titled "My Heart" . . . two stones from the desert, polished to a high finish by blowing sand in much the same way the action of sand water polishes stones at the seashore'. Queried about the abstracted grey-black forms against a rosy orange ground, O'Keeffe was quoted as saying: 'I thought they looked hard so I called the painting "My Heart," she smiled.'[21] Rich commented in the catalogue essay: 'Frequently when on a new tack the artist will express uncertainty as to where her "so-called mind" (as she humorously refers to it) is taking her. At seventy-two O'Keeffe can still surprise herself.'[22]

In fact, O'Keeffe followed her heart rather than her head to begin another reinvention. Her next major exhibition of the 1960s was slated for Fort Worth, Texas, then a regional arts centre known as 'Cowtown'; the Amon Carter Museum of Western Art was the site. The key to both choices, Worcester and Texas, had everything to do with curators whom she trusted. Rich had been 'one of the best men' since her first major solo show in Chicago in 1943, and held her in special regard until his death in 1976. The other trustworthy curator was James Johnson Sweeney, who had left the Museum of Modern Art in the late 1940s to serve as director of the Museum of Fine Arts in Houston. Sweeney worked with O'Keeffe for both Texas venues. Her newest project, a mural-scale painting of the sky, emerged from her world travels. In the ominous period just before Pearl Harbor, she had written of her delight in the view from an aeroplane: 'It is breath taking as one rises up over the world one has been living in – the Rio Grande – the mountains – then the pattern of rivers . . . The world all simplified and beautiful and clear cut in pattern like time and history will simplify and straighten out these times of ours.'[23]

In her 75th year she began to experiment with the idea *Sky Above Clouds I*, first exhibited in 1963 at the American Federation of the Arts in New York in its smallest, 4-foot-wide version. The occasion honoured the Brandeis University Creative Arts medallists from the past five years, and O'Keeffe had received the lifetime achievement Medal in Painting that year. The celebration highlighted fourteen artists, from O'Keeffe and Alexander Calder (the medal winner for sculpture in 1962) to Ellsworth Kelly (b. 1923), the younger Citation winner for painting in 1963. The exhibition offered O'Keeffe the opportunity to exhibit her latest efforts while in New York.[24] As for the *Sky*, she next tried the motif of wide sky with receding clouds in a 7-foot width, exhibiting at the Whitney Biennial of 1964.[25] Once spring of 1965 arrived, she was ready for the campaign to prepare the largest canvas of her career, *Sky Above Clouds IV*, at 24 feet wide, for her Texas opening in 1966.

Meanwhile, a critically acclaimed exhibition in autumn 1963, *American Modernism: The First Wave*, at the Rose Art Museum, inaugurated in 1961 on the Brandeis University campus, established O'Keeffe's growing historical recognition in the genealogy of abstract art. The show, curated by Sam Hunter, surveyed 'the swift and dramatic changes post-war abstract painting has worked in our image of American art'. Hunter's emphasis on the 'organic abstractions' of Dove and O'Keeffe underscored their opening to an expressive, emotional vein of painting, resisting Cubism's sway. Further, his analysis emphasized her important role: 'O'Keeffe in particular seemed able to invest abstract painting with new content and significant new form.'[26] The press drew attention to the young museum's thoughtful overview on looking back, 'a call of rebellion against the rebels'.[27] The artists on view were seen to link forward either to Pop art or, in O'Keeffe's case, to the gestural Color Field abstractionists such as Mark Rothko and Clyfford Still.

The spirit of O'Keeffe's original Texas watercolours and her love of big skies fuelled the daring work ahead, once more 'to paint it big'. She transformed her garage into an extended studio, and after first tacking up a preparatory drawing the length of the wall, prepared the canvas on stretchers for a very wide mural. She wrote about the making of this canvas in the greatest detail of any work in her autobiography of 1976. It seemed she had summoned her spirit animal, since she had to leap (or stand) on a table set up especially to reach the top areas of the canvas, to perch on a

Georgia O'Keeffe, *Above the Clouds I*, 1962/3, oil on canvas.

O'Keeffe touching up *Sky Above Clouds IV*, 1965, at Amon Carter Museum of Western Art, 1966.

chair atop the table and finally to rest seated on the floor in order to cover the entire immense canvas. Its execution involved careful planning, including priming the rough canvas and devising reinforced bars to stretch the wide painting taut on its frame, all with the help of a local sheepherder, Frank. At last, *Sky Above Clouds IV* was brought to completion before winter set in. And then it all had to be disassembled and rolled up on a drum for transport by truck across the state to Texas.[28]

Though O'Keeffe rarely smiled for the camera, in Texas she donned her painter's apron and touched up the edge of *Sky* with good humour. For the occasion at the Amon Carter Museum of Western Art in 1966, she created an exhibition of 98 works that reveals the emphatic O'Keeffe touch, documenting the charcoals of 1915 and then a rich display of her first watercolours to current work. In the catalogue, a stern O'Keeffe, 79 years old, posed in front of the *Sky* mural. For Todd Webb's formal portrait she wore the white kimono dress, fastened with a barely visible 'OK' pin, a gift from Calder (now in silver to match her hair). The catalogue essays, documenting her career from its origins to her final statement on her distrust of 'the word', reprise the Stieglitz method. There is no hint of curatorial voice or narrative text on her career. Instead, excerpts from former writings are featured: Marsden Hartley led off the sequence. His admiration for her work, much changed since 1921 and proclaimed in an essay of 1935, captured her intuitive spirit: 'O'Keeffe has never questioned the condition of delight – it is for her like her daily meal – or a walk in the world, alone.' A quote from a Canyon car mechanic nailed her early reputation in West Texas: 'I remember her well . . . Believe it or not, she could outwalk any man in this whole country.'[29]

Marking the national achievement in Texas and the longevity of her art, *Artforum* magazine marked the national achievement in Texas and the longevity of her art when O'Keeffe's art dominated the cover in May 1966. Now O'Keeffe shared the spotlight with a younger generation in the most avant-garde publication of the 1960s. The accompanying essay insightfully explored O'Keeffe's 'objects of quiet delight and contemplation' and asked: '[have] the scents of innovation of the last seven or eight years . . . drifted to New Mexico?'[30] The ambitious *Sky Above Clouds IV* created a serene, simplified world beyond, her own 'above world' meditation configured by solid oblong clouds that beckoned to her vision of walking across a most beautiful solid white sky, moving into a distant horizon of pale pink fading to white.

Soon O'Keeffe's exhibition of large, geometricized motifs drew further notice in New York, aided and abetted by Eugene Goossen, the curator who included her work in an exhibition at the Museum of Modern Art, *The Art of the Real* (1968), defining contemporary trends in Minimalism. Praising O'Keeffe as an artist whose stylistic ability allowed her 'to survive the prejudice against her sex in art', Goossen gave her an enhanced position employing an analogy popular in this era, claiming that O'Keeffe paintings, 'if blown up to the heroic size of the abstract expressionists, could pass easily for slightly nature-oriented examples of this later period'.[31] Goossen wrote the introduction to *Art of the Real*, where he illustrated *Blue Lines X* (1916), and paired the stark frontality of her *Lake George Window* (1929) with Ellsworth Kelly's *Window: Paris* (1949).[32]

O'Keeffe's last retrospective during her lifetime and her first solo show in New York since 1946 arrived in 1970. With intense advance planning and the curatorial assistance of Doris Bry, the Whitney Museum claimed O'Keeffe for new audiences. Luckily O'Keeffe coincided with another propitious cultural crossroads. In that period, the second wave of feminism gained a chorus of robust voices. Kate Millett's controversial book *Sexual Politics* had been published the previous year, and attacked the sexist, patriarchal underpinnings of famous authors from Freud to D. H. Lawrence.[33] In spring 1972 *Ms.* magazine published its first issue. The interest in consciousness-raising among youthful feminists determined to challenge the dominant male structures found an icon in O'Keeffe. She did not return the adoration. Nonetheless, many young admirers came to her paintings, where her direct extension of self into the candid revelations of the sensual response to flowers and nature resonated anew.

In fact, O'Keeffe disdained the direction of new feminism, and expressed her displeasure after Judy Chicago contacted her.[34] In Chicago's later installation piece, *The Dinner Party* (1979), O'Keeffe attained the prime place at the triangular table of the most fully achieved flower. Chicago made O'Keeffe's body analogous to the three-dimensional flower decorating the plates, once again equating anatomy with her identity. To the artist, it all appeared no different from the male critics of the 1920s. To an interviewer, she recounted that suffrage had been her women's issue, and she had enjoyed the National Woman's Party in the 1920s, because they 'went about their business in a dignified way'. O'Keeffe was more than aware that the battle for the Equal Rights Amendment, set before Congress in 1923, was failing. About the young ones, she sniffed: 'As for the feminists now, I get embarrassed with the way they go on. They would be better off if a lot of them stayed home and did their work.'[35]

When the Whitney retrospective opened in autumn 1970, there were few new works among the 121 paintings and drawings on view, but O'Keeffe's voice remained relevant, not only for the generation of Minimalist and Color Field painting. The abstract calligraphy of the evocative *Road Past the View* (1964), based upon a photograph she took with her Leica, a gift from photographer Todd Webb, inscribed the bend of the road following the Chama River away from her Abiquiu mesa. More rivers and roads followed in abstract patterning. From one window she wrote: 'I see the road toward Espanola, Santa Fe and the world.' The recent *Sky Above Clouds IV* (1965), the 24-foot-long mural, became a signature work of the late years, exhibited in the lobby of the Whitney, and was purchased for the Art Institute of Chicago. There it still hangs, dramatically encompassing the viewer's space over the large staircase. The painting *Black Rock with Blue III* (1970), a sculpturally rendered, organic treatment of the enlarged rock against the blue, seemed predictive of the pottery making that soon became her new pursuit. Bry chose a photograph of her own from 1951 for the frontispiece: O'Keeffe, with darker hair and sharp eyesight, peering incisively toward the title page.

O'Keeffe's vision remained central to her art and world, although her daily scrutiny of the 'wideness and wonder' began to deteriorate from macular degeneration. The turning point for her painting came in the year after the landmark retrospective when a blood clot burst in her left eye in 1971, leaving her with only peripheral vision. Her last work painted by herself alone, a horizontally banded colour field of blue, black and white, is titled *The Beyond* (1972).

John Bruce Hamilton, who had been employed by Ghost Ranch doing carpentry, came to her door in 1973 looking for work. Hamilton had recently moved to northern New Mexico, and had registered as a conscientious objector to avoid the Vietnam War draft. Born in Dallas, Texas, the young man, then called Juan, grew up in South America. He became fluent in Spanish when living for fifteen years in Peru with his parents, who worked among Native populations for the Presbyterian Church. Hamilton was 26 years old when he first met O'Keeffe and was working as a potter in his own studio in the nearby community of Barranco; he soon became essential to the daily operations of her studio. The artist quickly gave Hamilton greater responsibilities, and asked him to come with her on a trip to Morocco in 1974 with her neighbours, the Girards. At the same time, she gathered other young people around her, hiring a librarian and house painters (one was pulled into the studio to help her execute paintings), and helping young art historians who came seeking material on Stieglitz for their dissertations. In 1977 *Art News* profiled 'Georgia O'Keeffe at 90' at her Ghost Ranch home with Hamilton, who had assumed the role of assistant. He freely teased her as 'Mrs Stieglitz', eliciting a lively protest with her cane. With scenes of her home and the desert, the article also illustrated a new painting, *From a Day with Juan III*. The last years of O'Keeffe's life, the thirteen years from Hamilton's arrival at her doorstep until her death on 6 March 1986, were marked by a companionship that was both caring and argumentative.

O'Keeffe lived in the moment, and often noted that 'she did not look back.' It became most difficult of all to stop painting. In the summer of 1976 she described what she could still see: 'It's like there are little holes in my vision . . . I can't see straight on very well. But around the edge there are little holes where I can see quite clearly.' She once had keen eyesight and never wore glasses; many friends and helpers '[watched] her come up against her eyesight' and it became the deep, inherent frustration in her daily life.[36] Frances O'Brien felt that it all cost too great a price: 'If she only hadn't lost her sight like that, things would have been so different.'[37] Many close friends were riled by the ageing artist's stubborn self-interest as she approached 90, and Anita Pollitzer's book was definitively quashed just a year before her death in 1975. Several were asked to return paintings that once had been gifts.

All that she had accomplished up to 1970, including her iconic profile on the cover of *Life* magazine in March 1968 as a desert seer and pioneer of 'stark visions', marked her lifetime achievement. Now a popularly recognized icon of American art, new opportunities, even painting with the unacknowledged assistance of others, became irresistible. Her employee John Poling was invited to her studio one day when he was helping to paint her wooden gutters, and then was asked to gesso a canvas. As one thing led to another, he followed O'Keeffe's instruction. Only later did he recognize one of the works he helped to paint with her direction in the 1977 *Art News* article. The back of the canvas *From a Day with Juan I* is dedicated: 'For Juan with rattlesnakes / and love and affection / Georgia – July–27–1977'. These assisted paintings now are documented in the catalogue raisonné.[38]

Certain friends had known Doris Bry well, over the 25 years working for O'Keeffe as curator and artist's agent. Frances O'Brien and Doris Bry had been friends of O'Keeffe in the 1940s after Stieglitz's death and were allowed to stay in the 54 East 59th Street apartment while O'Keeffe began to oversee the estate and travel to New Mexico. Frances joked that they were a trio of three generations: 'O'Keeffe, O'Brien and O'Bry'. In 1977 the artist summarily fired Bry as her agent (she had earlier severed business with Halpert in 1963). She asked for the return of the paintings under Bry's supervision. To that end, she sued her long-standing representative in *O'Keeffe v. Bry*, filed on 8 August 1978, to which Bry then filed a counter-suit.[39] Her oldest friends became very uncomfortable with O'Keeffe's intransigence in Abiquiu, and Peggy Kiskadden drew the line about any future summer visits there. In a blistering reply to the generous Kiskadden, a friend since the 1930s, the artist summoned the destructive chaos of an angry fury: 'Even as an "Ancient Spirit" I have not been idle – and a young mind helps. So there we are – *Finished*.'[40]

As recalled in O'Keeffe's *New York Times* obituary, Bry's counter-claim against O'Keeffe was dramatically delivered to Juan Hamilton (the 'young mind' the artist relied on) late in 1978. The process server arrived at the gala opening of his first exhibition, at the Robert Miller Gallery in New York. Bry included Hamilton in her counter-claim against O'Keeffe's lawsuit for 'malicious interference', citing $13.25 million in loss of income and property.[41] The Whitney retrospective of 1970 had contributed to new highs in O'Keeffe's prices over the following decade, when Doris Bry was still managing her affairs.[42]

After many years of resisting bad press, and learning to use the popular media to great advantage, O'Keeffe (with Hamilton) agreed to an ill-advised interview with *People* magazine, and gossip circulated about their relationship. Hamilton's mellow statements blurred his complicated relationship to the elderly painter: 'There is prejudice against us because she is an older woman and I'm young and somewhat handsome.'[43] Some who observed them in the late years saw a 'flirtatious ambivalence', though others stated that Hamilton treated his work in Abiquiu and Ghost Ranch as a job; he married Anna Marie Erskine in 1980 and they had a family.

Hamilton travelled with O'Keeffe to New York. There she was captured on film at the MOMA bicentennial exhibition of 1976, *The Natural Paradise: Painting in America, 1800–1950*, where her painting *Orange and Red Streak* (1919) was on view. Later, the pair visited the Andy Warhol Factory in 1980, and appeared in a video segment of Andy Warhol TV with Paloma Picasso (now excerpted on the Warhol Museum's iPhone tour). O'Keeffe's Polaroid portrait was taken by Warhol, and became her diamond dust silkscreen, a negative image taken from a Polaroid that O'Keeffe disliked, in which she wears a black headscarf. The joint interview with Warhol for the September 1983 issue of *Interview* reveals the self-centered directness of O'Keeffe's speech as she aged. This paralleled the New York installation of the *Alfred Stieglitz* exhibition, planned by Hamilton with Sarah Greenough, curator of photography at the National Gallery of Art. Flora Miller Biddle, then president of the Whitney Museum of American Art, hosted a lunch at the ritzy Four Seasons during O'Keeffe's trip in 1983, and, observing the artist's difficulties with her vision, helped to feed her. While discussing the possibility of another Whitney show, Biddle found O'Keeffe's and Hamilton's 'new relationship . . . somewhere between a grandmother-grandson and two lovers'.[44]

Without Hamilton's input, O'Keeffe might not have completed all the major projects that defined her work and career as she passed the milestone of 90 years. In 1974 she had contacted a publisher: 'I myself, am writing about what I have done.'[45] She proposed an autobiography, first started in the 1940s with the encouragement of the artist William Einstein, to be illustrated with large-scale images of her work for a de luxe portfolio book. Hamilton spent the summer of 1976 in New York, checking all the colour proofs. When the de luxe edition of *Georgia O'Keeffe* was published in 1976, it sold 22,000 copies in one month.

Significantly, the artist gives Stieglitz only passing notice in the entire text, and little credit for her successful start in New York. Like a Buddhist master, O'Keeffe created enigmatic parallel commentaries, placed in sparse blocks of text, opposite images of her paintings. The words at first seem to have little to do with certain paintings. One senses that there is a game afoot, and far more is being held back than is written.[46]

Many of O'Keeffe's paintings, pastels and drawings were not to be seen by the public until well after her death. The book's images, just 108 works, represented just over 5 per cent of her lifetime production. True, the artist highlighted both superb and difficult examples of her work, but restricted the public from seeing it all. Just as Stieglitz had thrown out what he considered mediocre prints or old negatives, in later years she destroyed batches of paintings that she deemed unworthy.[47] Specialists and scholars waited more than twenty years after her death in 1986 for the definitive two-volume catalogue raisonné meticulously assembled by Barbara Buhler Lynes, when the entirety of O'Keeffe's artistic production could be measured.

Perry Miller Adato, commissioned by PBS to create a documentary for the *American Masters* series, contacted O'Keeffe and was granted the rare privilege of filming her in her Ghost Ranch home and walking the desert paths beside her in her beloved Piedra Lumbre. Prodding O'Keeffe to tell certain of her stories, Adato revealed the humorous, convivial side of the artist. O'Keeffe described the success of her career, but particularly relished a metaphor of walking on a knife's edge, where she might fall off in either direction at crucial moments. Adato walked across the tough hills of the Black Place with her, an arduous trip by car and foot, for part of her filmed interview and documentary account, the last extended record of O'Keeffe speaking on film. In 1977 O'Keeffe memorably reiterated her sense of good fortune with humility: 'I don't think I have a great gift. It isn't just talent. You have to have something else. You have to have a kind of nerve.' She added: 'and a lot of very, very hard work'.[48]

In 1978 she prepared a group of 51 of the original Stieglitz prints of herself, which she allowed to be exhibited with her name for the first time (reprising the images of the Stieglitz exhibition in 1921, 'A Woman'). The resulting exhibition in New York, *Alfred Stieglitz: A Portrait of Georgia O'Keeffe*, became the sensation of the season with a banner fluttering from the facade of the august Metropolitan Museum of Art on Fifth Avenue. The chronology of the photographs themselves performed a slow striptease of Miss O'Keeffe, from schoolteacher to the ardent young artist paired with her work, and the startling, classically inspired nude torsos. The *New Yorker* critic Janet Malcolm captured the revelatory power of the O'Keeffe photos 50 years on: 'Innocently opening the [exhibition] book . . . is a little like taking a drive in the country and suddenly coming upon Stonehenge'.[49] The series included symbols of O'Keeffe's hard-gained independence, such as her hand against the v8 icon on her gleaming Ford hubcap, or holding a skull in the 1930s. To her librarian of the 1970s, O'Keeffe slyly pulled open a drawer and showed her one of the nude photographs from early years: 'Look what you come to if you let yourself be photographed like this.'[50]

On 8 August 1984 O'Keeffe signed a codicil to her will, giving the control of the disposition of her entire estate to Hamilton. Wrapped in the warm blankets of Sol y Sombra, with around-the-clock nursing in the last years, she lived in the large house, near Santa Fe medical facilities, purchased by Hamilton for her and for his family in the upstairs floors. O'Keeffe missed her Abiquiu home and slowly drifted away from life, her visual acuity long gone. Georgia O'Keeffe died alone in the St Vincent hospital in Santa Fe on 6 March 1986, at the age of 98.

After the artist's death, legal actions by her few living relatives came swiftly. The lawsuit brought against Hamilton requested control of the estate; he quickly settled the case by the autumn of 1987, saying that there had been too many lawsuits in Miss O'Keeffe's last years.[51] The resolution of the estate led to the creation of the Georgia O'Keeffe Foundation, a board constituted of family members, art historians and Hamilton, which carefully dispersed the remainder of O'Keeffe's paintings to a wide-ranging list of American museums, beginning with the short list O'Keeffe had designated in her last will of 1979. Once the O'Keeffe Museum was founded in 1997, by the generous philanthropy of Anne Tandy Marion and the Burnett Foundation, the O'Keeffe Foundation board, convened by court order, completed its mission and dissolved in 2006. At that time, all remaining property left in the estate was turned over to the Georgia O'Keeffe Museum in Santa Fe, a centre for exhibitions, education and scholarly research on O'Keeffe's life, art and the history of American modernism.

Epilogue: Ancient Spirit

In many ways, the isolated austerity of O'Keeffe's late life in the desert emulates the saintly pursuit of self-abnegation and meditation, and so too the artist – like many ascetics before her – had once embraced the sensuous life. Without a doubt the critics in her early career tormented her. The art critic Henry McBride had written a jesting provocation at the beginning of her long career that O'Keeffe should get herself to a nunnery. Silence, relentlessness and 'aloneness' gave a certain measure of peace, as did the vast grandeur of her home land-scape. Her artistic pursuit presents polar opposites, first abstraction and then the turn to realism, the magnified details of floral still-life to the examination of bones and the rocks of the Southwest. Her path led inexorably to immersion in sky and land in late life, the landscape becoming more than 'The source of her imagery . . . the source of her power', as James Turrell, the artist of space sculpting light of the Roden Crater in Arizona, has written.[1] O'Keeffe welcomed many pilgrims to her late-life retreat, and others came knocking, unbidden.

As young artists, Turrell and his companion visited O'Keeffe during a road trip across Route 66, starting from Los Angeles and going to the Grand Canyon, before they turned towards Abiquiu. Thinking that they must pay homage to the artist who embraced the strange beauty of the desert, 'who was decidedly heroic . . . one who recognized the importance of not cutting off access to one's source', they found that O'Keeffe was not at home. They were able to speak with her only briefly after a long wait, and then 'knew to go'. The immediate environment around her at Ghost Ranch, markedly different from Abiquiu, caused the artists to sense '[when] the red returns, a power beyond just view is felt'. These pilgrims, despite O'Keeffe's quiet signs that they should leave, felt touched by a 'light giddy emotion'.[2]

The cliffs, the sunsets from the rooftop of her house, the direct view of the Pedernal each day, both enriched and isolated her within the desert retreat. After the renovation of her Abiquiu house, where she spent the colder months near her well-irrigated garden, her residence put her alongside neighbours who needed educational support, and also with those who practised the secretive Penitente rituals. In her disdain for any obvious trappings of wealth (though her paintings' success entangled her with increased financial security), she followed her love of tending the garden, harvesting a yearly bounty of apricots and fresh vegetables, and the daily ritual of walking in the landscape.

The artist knew her neighbours, and made sure to contribute to their well-being. She generously supported the village with donations to their school and community services. The Penitente *morada*, built in the 1700s, was the group's windowless assembly room or chapel, so that Penitente processions and ritual remained the most prominent symbol of Catholicism. As the *morada* was just a short walk up the hill from her house. O'Keeffe observed their public ritual, and sometimes participated in street processions. She wrote to a friend, Frances O'Brien, in 1950: 'Today is Santa Thomas – and the town is dancing. First a dance pretending to be tipsy. Then later dancing because they are.'[3] Observing more village burials, she related:

> We have had two or three funerals. The men of the town . . . walk singing – a real kind of a cry of sorrow . . . The procession goes up the hill opposite me. It is a sad wonderful sort of sound – and a sorrowing sight.
>
> I would like them to sing that way when I die.[4]

In the 1960s O'Keeffe began to visit the Benedictine monks at the Monastery of Christ in the Desert, closer to Ghost Ranch. The brethren built a George Nakashima-designed chapel in 1961 on federally protected lands. The simple adobe chapel, its high campanile echoing the rising red cliffs around the structure, the landscape a geological counterpart to the one at Ghost Ranch, still draws pilgrims to Vespers, with the monks' chanting and silent meditation, and to the Easter Vigil.

O'Keeffe recalled being 'in love with the Catholic church' as a child, and one of her friends ironically described her as having 'a strong weakness for the Catholic faith'.[5] It was always to Frances O'Brien that O'Keeffe directed her most detailed accounts of religious matters, and whom the artist understood had 'a Catholic soul'.[6]

Her reflections on religion became focused on the simplicity of Buddhist contemplation in late years. Her interest in Asian art had long been an underpinning of her painting, and her interest was fuelled by reflection and study of its tradition. As she said:

Georgia O'Keeffe, *My Front Yard, Summer*, 1941, oil on canvas.

'I like the art that came out of Buddhism much more than the art that came out of the Catholic Church . . . There is a tranquility and peace in Buddhist art that I don't find in Catholic Art.'[7]

O'Keeffe always thought ahead, as in all ways she addressed practical matters. As she neared the age of 90, she decided upon cremation and wished to be 'scattered out near the cliffs where she can become part of the grass and the trees'.[8] This came to pass when Juan Hamilton scattered her ashes from the top of the Pedernal in 1986.

Her observations on Buddhism post-date her meeting with Father Thomas Merton (1915–1968), who kept a journal as he travelled from his Trappist monastery in Kentucky, where he devoted his entire priesthood to writing. He published seven books, and had written *The Way of Chuang-Tzu* just three years earlier, in 1965. His first trip in the spring of 1968 took him to San Francisco, and then on to Albuquerque. Merton's destination was northern New Mexico and the Monastery of Christ in the Desert, and there he met O'Keeffe. He became interested in photography in the early 1960s, and his camera becoming a means of exploring the common objects of daily life and nature – such as tree roots, rocks and motifs similar to those found in O'Keeffe paintings. He visited her at Ghost Ranch, and photographed a diagonally cropped angle of her house, so that its back corner balanced the rising profile of the Pedernal. His amateur efforts convey a sense of the mountain as central to O'Keeffe's world. In fact, one visitor heard Father Merton express exactly this sense of awe, the 'sacred about this'.[9] Merton and O'Keeffe were captured by an unidentified photographer, with the artist facing the camera, her arms crossed over her white dress; Merton stands in profile, his head slightly bowed in her direction. He noted about the painter: 'a woman of extraordinary quality, live, full of resiliency, awareness, quietness. One of the few people one ever finds in this country at least who quietly does everything right. Perfection of her house & patio on ghost ranch, low, hidden in desert rocks and vegetation.'[10]

Thomas Merton's stay at the monastery was brief, only a few days, and he anticipated meeting O'Keeffe again; he noted in his daybook with regret that she could not come for a planned lunch. Merton was singled out by O'Keeffe's friend O'Brien as stimulating new interest in Catholicism, due to his espousal of Asian beliefs and inclusive views on meditative religious practice. Whatever the priest's brief visit and influence might have meant for her, O'Keeffe continued to celebrate the ritual of the Benedictine monks and the Easter services with Latin chants.

She brought other pilgrims, interviewers and young people to the monastery. If monastic practice paralleled aspects of her late life, O'Keeffe enjoyed friendly visits to the Benedictines. She invited her *New Yorker* interviewer, Calvin Tomkins, in 1974 to go with her; her assistant painter-repairman John Poling in his Volkswagen Beetle in 1976 described a visit over the remote road to the chapel; and a young librarian she hired in 1973 was invited to the Easter service. She described a pre-dawn trip that gives a context to O'Keeffe's demanding ritual:

> [She] got up at 2:30 in the morning to take me to Easter sunrise service, to the Monastery of Christ in the Desert, she dressed me in one of her big black heavy cloaks, and we were twins, she was dressed in black from neck to the floor. We sat in the back of her bus, and rode for miles in the dark.[11]

O'Keeffe advised her companion that it was 'best to sit like a sack of potatoes' during the bouncy ride. Once the pilgrims arrived at the chapel, the monks filed into the sculpted adobe space, chanting a cappella hymns of praise. Merrill observed: 'All candlelight, [O'Keeffe] feels medieval and Oriental all at the same time . . . she was very still . . . no agitation . . . she takes command wherever.'

O'Keeffe unexpectedly opened up her otherwise silent views on religion in an interview in 1976: 'I feel I'm a very religious person – religion to me means respect for people – but I'm not in a religion.'[12]

From her rooftop at Ghost Ranch, where she climbed up by ladder, she looked out towards the Pedernal and discovered its spirit animal, embedded in the rock: 'the world all round – the miles of cliff behind, the wide line of low mountains with a higher narrow flat top. It is very beautiful – tree-covered with a bare spot in the shape of a leaping deer near the top.'[13] The *koan* of this particular passage, opposite an illustration of the painting *Ladder to the Moon* in her autobiography, is that we cannot see this shape in the darkened silhouette of mountains. She is describing a scene in her mind's eye as her vision failed: the work about disembodied upward flight. In much earlier work, made more than 30 years previously, there are several views of the Pedernal in full light, straight on, with the profile of its leaping deer. She had discovered the animals anthropomorphized in 'her' mountain, just as the Native American danced with headdresses made of antlers, or jumped and rhythmically pounded the earth to draw down the agrarian necessities of rain from the mountains, to celebrate sun and harvest, to repel the demonic fear of snakes and lightning. These associations never left her, and indeed O'Keeffe's spirit world did not stop with her death in 1986. The very year of her passing, an exhibition entitled *The Spiritual in Art: Abstract Painting, 1890–1985*, held at the Los Angeles County Museum of Art, contained one of the most incisive set of essays on the place of twentieth-century abstract pioneers. Beginning from the famous inventions of Wassily Kandinsky, the catalogue and exhibition definitively added Georgia O'Keeffe to the historical canon.[14]

Twenty years later, a very different 'transmigration of bone' (in Marsden Hartley's felicitous phrase) from her elevated, floating elk, deer, ram and antelope skulls occurred. A new creature had been discovered by scientists in the field of palaeontology. This resulted from the original *Coelophysis* discovery in 1947 by Dr Edwin Colbert, premier palaeontologist of the American Museum of Natural History in New York, who had packed the fruitful 200-million-year-old yield of Ghost Ranch in plaster and shipped the remains back to New York for further study. Long after the deaths of nonagenarians Colbert and O'Keeffe, a quite different sort of prehistoric creature turned out to have been preserved along with the *Coelophysis* bones of the summer expeditions in 1947–8. That is to say, one of the *Coelophysis* had devoured another creature, whose bones were interred in the cavity of the articulated skeleton. The creature, whose fossilized remains had never before been identified, related to the archosaurs of the Triassic period, was once a 6-foot-long reptile, a forerunner of crocodiles. It had roamed the ancient tropical sea that covered Ghost Ranch. The discovery of the archosaur in January 2006 by scientists, led by Sterling Nesbitt, led to the naming of the skeletal remains.[15]

The scientists chose *Effigia okeeffeae*, or 'O'Keeffe's Ghost', in honour of the artist's deep interest in both her 'modern' bones and the prehistoric geology of Ghost Ranch. The designation now exists as her memorial in the study of palaeontology, a lasting recognition of her inquisitive spirit. The archosaur caps O'Keeffe's long legacy as both ancient spirit and modernist artist. In ways that she could never have imagined, her paintings of bones and the land express an immortality that most certainly outlives death itself.

References

All O'Keeffe paintings and watercolours are here referenced with the numbers assigned as 'CR' in B. B. Lynes, *Georgia O'Keeffe: A Catalogue Raisonné*, 2 vols (New Haven, CT, and London, 1999).

Introduction: Pioneer, Independent Spirit, Visionary

1 *Georgia O'Keeffe*, exh. cat., Amon Carter Museum of Western Art, Fort Worth, TX (1966), p. 23.
2 O'Keeffe to Stieglitz, 15 March 1917, in S. Greenough, *My Faraway One: Selected Letters of Georgia O'Keeffe and Alfred Stieglitz*, vol. I: *1915–1933* (New Haven, CT, and London, 2011), p. 124.
3 *Georgia O'Keeffe: Exhibition Catalogue*, exh. cat., An American Place, New York (1939), Beinecke Rare Book and Manuscript Library, Yale University, Yale Collection of American Literature, Alfred Stieglitz/Georgia O'Keeffe Archive, MSS 85, Box 118.
4 G. O'Keeffe, *Georgia O'Keeffe* (New York, 1976), n.p., opposite no. 55, *Green Grey Abstraction* (1931).
5 E. H. Turner, *Georgia O'Keeffe: The Poetry of Things*, exh. cat., Phillips Collection, Washington, DC (1999).
6 D. C. Rich, *Georgia O'Keeffe*, exh. cat., Art Institute of Chicago, Chicago, IL (1943). *Georgia O'Keeffe*, typescript, Museum of Modern Art, New York, May–October 1946; no catalogue published. J. J. Sweeney Papers, Museum of Modern Art Archives, New York.
7 O'Keeffe to Mrs Franklin Roosevelt, 10 February 1944. J. Cowart, S. Greenough and J. Hamilton, *Georgia O'Keeffe:*

Art and Letters, exh. cat., National Gallery of Art, Washington, DC (1987), p. 235.

8 P. Plagens, 'A Georgia O'Keeffe Retrospective in Texas', *Artforum* (May 1966), pp. 27–30.

9 E. C. Goossen, 'O'Keeffe', *Vogue* (1 March 1967).

10 J. D. Katz et al., *Hide/Seek: Difference and Desire in American Portraiture*, exh. cat., National Portrait Gallery, Washington, DC (2010), plate 35, *Goat's Horn with Red*, pp. 142–3.

11 Georgia O'Keeffe to Dr Albert Barnes, 18 December 1930. Presidents' Files, Albert C. Barnes Correspondence, The Barnes Foundation Archives, Merion, Pennsylvania. Reprinted with permission.

12 *Georgia O'Keeffe: A Portrait*, exh. cat., Metropolitan Museum of Art, New York (1978), n.p. (introduction by O'Keeffe).

13 O'Keeffe, *Georgia O'Keeffe*, n.p., opposite *Ranchos Church* (1930).

14 O'Keeffe to Sherwood Anderson, Lake George, September 1923, cited in Cowart, Greenough and Hamilton, *Georgia O'Keeffe: Art and Letters*, pp. 174–5.

1 Family Untied: An Artistic Education

1 G. O'Keeffe, *Georgia O'Keeffe* (New York, 1976), n.p.

2 Anita Pollitzer, *A Woman on Paper: Georgia O'Keeffe* (New York, 1988), p. 55. This was published two years after Georgia O'Keeffe's death in 1986, because the artist withheld permission to use any quotes from her correspondence with Anita Pollitzer. Pollitzer worked on the biography extensively in the 1950s, revising it later according to O'Keeffe's line edits.

3 Ibid., p. 1.

4 R. Robinson, *Georgia O'Keeffe: A Life* (New York, 1989), p. 7 n. 7, citing details on the *Mayflower* genealogy.

5 Ibid., pp. 10, 15.

6 Ibid., p. 10.

7 L. Lisle, *Portrait of an Artist: A Biography of Georgia O'Keeffe* (New York, 1980), p. 7.

8 Pollitzer, *A Woman on Paper*, p. 58; Robinson, *Georgia O'Keeffe*, p. 22.

9 Lisle, *Portrait of an Artist*, p. 7, citing *Sun Prairie Countryman*, November 1887.

10 Pollitzer, *A Woman on Paper*, pp. 58–9.

11 Interview for *Good Morning America* (November 1976), Laurie Lisle Research Documents, Archives of American Art, Washington, DC.

12 Lisle, *Portrait of an Artist*, p. 19; cited also in Robinson, *Georgia O'Keeffe*, p. 22.

13 O'Keeffe to Stieglitz, 13 November 1916. S. Greenough, ed., *Alfred Stieglitz: The Key Set: The Alfred Stieglitz Collection of Photographs*, 2 vols (Washington, DC, 2002), vol. I, p. 70.

14 Robinson, *Georgia O'Keeffe*, pp. 9–11. Andy Warhol, 'Georgia O'Keeffe and Juan Hamilton', *Interview*, September 1983, Reader's Proof copy, n.p. Beinecke Rare Book and Manuscript Library, Yale University, Yale Collection of American Literature, Alfred Stieglitz/Georgia O'Keeffe Archive, MSS 85, Box 217.

15 S. Greenough, ed., *My Faraway One: Selected Letters of Georgia O'Keeffe and Alfred Stieglitz*, vol. I: *1915–1933* (New Haven, CT, and London, 2011), p. 69 n. 147. O'Keeffe was sixteen years old in November 1903, long before she left home for professional training. By the time her mother was quite ill, in 1910, she was a young adult, 23 years old, and stayed to care for her younger siblings.

16 Frances O'Brien interviews conducted by Nancy Wall, 1986–7, Frances O'Brien Papers, Georgia O'Keeffe Museum.

17 Audio interview with Catherine O'Keeffe Klenert (1977), Laurie Lisle Research Documents, Archives of American Art, Washington, DC.

18 William S. Pollitzer (d. 2002) shared photocopies of the original O'Keeffe edits to Pollitzer's manuscript with the author.

19 O'Keeffe to Stieglitz, 13 November 1916, in Greenough, ed., *My Faraway One*, p. 70.

20 Warhol, 'Georgia O'Keeffe and Juan Hamilton'.

21 O'Keeffe to Stieglitz, 13 November 1916, in Greenough, ed., *My Faraway One*, pp. 68–9.

22 B. B. Lynes, *Georgia O'Keeffe: A Catalogue Raisonné*, 2 vols (New Haven, CT, and London, 1999), CR 32, untitled oil.

23 M. Braggiotti, 'Her Worlds are Many', *New York Post* (16 May 1946). M. L. Kotz, 'O'Keeffe at 90: Filling Space in a Beautiful Way', *Art News* (December 1977), p. 40.

24 Robinson, *Georgia O'Keeffe*, p. 19. District Five schoolhouse, called the Town Hall School, was on the Totto property.

25 O'Keeffe, *Georgia O'Keeffe*, n.p.

26 Lisle, *Portrait of an Artist*, p. 25, records that the O'Keeffes received $12,000 for the farmland in Wisconsin, and spent $3,500 on the new house in Williamsburg, Virginia.

27 Pollitzer, *A Woman on Paper*, p. 71. Photograph of the Wheatland house on pp. 72–3.

28 Robinson, *Georgia O'Keeffe*, pp. 40–42.

29 Ibid., p. 42 n. 5, citing Christine McRae Cocke, 'Georgia O'Keeffe as I Knew Her', *The Angeleus*, November 1934.

30 Lisle, *Portrait of an Artist*, p. 29.

31 Ibid., pp. 29–30, citing Cocke, 'Georgia O'Keeffe as I Knew Her'.

32 F. H. Hurt, 'The Virginia Years of Georgia O'Keeffe', *Commonwealth: The Magazine of Virginia*, XLVII/9 (October 1980), pp. 24–39. These pages illustrate her *Mortar Board* ink drawings and caricatures of the teachers.

33 Robinson, *Georgia O'Keeffe*, p. 49.

34 A. P. Wagner, '"Living on Paper": Georgia O'Keeffe and the Culture of Drawing and Watercolor in the Stieglitz Circle', dissertation submitted, University of Maryland, 2005, p. 130.

35 O'Keeffe, *Georgia O'Keeffe*, n.p.

36 Lisle, *Portrait of an Artist*, p. 34; Robinson, *Georgia O'Keeffe*, p. 53.

37 Lynes, *Georgia O'Keeffe*, CR 29.

38 O'Keeffe to Stieglitz, Canyon, Texas, 4 November 1916, in Greenough, ed., *My Faraway One*, p. 60.

39 Pollitzer, *A Woman on Paper*, p. 75.

40 Robinson, *Georgia O'Keeffe*, p. 60, citing Kotz, 'O'Keeffe at 90', p. 44.

41 Wagner, '"Living on Paper"', pp. 134–5 n. 71.

42 Robinson, *Georgia O'Keeffe*, p. 74. Pollitzer, *A Woman on Paper*, photograph of William Merritt Chase in his Art Students League class, pp. 88–9.

43 H. A. Read, 'Georgia O'Keeffe: Woman Artist whose Art is Sincerely Feminine', *Brooklyn Sunday Eagle Magazine* (6 April 1924), p. 4.

44 O'Keeffe to Anita Pollitzer, October 1915. Earlier prize drawings and quick portrait sketches were either given or thrown away; 'don't

expect to get any of it out ever again . . . I feel disgusted with it all
and am glad I'm disgusted.'

45 O'Keeffe, *Georgia O'Keeffe*, n.p. Cited in Robinson, *Georgia O'Keeffe*,
  p. 70, who contextualizes this famous first meeting by stating that
  Stieglitz and O'Keeffe first met on 2 January 1908.

46 Ibid., n.p.

47 Read, 'Georgia O'Keeffe', p. 4.

48 Pollitzer, *A Woman on Paper*, p. 101.

49 Ibid., pp. 77–8.

50 O'Keeffe to Stieglitz, 13 November 1916, in Greenough, ed.,
  My Faraway One, p. 69.

51 C. Tomkins, 'Profiles: The Rose in the Eye Looked Pretty Fine',
  New Yorker (4 March 1974), p. 66.

52 Pollitzer, *A Woman on Paper*, p. 107.

53 F. Stoker, *Georgia O'Keeffe in Canyon* (Canyon, TX, 1990), p. 5. Pollitzer,
  A Woman on Paper, pp. 107–8; Wagner, '"Living on Paper"', p. 147.

54 Robinson, *Georgia O'Keeffe*, p. 101.

55 K. Kuh, *The Artist's Voice: Talks with Seventeen Artists* (New York, 1962),
  p. 189.

56 Ibid., p. 190.

57 O'Keeffe to Pollitzer, autumn 1915, Beinecke Rare Book and Manuscript
  Library, Yale University, Yale Collection of American Literature,
  Alfred Stieglitz/Georgia O'Keeffe Archive, Series VIII, Box 208.

58 Lisle, *Portrait of an Artist*, pp. 73–4, based her description of the
  dramatic death of Ida O'Keeffe on the account of a neighbour, Ethel
  Holsinger. Audio interview with Catherine O'Keeffe Klenert (1977),
  Laurie Lisle Research Documents, Archives of American Art,
  Washington, DC.

59 Claudia O'Keeffe to Georgia O'Keeffe, 11 November 1918.
  Stieglitz/O'Keeffe Archive, MSS 85, Box 206.

2 Breakthrough: 'Charcoal Landscapes'

1 A. Pollitzer, 'That's Georgia!', *Saturday Review of Literature* (4
  November 1950), p. 41; Pollitzer, *A Woman on Paper: Georgia O'Keeffe*
  (New York, 1988), p. 1. Pollitzer states that they met at the Art

Students League, but this is an error, clarified by many sources, cf. her *Saturday Review* article, above.

2 Pollitzer, 'That's Georgia!', p. 41.
3 The full collection of O'Keeffe–Pollitzer letters is held in the Beinecke Rare Book and Manuscript Library, Yale University, Yale Collection of American Literature, Alfred Stieglitz/Georgia O'Keeffe Archive (hereafter: Stieglitz/O'Keeffe Archive), MSS 85, Boxes 208–9. The letters are reprinted in C. Giboire, ed., *Lovingly, Georgia: The Complete Correspondence of Georgia O'Keeffe and Anita Pollitzer* (New York, 1990); selected letters are published in the Pollitzer biography, *A Woman on Paper* (New York, 1988). Cf. N. Scott, 'The O'Keeffe–Pollitzer Correspondence, 1915–17', *Source*, III/1 (Fall 1983), pp. 34–42. The complete correspondence begins on 10 June 1915 and ends in 1973.
4 O'Keeffe to Barnes, March 1930, Barnes Foundation Archives, Merion, Pennsylvania.
5 S. Greenough, *Modern Art and America: Alfred Stieglitz and his New York Galleries*, exh. cat., National Gallery of Art, Washington, DC (2001), p. 24 n 3. De Zayas titled a caricature of Stieglitz 'Accoucheur d'idées', published in *Camera Work* (April 1912).
6 Greenough, *Modern Art and America*, pp. 277–311.
7 O'Keeffe to Stieglitz, 21 December 1916, in S. Greenough, ed., *My Faraway One: Selected Letters of Georgia O'Keeffe and Alfred Stieglitz*, vol. I: *1915–1933* (New Haven, CT, and London, 2011), p. 94.
8 G. O'Keeffe, introduction, in *Georgia O'Keeffe: A Portrait by Alfred Stieglitz*, exh. cat., Metropolitan Museum of Art, New York (1978), n.p. See Edmund Wilson, *American Earthquake* (New York, 1957), p. 102.
9 Pollitzer to O'Keeffe, 23 October 1915, in Pollitzer, *A Woman on Paper*, p. 33.
10 E. H. Turner, 'O'Keeffe as Abstraction', in *Georgia O'Keeffe: Abstraction*, ed. B. Haskell, exh. cat., Whitney Museum of American Art, New York (New Haven, CT, and London, 2009), p. 65.
11 O'Keeffe to Pollitzer, Charlottesville, Virginia, June 1915, 25 August 1915, in Pollitzer, *A Woman on Paper*, pp. 6, 12–13.
12 Pollitzer to O'Keeffe, 10 June 1915, ibid., pp. 3–6. A. Stieglitz, ed. *Camera Work*, XXXIV–XXXV (April–July 1911). The issue comprised four Steichen photographic montages of Auguste Rodin and his

sculpture of Balzac; there were also two gravures and seven coloured collotypes of the Rodin drawings, first shown at 291 in 1908.

13 A. P. Wagner, '"Living on Paper": Georgia O'Keeffe and the Culture of Drawing and Watercolor in the Stieglitz Circle', PhD dissertation, University of Maryland, 2005, p. 145.

14 O'Keeffe to Pollitzer, October 1915, in Pollitzer, *A Woman on Paper*, p. 30.

15 Ibid. For longer excerpt, see Giboire, ed., *Lovingly, Georgia*, p. 48.

16 O'Keeffe to Pollitzer, September 1915, in Pollitzer, *A Woman on Paper*, p. 15.

17 Arthur W. Macmahon to O'Keeffe, 16 September 1915, Stieglitz/O'Keeffe Archive, MSS 85, Box 201.

18 O'Keeffe to Pollitzer, Charlottesville, 21 June 1916, Stieglitz/O'Keeffe Archive, MSS 85, Box 208. This letter was written during O'Keeffe's period of mourning in the month after her mother's death on 2 May 1916.

19 Pollitzer to O'Keeffe, 3 October 1915, in Pollitzer, *A Woman on Paper*, p. 18.

20 O'Keeffe to Pollitzer, October 1915, ibid., p. 29.

21 A. J. Eddy, *Cubists and Post-Impressionism* (Chicago, IL, 1914). O'Keeffe later recalled seeing an early abstraction by Arthur Dove, *Based on Leaf Forms* (now lost), a colour plate in the book. The text opposite the Dove page encourages artists to look at the methods of Chinese painting.

22 O'Keeffe to Pollitzer, 26 October 1915, in Pollitzer, *A Woman on Paper*, p. 33.

23 O'Keeffe to Pollitzer, October 1915, ibid., p. 28.

24 O'Keeffe to Stieglitz, 14 August 1915, in Greenough, ed., *My Faraway One*, p. 3. O'Keeffe describes the folio periodical *291*, IV (June 1915).

25 O'Keeffe to Pollitzer, November 1915, in Giboire, ed., *Lovingly, Georgia*, p. 77.

26 Macmahon to O'Keeffe, 15 November 1915, Stieglitz/O'Keeffe Archive, MSS 85, Box 201.

27 Macmahon to O'Keeffe, 30 November 1915, ibid.

28 O'Keeffe to Pollitzer, November 1915, in Pollitzer, *A Woman on Paper*, p. 39.

29 O'Keeffe to Pollitzer, 13 December 1915, ibid., pp. 39–40.

30 Pollitzer to O'Keeffe, December 1915, ibid., p. 40.

31 Pollitzer to O'Keeffe, 20 and 30 December 1915, in Giboire, ed., *Lovingly, Georgia*, pp. 107, 111.

32 Macmahon to O'Keeffe, telegram, 24 December 1915, Stieglitz/O'Keeffe Archive, MSS 85, Box 201.

33 Ibid.

34 Pollitzer, *A Woman on Paper*, p. xxiii.

35 Pollitzer to O'Keeffe, postmarked 1 January 1916, Stieglitz/O'Keeffe Archive, MSS 85, Box 208. The letter was written late at night on New Year's Eve, 31 December 1915, with the postmark bearing the date it was mailed, 1 January 1916. The letter has been misdated for decades, and conflated with Stieglitz's birthday on 1 January. Stieglitz's keen memory for dates and special anniversaries would not have confused the epiphanic discovery of O'Keeffe as having been in November if the events had occurred on his birthday. Cf. *New Yorker* (6 July 1929); and Dorothy Norman, *Alfred Stieglitz: An American Seer* (New York, 1973), which represent accounts that blurred, then mythologized, accounts of the first encounter with O'Keeffe's art.

36 Scott, 'The O'Keeffe–Pollitzer Correspondence, 1915–17', p. 40 n. 3, clarifies the reasons for omitting or bracketing the phrase: 'written only in pencil, between the lines . . . and thus may represent her afterthought'. Wagner, '"Living on Paper"', p. 236 n. 175, discusses the various scholars' interpretations of the famous phrase.

37 Pollitzer to O'Keeffe, 1 January 1916 (postmark). Pollitzer, *A Woman on Paper*, reproduces first page of the letter, p. 45. Stieglitz/O'Keeffe Archive, Box 208. The Archive's Finding Aids note (p. 13) that Doris Bry noted dates on most of the letters, as is the case here, by postmark. This work was undertaken after Stieglitz's death, during the late 1940s.

38 O'Keeffe to Pollitzer, Columbia, South Carolina, 4 January 1916. In the long letter, she confides: 'but I'm terribly afraid the bubble will break'. In Giboire, ed., *Lovingly, Georgia*, pp. 117–18.

39 F. Dell, *Women as World Builders* (Chicago, IL, 1913), p. 10.

40 Pollitzer, *A Woman on Paper*, pp. 48–9.

41 Macmahon to O'Keeffe, January 1916; telegram, New York, 29 February 1916. Stieglitz/O'Keeffe Archive, MSS 85, Box 201.

42 O'Keeffe to Pollitzer, February 1916, in Giboire, ed., *Lovingly, Georgia*, p. 152. Pollitzer generously arranged for O'Keeffe to live with her uncle Sigmund Pollitzer and his wife, on East 60th Street.

43 Pollitzer, *A Woman on Paper*, pp. 48–9.

44 Stieglitz to O'Keeffe, 20 January 1916, in Greenough, ed., *My Faraway One*, p. 3.

45 O'Keeffe to Stieglitz, 1 February 1916, ibid., p. 4.

46 Greenough, ed., *My Faraway One*, p. xiv. O'Keeffe's final will prohibited access to these letters until twenty years after her death, so that the material became public only in 2006.

47 O'Keeffe to Stieglitz, 3 May 1916, in Greenough, ed., *My Faraway One*, p. 5.

48 O'Keeffe to Stieglitz, 21 and 28 May 1916, ibid., pp. 6–8.

49 Stieglitz to O'Keeffe, 6 May 1916; and O'Keeffe to Stieglitz, 8 May 1916, ibid., p. 6.

50 P. M. Adato, *Georgia O'Keeffe: American Masters* (1977), documentary, PBS, Educational Broadcasting, broadcast November 1977.

51 Norman, *Alfred Stieglitz*, p. 131. Wagner, '"Living on Paper"', pp. 253–4, relates the full story in context.

52 The dates of the first O'Keeffe group exhibition at 291 Fifth Avenue were 23 May–18 June 1916. K. Pyne, *Modernism*, p. 170 n. 120.

53 Stieglitz to O'Keeffe, 16 and 31 July 1916, in Greenough, ed., *My Faraway One*, pp. 15, 17.

54 *Camera Work*, XLVIII (1916), p. 12.

55 Pollitzer to Stieglitz, 3 July 1915, in Giboire, ed., *Lovingly, Georgia*. For Marin, see *291* (1915), which Pollitzer requested to be mailed directly to O'Keeffe in South Carolina. For Van Gogh and the *Cypresses*, see *Camera Work*, special number (June 1913); and Lisa Mintz Messinger, *Stieglitz and his Artists: Matisse to O'Keeffe*, exh. cat., Metropolitan Museum of Art, New York (New Haven, CT, and London, 2011), p. 194.

56 Wagner, '"Living on Paper"', p. 162. The show was titled *Exhibition of Recent Drawings and Paintings by Picasso and by Braque of Paris* and ran from 9 December 1914 to 11 January 1915.

57 H. Tyrell, 'New York Art Exhibitions and Gallery News', *Christian Science Monitor* (2 June 1916). Cited in Barbara B. Lynes, *O'Keeffe, Stieglitz and the Critics, 1916–29* (Chicago, IL, 1989), pp. 166–7.

58 Pollitzer to O'Keeffe, 20 August 1916. *American Art News* (May 1916), notice inserted in letter. Giboire, ed., *Lovingly, Georgia*, p. 176.

59 O'Keeffe to Stieglitz, 22 November 1916, in Greenough, ed., *My Faraway One*, pp. 79–80. B. B. Lynes, *Georgia O'Keeffe: A Catalogue Raisonné*, 2 vols (New Haven, CT, and London, 1999), CR 64.

60 O'Keeffe to Stieglitz, 24 and 30 November 1916, in Greenough, ed., *My Faraway One*, pp. 79, 84. O'Keeffe references the exhibition of *Blue Lines x* in a November group show at 291, with works by Marin, Dove and Walkowitz also on view.

61 Stieglitz to O'Keeffe, 26 August 1916 and 20 September 1916, ibid., pp. 20, 29. Stieglitz to O'Keeffe, 18 November 1916: Stieglitz describes the group exhibition where he includes her works for the first time at 291 with those of his modernist Americans, ibid., p. 50. Stieglitz to O'Keeffe, 30 April 1917: Stieglitz relates that a visitor found 'whiteness' [and] 'a religious sense of purity' in *Two Lines* and her *Self-portrait* (Lynes, *Georgia O'Keeffe*, CR 99), ibid., p. 144.

62 H. Tyrell, 'New York Art Exhibition and Gallery Notes: Esoteric Art at "291"', *Christian Science Monitor* (4 May 1917), p. 10, cited in Lynes, *O'Keeffe, Stieglitz and the Critics*, p. 168. For the confusion of title, cf. R. Robinson, *Georgia O'Keeffe: A Life* (New York, 1989), p. 179.

63 Pollitzer to O'Keeffe, 1916, in Giboire, ed., *Lovingly, Georgia*, pp. 195–6.

64 O'Keeffe to Stieglitz, 25 July and 26 August 1916, in Greenough, ed., *My Faraway One*, pp. 15 and 23.

65 Pollitzer to O'Keeffe, 1916, in Giboire, ed., *Lovingly, Georgia*, pp. 221–2.

66 O'Keeffe to Stieglitz, 26 August 1916, in Greenough, ed., *My Faraway One*, p. 23.

67 Stieglitz to O'Keeffe, 31 July 1916, ibid., p. 17.

3 Painting in Canyon: 'Between Heaven and Earth'

1 O'Keeffe to Stieglitz, 15 March 1917, in S. Greenough, *My Faraway One: Selected Letters of Georgia O'Keeffe and Alfred Stieglitz*, vol. I: *1915–1933* (New Haven, CT, and London, 2011), p. 124. The letters from O'Keeffe's time in Canyon, ibid., pp. 26–299, reflect the hundreds of letters, notes and telegrams exchanged by Stieglitz and O'Keeffe during the period in Texas from September 1916 to June 1918. These form a part of the Beinecke Rare Book and Manuscript Library, Yale University, Yale Collection of American Literature,

Alfred Stieglitz/Georgia O'Keeffe Archive, MSS 85, series 1 (hereafter: Stieglitz/O'Keeffe Archive). Alfred Stieglitz: Correspondence, Stieglitz/O'Keeffe Letters, 1916–46: Boxes 58–80; Stieglitz letters to O'Keeffe dated 1916–July 1946: Boxes 81–95, O'Keeffe letters to Stieglitz, August 1915–July 1946. The Canyon letters are held in eight archival boxes: 58–62; 81–3. All letters have been digitized.

2 O'Keeffe to Stieglitz, 3 September 1916, in Greenough, *My Faraway One*, p. 26.

3 G. O'Keeffe, *Georgia O'Keeffe* (New York, 1976), n.p.

4 O'Keeffe to Stieglitz, 30 November 1916, ibid., p. 84. B. B. Lynes, *Georgia O'Keeffe: A Catalogue Raisonné*, 2 vols (New Haven, CT, and London, 1999), CR 128–30.

5 O'Keeffe to Stieglitz, 11 October 1916, in Greenough, ed., *My Faraway One*, p. 42.

6 O'Keeffe to Stieglitz, 3 September 1916. Greenough, ed., *My Faraway One*, p. 26.

7 F. Stoker, *O'Keeffe in Canyon* (Canyon, TX, 1990), pp. 10–11.

8 O'Keeffe to Stieglitz, 11 October 1916, in Greenough, ed., *My Faraway One*, p. 42 n. 93. Stieglitz's letter, dated 1–7 October, was 33 pages long.

9 O'Keeffe to Stieglitz, 22 November 1916, ibid., p. 80.

10 O'Keeffe to Stieglitz, 10(?) January 1917, ibid., p. 100.

11 O'Keeffe to Stieglitz, 3 September 1916, ibid., p. 26.

12 O'Keeffe to Pollitzer, September 1916 (written after 11 September 1916: O'Keeffe describes teaching two courses in beginner's design, and another on costume design; she added another on interior design in November 1916), in C. Giboire, *Lovingly, Georgia: The Complete Correspondence of Georgia O'Keeffe and Anita Pollitzer* (New York, 1990), pp. 187–8.

13 Stoker, *O'Keeffe in Canyon*, p. 7; West Texas State Bulletin notes, pp. 40–41; E. H. Turner, *Georgia O'Keeffe: The Poetry of Things*, exh. cat., Phillips Collection, Washington, DC (1999), p. 50, illus. 33.

14 O'Keeffe to Pollitzer, December 1916, in Giboire, ed., *Lovingly, Georgia*, pp. 226–7. Willard Huntington Wright (1888–1939) was the brother of artist Stanton Macdonald-Wright, the abstract Synchromist painter of the Stieglitz circle, much admired by O'Keeffe.

15 C. Tomkins, 'The Rose in the Eye . . .', *New Yorker* (4 March 1974), p. 42.

16 O'Keeffe to Pollitzer, January 1917, in Giboire, ed., *Lovingly, Georgia*, pp. 238–9.

17 O'Keeffe to Pollitzer, January 1917, ibid.

18 O'Keeffe to Stieglitz, 18 October 1917, in Greenough, ed., *My Faraway One*, p. 199.

19 O'Keeffe to Stieglitz, 26 October 1916, ibid., p. 49 n. 111, for the full inscription by Stieglitz in the edition of Goethe, *Faust: A Tragedy*, ed. Bayard Taylor (1912), from the Book Room in O'Keeffe's house in Abiquiu, New Mexico. 'I have lived – When I was NINE I discovered Faust. / It gave me quiet then. – / I knew not why. – But it – Gave me quiet. And I / Have lived since then – much / & hard – & in consequence / suffered so that I could not / suffer anymore. Faust / quieted me in such despairing / moments – always / And as I grew it seemed to / Also grow. It is a Friend: / – Like the Lake. – To one who without knowing it has given me much at a time when I needed Faust & Lake. 1916.'

20 O'Keeffe to Stieglitz, 26 October 1916, in Greenough, ed., *My Faraway One*, p. 50, n. 112.

21 Stieglitz to O'Keeffe, 26 October 1916, ibid., pp. 47–8.

22 O'Keeffe to Stieglitz, 31 October 1916, ibid., pp. 57–8.

23 Stieglitz to O'Keeffe, 26 March 1917, ibid., pp. 124–5.

24 O'Keeffe to Stieglitz, 26 October 1916, ibid., p. 50.

25 O'Keeffe to Stieglitz, 15 March 1917, ibid., p. 124.

26 O'Keeffe, *Georgia O'Keeffe*, n.p.

27 O'Keeffe to Pollitzer, n.d., Stieglitz/O'Keeffe Archive, Series VIII, Box 208, cited in N. Scott, 'The O'Keeffe–Pollitzer Correspondence, 1915–17', *Source*, III/1 (Fall 1983), p. 34.

28 W. M. Fisher, 'The Georgia O'Keeffe Drawings and Paintings at 291'; reprinted in *Camera Work*, 49–50 (June 1917).

29 H. Tyrell, 'New York Art Exhibition and Gallery Notes: Esoteric Art at "291"', *Christian Science Monitor* (4 May 1917). Cited in B. B. Lynes, *O'Keeffe, Stieglitz and the Critics, 1916–29* (Chicago, IL, 1989), pp. 167–8.

30 O'Keeffe to Stieglitz, 9 May 1917, in Greenough, *My Faraway One*, p. 148.

31 O'Keeffe to Stieglitz, 29 May 1917, ibid., p. 150 n. 315.

32 A. Macmahon to O'Keeffe, [June?] 1917, Stieglitz/O'Keeffe Archive, MSS 85, Box 201.

33 A. Macmahon to O'Keeffe, May 1917 and 12 June 1917, ibid.

34 O'Keeffe to Pollitzer, 20 June 1917, in Giboire, ed., *Lovingly, Georgia*, pp. 254–6.

35 O'Keeffe to Stieglitz, 1 June 1917, in Greenough, ed., *My Faraway One*, p. 153.

36 O'Keeffe to Stieglitz, 15 March 1917, ibid., p. 122 n. 263.

37 O'Keeffe to Stieglitz, 24 April 1917, ibid., p. 139.

38 O'Keeffe to Stieglitz, 1 May 1917, ibid., p. 144.

39 O'Keeffe to Stieglitz, 29 November and 2 December 1917, ibid., pp. 216–17. On 2 December she wrote: 'Soldiers – my brother – his side partner – both engineers – What it is all doing to them is astounding to me – I seemed to feel like adopting his friend as a brother on sight.'

40 O'Keeffe to Stieglitz, 8 February 1918, ibid., p. 251. Cited article 'Attacked Tuesday at Dusk', *New York Times* (8 February 1918).

41 O'Keeffe to Stieglitz, 8 February 1918, ibid. '*Tuscania*'s Captain Saw an Ill Omen' and 'Thinks Destroyer Sank the U-boat', *New York Times* (8 February 1918). Both articles reported on the rescue operation by the British and secondary attacks to bring down the German submarine.

42 O'Keeffe to Stieglitz, 14 December 1917, in Greenough, ed., *My Faraway One*, p. 223.

43 O'Keeffe to Stieglitz, 11 March 1917, ibid., pp. 119–21.

44 Ibid.

45 O'Keeffe to Pollitzer, Canyon, Texas, September 1916, in Giboire, ed., *Lovingly, Georgia*, p. 186.

46 Lynes, *Georgia O'Keeffe*, CR 155, *Special No. 21* [*Palo Duro Canyon*, oil on board]; preceding *Special No. 21*, a series of drawings from the canyon: CR 135–153, and a charcoal, CR 154.

47 Greenough, ed., *My Faraway One*, p. 167 n. 357.

48 O'Keeffe to Stieglitz, 4 and 8 February 1918, ibid., p. 250. Seven *Camera Work* issues arrived as well as Van Gogh's *Letters of a Post-Impressionist: Being the Familiar Correspondence of Vincent Van Gogh* (Boston, MA, 1913).

49 O'Keeffe to Stieglitz, 14 February 1918, in Greenough, ed., *My Faraway One*, p. 254.

50 O'Keeffe to Stieglitz, 18 February 1917, ibid., p. 200 n. 417.

51 Lynes, *Georgia O'Keeffe*, CR 189–94.

52 Stieglitz to O'Keeffe, 9 May 1918, in Greenough, ed., *My Faraway One*, p. 286.

53 Ibid.

54 O'Keeffe to Stieglitz, Waring, Texas, 30 April 1918, in Greenough, ed., *My Faraway One*, p. 278.

55 Stieglitz to O'Keeffe, 9 May 1918, ibid., pp. 286–7. Stieglitz cites 'jury duty' and the 'situation at home' as reasons he could not leave New York.

56 O'Keeffe to Stieglitz, 14 December 1917, ibid., p. 223.

57 O'Keeffe to Stieglitz, 21 May 1918, ibid., p. 290.

58 Tomkins, 'The Rose in the Eye . . .', p. 42.

4 A Portrait: Woman

1 O'Keeffe to Stieglitz, San Antonio, Texas, 3 June 1918, in S. Greenough, ed., *My Faraway One: Selected Letters of Georgia O'Keeffe and Alfred Stieglitz*, vol. I: *1915–1933* (New Haven, CT, and London, 2011), p. 298.

2 Paul Strand to Stieglitz, 1 June 1918, ibid., p. 298 n. 567.

3 H. Drohojowska-Philp, *Full Bloom: The Art and Life of Georgia O'Keeffe* (New York, 2004), p. 169; Strand to Stieglitz, 13 September 1918, cited in R. Whelan, *Alfred Stieglitz: A Biography* (Boston, MA, 1995), p. 398 n. 6.

4 R. Robinson, *Georgia O'Keeffe: A Life* (New York, 1989), p. 218 n. 6. Robinson quotes Alexis O'Keeffe's letter to her sister Catherine, describing his distaste for his older sister's living circumstances in autumn 1918, having found her living with an elderly man in a New York garret. Audio interview with Catherine O'Keeffe Klenert (1977), Laurie Lisle Research Documents, Archives of American Art, Washington, DC. Klenert related that Alexis was brought home 'on a cot' and recuperated for one year.

5 Stieglitz to Strand, 27 April 1919, cited in K. Pyne, *Modernism and the Feminine Voice: O'Keeffe and the Women of the Stieglitz Circle*, exh. cat., Georgia O'Keeffe Museum (Berkeley, CA, 2007), p. 216 n. 38.

6 O'Keeffe to Stieglitz, 14 June 1918, in Greenough, ed., *My Faraway One*, p. 302.

7 Stieglitz to O'Keeffe, 15 June 1918, ibid., pp. 302–3.

8   Stieglitz to O'Keeffe, 5 August 1929, ibid., p. 506.

9   Stieglitz to Marie Rapp, July 1918, cited ibid., p. 307 n. 571. S. D. Lowe,
    Stieglitz: A Memoir/Biography (New York, 1983), p. 217.

10 Whelan, *Alfred Stieglitz*, pp. 399–400.

11 Alfred Stieglitz to Sadakichi Hartmann, 27 April 1919. Cited in
    S. Greenough and J. Hamilton, *Alfred Stieglitz*, exh. cat., National
    Gallery of Art, Washington, DC (1983), p. 205. K. Hoffman, *Alfred
    Stieglitz: A Legacy of Light* (New Haven, CT, and London, 2011), p. 105,
    confirms that Stieglitz made more than 100 photographs in the first
    two years, and states that 50 of the series were created during their
    first months together.

12 *Georgia O'Keeffe: A Portrait by Alfred Stieglitz*, exh. cat., Metropolitan
    Museum of Art, New York (1978), n.p. (introduction by G. O'Keeffe).

13 A. Pollitzer, *A Woman on Paper: Georgia O'Keeffe* (New York, 1988),
    p. 188: 'Stieglitz had the idea for some time, long before he knew
    Georgia, of doing a series of photographs on woman – not woman
    stylishly gowned or languorously draped – but woman.'

14 'Introduction', in *Georgia O'Keeffe: A Portrait*, n.p.: 'The camera always
    stood near the wall – a box maybe a foot square and four or five inches
    thick. It stood on its rickety tripod with the black headcloth over it . . .
    At a certain time of day the light was best for photographing – so at
    that time we usually tried to be in Elizabeth's studio.'

15 Lowe, *Stieglitz*, p. 433. Appendix II: Exhibition arranged by Stieglitz
    at the Anderson Galleries, 489 Park Avenue (7–14? February 1921):
    *Stieglitz 146 photographs '(128 never exhibited before, 78 done since July
    1918). Demonstration of Portraiture, A Woman 1918–20.'*

16 'Introduction', in *Georgia O'Keeffe: A Portrait*, n.p.

17 Ibid.

18 Lowe, *Stieglitz*, pp. 217–18.

19 Stieglitz to O'Keeffe, 5 August 1929, in Greenough, ed., *My Faraway
    One*, p. 506. Stieglitz writes that soon it will be 9 August: 'eleven years
    since you gave me your virginity'.

20 Ibid.

21 Drohojowska-Philp, *Full Bloom*, p. 185 n. 23.

22 'Introduction', in *Georgia O'Keeffe: A Portrait*, n.p.

23 E. B. Coe, *Modern Nature: Georgia O'Keeffe and Lake George*, exh. cat.,
    The Hyde Collection, Glen Falls, New York (2013). B. B. Lynes, *Georgia

O'Keeffe: Catalogue Raisonné, 2 vols (New Haven, CT, and London, 1999), CR 289–91. *Lake George, Coat and Red*, 1919, and *Series 1, no. 10 and 10A*, 1919, were among O'Keeffe's first oils at Lake George.

24 Stieglitz to Paul Strand, 23 January 1919, cited in Whelan, *Alfred Stieglitz*, p. 407 n. 15.

25 Leo Janos, 'O'Keeffe at Eighty-four', *The Atlantic* (December 1971), p. 115; Pollitzer, *A Woman on Paper*, p. 165.

26 Pollitzer, *A Woman on Paper*, p. 175.

27 Arthur Dove to Stieglitz, 16 September 1919, cited in B. Haskell, ed., *O'Keeffe: Abstraction*, exh. cat., Whitney Museum of American Art, New York (New Haven, CT, 2011), p. 71.

28 Lynes, *Georgia O'Keeffe*, CR 286; collection of Helen Torr Dove, until 1949.

29 Stieglitz to Paul Strand, 5 January 1919, cited in S. W. Peters, *Becoming O'Keeffe: The Early Years* (New York, 1991), p. 149.

30 Whelan, *Alfred Stieglitz*, p. 407. The first exhibition of Stieglitz's photographs of O'Keeffe, in March 1919, was arranged by Aline Liebman, a friend, artist and later collector of O'Keeffe's art, at the Young Women's Hebrew Association.

31 S. Greenough, ed., *Alfred Stieglitz: The Key Set: The Alfred Stieglitz Collection of Photographs*, 2 vols (Washington, DC, 2002).

32 O'Keeffe to Stieglitz, 15 March 1918, cited in Haskell, ed., *O'Keeffe: Abstraction*, p. 66.

33 Stieglitz to O'Keeffe, 9 January 1918, in Greenough, ed., *My Faraway One*, p. 233.

34 Pyne, 'The Feminine Voice and the Woman-child', *Modernism and the Feminine Voice*, pp. 119–24.

35 Stieglitz to Stanton Macdonald-Wright, 9 October 1919. Cited in D. Norman, *Alfred Stieglitz: An American Seer* (New York, 1973), p. 138.

36 Ibid., p. 137.

37 R. Cozzolino, 'PAFA and Dr Barnes', *American Art*, XXVII/3 (Fall 2013), pp. 20–26, fig. 2.

38 L. M. Messinger, *Stieglitz and his Artists: Matisse to O'Keeffe*, exh cat., Metropolitan Museum of Art, New York (New Haven, CT, and London, 2011), p. 207. Lynes, *Georgia O'Keeffe*, CR 258, Whitney Museum of American Art, New York.

39 F. Dell, *Women as World Builders* (Chicago, IL, 1913), pp. 49–50.

40 Pyne, *Modernism and the Feminine Voice*, p. 236 n. 67.

41 C. S. Merrill, *Weekends with O'Keeffe* (Albuquerque, NM, 2010), p. 4.

42 Lowe, *Stieglitz*, p. 441.

43 Ibid., p. 433. Stieglitz detailed all the names of sitters who were included in his portfolio of the *Demonstration of Portraiture*, until the final group, which bore the title *A Woman, 1918–20*. B. Haskell and S. Nicholas, 'Georgia O'Keeffe: A Contextual Chronology', in *Georgia O'Keeffe*, ed. Haskell, p. 212. Current scholarship has established that there were 45 photographs of O'Keeffe on view.

44 Stieglitz to Anne Brigman, 24 December 1919. Cited in Pyne, *Modernism and the Feminine Voice*, p. 113.

45 T. A. Carbone, 'Body Language', in *Youth and Beauty: Art of the American Twenties*, exh. cat., Brooklyn Museum of Art, New York (2011), p. 47.

46 Henry McBride, 'O'Keeffe at the Museum', *New York Sun* (18 May 1946), p. 9.

47 Pyne, *Modernism and the Feminine Voice*, p. 239 n. 73.

48 P. Rosenfeld, 'Stieglitz', *The Dial* (April 1921), pp. 408–9.

49 Whelan, *Alfred Stieglitz*, p. 418; H. McBride, 'Modern Art', *The Dial*, vxx (January 1921), pp. 113–14.

50 M. Hartley, 'Some Women Artists in Modern Painting', in *Adventures in the Arts* (New York, 1921), p. 116.

51 P. Rosenfeld, 'American Painting', *The Dial*, vxxi (December 1921), pp. 666–70. Cited in Lynes, *Georgia O'Keeffe*, no. 6, p. 171.

52 Lynes, *Georgia O'Keeffe*, CR 283–5.

53 Rosenfeld, 'American Painting', p. 665.

54 Ibid.

55 P. Rosenfeld, 'The Paintings of Georgia O'Keeffe: The Work of the Young Artist Whose Canvases are to be Exhibited in Bulk for the First Time this Winter', *Vanity Fair*, xviii (July 1922), pp. 56, 112, 114.

56 'The Female of the Species Achieves a New Deadliness: Women Painters of America Whose Work Exhibits Distinctiveness of Style and Marked Individuality', *Vanity Fair*, xix (July 1922), p. 50.

5 New York: 'The Nimbus of Lustre'

1 Alfred Stieglitz Collection, exhibition brochure, Anderson Galleries, New York, 29 January–10 February 1923. C. Eldredge, *Georgia O'Keeffe: American and Modern*, exh. cat., Hayward Gallery, London (New York, 1993), pp. 158–9.

2 B. B. Lynes, *Georgia O'Keeffe: Catalogue Raisonné*, 2 vols (New Haven, CT, and London, 1999), CR 283–7. Seven pastels remain from the work of May 1922 in the catalogue raisonné.

3 G. O'Keeffe, 'To *MSS*, and its 33 Subscribers', *MSS*, IV (December 1922), cited in Lynes, *Georgia O'Keeffe*, p. 182.

4 R. Whelan, *Alfred Stieglitz: A Biography* (Boston, MA, 1995), p. 438. He notes that O'Keeffe made $3,000 from sales at the 1923 exhibition. R. Robinson, *Georgia O'Keeffe: A Life* (New York, 1989), p. 254, for reference to twenty pieces sold.

5 O'Keeffe to Henry McBride, February 1923, p. 171, cited in J. Cowart, S. Greenough and J. Hamilton, *Georgia O'Keeffe: Art and Letters*, exh. cat., National Gallery of Art, Washington, DC (1987).

6 O'Keeffe to Mitchell Kennerley, Autumn 1922, cited ibid., p. 170.

7 Georgia O'Keeffe, statement in *Alfred Stieglitz Present One Hundred Pictures* (New York, 29 January–10 February 1923), cited in B. Lynes, *O'Keeffe, Stieglitz and the Critics, 1916–29* (Chicago, IL, 1989), no. 11, p. 184.

8 Lynes, *Georgia O'Keeffe*, CR 181–4, 186–7. Stieglitz to O'Keeffe, 17 August 1917, in S. Greenough, ed., *My Faraway One: Selected Letters of Georgia O'Keeffe and Alfred Stieglitz*, vol. I: *1915–1933* (New Haven, CT, and London, 2011), p. 186.

9 S. D. Lowe, *Stieglitz: A Memoir/Biography* (New York, 1983), pp. 24–7.

10 O'Keeffe to Stieglitz, 3 May 1922, in Greenough, ed., *My Faraway One*, p. 318.

11 Guanyin, *Bodhisattva of Compassion*, carved limestone, Museum of Fine Arts, Boston. Originally: the Old Stone Buddha Monastery (Gu Shi-fo Si) near Xi'an, Shanxi Province, China.

12 El Greco, *Fray Felix Paravicino* (1609), Museum of Fine Arts, Boston.

13 O'Keeffe to Stieglitz to O'Keeffe, Boston, Massachusetts, May 1922, cited in *Georgia O'Keeffe: Abstraction*, ed. B. Haskell, exh. cat., Whitney Museum of American Art, New York (2009), p. 197.

14 O'Keeffe to Stieglitz, 4 May 1922, in Greenough, ed., *My Faraway One*, p. 324. She and Stieglitz shared pet names for genitalia; hers was Fluffy and his was 'Little Man'.

15 O'Keeffe to Stieglitz, 8 May 1922, ibid., p. 328.

16 O'Keeffe to Stieglitz, 11 May 1922, ibid., p. 331.

17 Lynes, *Georgia O'Keeffe*, CR 385–6. Metropolitan Museum of Art, New York, and Museum of Fine Arts, Boston.

18 O'Keeffe to Stieglitz, 16 May 1922, in Greenough, ed., *My Faraway One*, pp. 333–4.

19 Alfred Stieglitz, *Music: A Sequence of Ten Cloud Photographs and Songs of the Sky*. Noteworthy in this series is *Portrait of Georgia, no. 3 – Songs of the Sky*, J. Paul Getty Museum. See K. Hoffman, *Stieglitz: A Legacy of Light* (New Haven, CT, and London, 2011), fig. 159.

20 H. A. Read, 'Georgia O'Keeffe's Show: An Emotional Escape', *Brooklyn Daily Eagle* (11 February 1923), p. 2b, cited in Lynes, *O'Keeffe, Stieglitz and the Critics*, p. 191.

21 Ibid.

22 H. McBride, 'Art News and Reviews: Woman as Exponent of the Abstract: Free without the Aid of Freud', *New York Herald* (4 February 1923), Sec. 7, p. 7, cited in Lynes, *O'Keeffe, Stieglitz and the Critics*, pp. 187–9.

23 Ibid. Cf. interview notes for *Good Morning America* (ABC News, November 1976), Laurie Lisle Research Documents, Archives of American Art, Washington, DC.

24 A. Brook, 'February Exhibitions: Georgia O'Keefe', *The Arts*, III (February 1923), pp. 130, 132.

25 Herbert J. Seligmann, 'Georgia O'Keeffe, American', *MSS* (March 1923), p. 5.

26 Lowe, *Stieglitz*, pp. 262–3. Emmy Stieglitz died in 1953, and their daughter Kitty in 1971, ibid., p. 92: Flora Stieglitz Stern, Alfred's beloved sister, had died from childbirth complications in 1890.

27 Stieglitz to O'Keeffe, 6 July 1929, in Greenough, ed., *My Faraway One*, p. 457.

28 Stieglitz to O'Keeffe, 26 May 1918, ibid., p. 296.

29 O'Keeffe to Stieglitz, 23 September 1923, ibid., p. 350. L. Eilshemius: 'first show's overemphasis of abstract puzzles was reduced to only three'. Cited in Lynes, *O'Keeffe, Stieglitz and the Critics*, no. 24, p. 200.

O'Keeffe to Sherwood Anderson, 11 February 1924, cited in Cowart, Greenough and Hamilton, *Georgia O'Keeffe*, p. 176.

30 Anon., 'I Can't Sing, So I Paint! Say Ultra Realistic Artist; Art is Not Photography – It is Expression of Inner Life! Miss Georgia O'Keeffe Explains Subjective Aspect of her Work', *New York Sun* (5 December 1922), p. 22, cited in Lynes, *O'Keeffe, Stieglitz and the Critics*, p. 180.

31 H. A. Read, 'News and Views on Current Art: Georgia O'Keefe [*sic*] again Introduced by Stieglitz at the Anderson Galleries', *Brooklyn Daily Eagle* (9 March 1924), p. 2. Cited in Lynes, *O'Keeffe, Stieglitz and the Critics*, p. 201.

32 H. A. Read, 'Georgia O'Keeffe: Woman Artist Whose Art is Sincerely Feminine', *Brooklyn Sunday Eagle Magazine* (6 April 1924), p. 4, cited in Lynes, *O'Keeffe, Stieglitz and the Critics*, pp. 211–14.

33 H. McBride, 'Stieglitz–O'Keefe [*sic*] Show at the Anderson Galleries', *New York Herald* (9 March 1924). Cited in Lynes, *O'Keeffe, Stieglitz and the Critics*, pp. 199–201.

34 Interview notes for *Good Morning America*, Laurie Lisle Research Documents.

35 Ibid.

36 O'Keeffe to Henry McBride, February 1923, cited in Cowart, Greenough and Hamilton, *Georgia O'Keeffe*, p. 172.

37 K. Kuh, *The Artist's Voice: Talks with Seventeen Artists* (New York, 1962), p. 191. Lynes, *Georgia O'Keeffe*, CR 483.

38 A. Chave, 'Who Will Paint New York?', in *From the Faraway Nearby: Georgia O'Keeffe as Icon*, ed. C. Merrill and E. Bradbury (Reading, MA, 1992), p. 74.

39 O'Keeffe to Stieglitz, 26 September 1923. Haskell, ed., *O'Keeffe: Abstraction*, p. 70, pl. 73: *Pink Moon and Blue Lines* (1923). Lynes, *Georgia O'Keeffe*, CR 406.

40 G. O'Keeffe, *Georgia O'Keeffe* (New York, 1976), n.p.

41 O'Keeffe, 'To *MSS*, and its 33 Subscribers', cited in Lynes, *O'Keeffe, Stieglitz and the Critics*, p. 182.

42 K. Hoffman, *Alfred Stieglitz: A Legacy of Light* (New Haven, CT, and London, 2011), pp. 202–6.

43 F. O'Brien, 'Americans We Like', *The Nation* (1926), cited in Lynes, *O'Keeffe, Stieglitz and the Critics*, p. 269.

44 L. Sabine, 'Record Price for Living Artist: Canvases of Georgia O'Keeffe', *Brooklyn Sunday Eagle Magazine* (27 May 1928), p. 11, cited in Lynes, *O'Keeffe, Stieglitz and the Critics*, no. 79, p. 288.

45 V. Fryd, 'Georgia O'Keeffe's *Radiator Building*', *Winterthur Portfolio*, xxxv/4 (Winter 2000), pp. 269–89.

46 Chave, 'Who Will Paint New York?', p. 72.

47 M. Pemberton, 'About Town', *New Yorker* (20 February 1926), cited in S. Pemberton, *Portrait of Murdock Pemberton: The New Yorker's First Art Critic* (Enfield, NH, 2011), p. 189.

48 Ibid.

49 B. Novak, 'Georgia O'Keeffe and American Intellectual and Visual Traditions', in *The Georgia O'Keeffe Museum*, ed. G. King (New York, 1997), pp. 73–97.

50 Jennifer Gross, ed., *The Société Anonyme: Modernism for America*, exh. cat., Yale University Art Gallery (New Haven, CT, and London, 2006), p. 81 fig. 7.

51 H. Seligmann, *Alfred Stieglitz Talking* (New Haven, CT, 1966), pp. 128–9.

52 O'Keeffe to Stieglitz, 26 February and 1 and 28 March 1926. Beinecke Rare Book and Manuscript Library, Yale University, Yale Collection of American Literature, Alfred Stieglitz/Georgia O'Keeffe Archive, MSS 85, Box 84.

53 E. A. Jewell, 'Art in Review: Georgia O'Keeffe's Paintings Offer Five-year Retrospective at An American Place', *New York Times* (13 January 1933).

54 H. McBride, 'Georgia O'Keefe's [*sic*] Recent Work', *New York Sun* (14 January 1928), p. 8, cited in Lynes, *O'Keeffe, Stieglitz and the Critics*, no. 70, pp. 274–5.

55 B. Robertson, in E. B. Coe, *Modern Nature: Georgia O'Keeffe and Lake George*, exh. cat., The Hyde Collection, Glen Falls, New York (2013), p. 78.

56 L. Kalonyme, 'Fifty Recent Paintings by Georgia O'Keeffe', The Intimate Gallery, New York, 11 February–3 April 1926, cited in Lynes, *O'Keeffe, Stieglitz and the Critics*, p. 252.

57 E. A. Jewell, 'Georgia O'Keeffe, Mystic', *New York Times* (22 January 1928), p. 12, cited in Lynes, *O'Keeffe, Stieglitz and the Critics*, no. 72, pp. 276–8.

58 Jewell, 'Art in Review: Georgia O'Keeffe's Paintings'.

59 Robinson, *Georgia O'Keeffe*, p. 304 n. 53. The date of O'Keeffe's second procedure at Mount Sinai Hospital was noted by Helen 'Reds' Torr, the wife of Arthur Dove, in her diary on 30 December 1927.

60 Stieglitz to O'Keeffe, 6 July 1929, p. 462, in Greenough, ed., *My Faraway One*. Stieglitz's passionate letter of love for Georgia, from the next summer, reveals that he had found out that she discussed the third surgery with her sister only: 'Ida told me all about all about Berg & the operation he wanted to make'.

61 O'Keeffe, *Georgia O'Keeffe*. Lynes, *Georgia O'Keeffe*, CR 574.

62 M. P. [Pemberton], 'In the Galleries', *New Yorker* (10 March 1928), p. 77.

63 O'Keeffe to Stieglitz, 9 July 1929, in Greenough, ed., *My Faraway One*, p. 469.

64 O'Keeffe to Stieglitz, 2 June 1928, ibid., p. 385.

65 O'Keeffe to Stieglitz, 12 July 1928, ibid., p. 389.

66 Robinson, *Georgia O'Keeffe*, p. 308 n. 71.

67 Ibid., p. 386, citing letter of 29 October 1931 to Catherine O'Keeffe Klenert.

68 A. Stieglitz, 'O'Keeffe and the Lilies', letter to the editor, *Art News* (21 April 1928), cited in Lynes, *O'Keeffe, Stieglitz and the Critics*, p. 285.

69 J. Moore, 'The Pale Beauty of Priceless Flowers', in *Georgia O'Keeffe and the Calla Lily in American Art, 1860–1940*, exh. cat., Georgia O'Keeffe Museum (Santa Fe, NM, 2002), pp. 38–57.

70 H. McBride, 'Paintings by Georgia O'Keefe [*sic*]', *New York Sun* (9 February 1929), p. 7, cited in Lynes, *O'Keeffe, Stieglitz and the Critics*, p. 295.

71 'Paul Strand: New Photographs', exh. pamphlet, The Intimate Gallery, New York, 19 March–7 April 1929. Cited in R. Busselle and T. W. Stack, *Paul Strand: Southwest* (New York, 2004), p. 79.

72 Ibid., pp. 76–7.

6 New Mexico: 'I Feel Like Bursting'

1 Stieglitz to O'Keeffe, 6 July 1929, in S. Greenough, ed., *My Faraway One: Selected Letters of Georgia O'Keeffe and Alfred Stieglitz*, vol. I: *1915–1933* (New Haven, CT, and London, 2011), p. 460.

2 R. Busselle and T. W. Stack, *Paul Strand: Southwest* (New York, 2004), p. 74.

3 B. B. Lynes, *Georgia O'Keeffe: Catalogue Raisonné*, 2 vols (New Haven, CT, and London, 1999), CR 616.

4 O'Keeffe to Stieglitz, 30 April 1929, in Greenough, ed., *My Faraway One*, p. 411.

5 Rebecca Strand to Paul Strand, 2 May 1929, cited in Busselle and Stack, *Paul Strand: Southwest*, p. 86.

6 M. D. Luhan, *Lorenzo in Taos* (New York, 1932), pp. 3–28, 35–41. See also M. D. Luhan, *Edge of Taos Desert: An Escape to Reality* (Albuquerque, NM, 1987), p. 35; original edition, *Intimate Memories*, vol. IV (1937). L. P. Rudnick, *Mabel Dodge Luhan: New Woman, New Worlds* (Albuquerque, NM, 1984). Mabel Luhan changed the spelling of her name from the Spanish 'Lujan' that her husband, Tony Lujan, retained. The different spelling of their names is used here accordingly.

7 O'Keeffe to Stieglitz, 30 April 1929, 2 May 1929, in Greenough, ed., *My Faraway One*, pp. 411–12.

8 P. M. Adato, *Georgia O'Keeffe: American Masters* (1977), documentary, PBS, Educational Broadcasting, broadcast November 1977.

9 R. Larson and C. Larson, *Ernest L. Blumenschein: The Life of an American Artist* (Norman, OK, 2013), p. 96.

10 Busselle and Stack, *Paul Strand: Southwest*, p. 77.

11 S. Schwartz, 'When New York Went to New Mexico', *Art in America*, LXIV/4 (July–August 1976), pp. 93–7.

12 H. McBride, 'O'Keeffe in Taos', *New York Sun* (8 January 1930), cited in McBride, *The Flow of Art* (New York, 1975), p. 262.

13 O'Keeffe to Stieglitz, 10 and 30 May 1929, in Greenough, ed., *My Faraway One*, pp. 419, 429.

14 Interview notes for *Good Morning America* (ABC News, November 1976), Laurie Lisle Research Documents, Archives of American Art, Washington, DC.

15 McBride, *The Flow of Art*, p. 261.

16 G. O'Keeffe, *Georgia O'Keeffe* (New York, 1976), n.p.; Lynes, *Georgia O'Keeffe*, CR 667.

17 O'Keeffe to Stieglitz, 30 June 1929, in Greenough, ed., *My Faraway One*, p. 448.

18 Rudnick, *Mabel Dodge Luhan*, p. 188.

19 O'Keeffe to Stieglitz, 7 May 1929, in Greenough, ed., *My Faraway One*,
    p. 417. 'Tony is much interested in your letters to me – He can't read'.
    O'Keeffe to Stieglitz, 24 June 1929, ibid., p. 440.

20 R. Robinson, *Georgia O'Keeffe: A Life* (New York, 1989), pp. 330, 332.

21 O'Keeffe to Stieglitz, 3–4 May 1929, in Greenough, ed., *My Faraway
    One*, p. 415.

22 O'Keeffe to Stieglitz, 21 May 1929, ibid., p. 424. Lynes, *Georgia
    O'Keeffe*, CR 686, *Trees at Glorieta, New Mexico*.

23 O'Keeffe to Stieglitz, 29 May 1929, in Greenough, ed., *My Faraway
    One*, p. 428. Lynes, *Georgia O'Keeffe*, CR 662, *Ranchos De Taos Church*,
    Phillips Collection, Washington, DC.

24 O'Keeffe to Stieglitz, 29 May 1929, in Greenough, ed., *My Faraway
    One*, pp. 428–9. Lynes, *Georgia O'Keeffe*, CR 666.

25 Lynes, *Georgia O'Keeffe*, CR 650.

26 O'Keeffe to Stieglitz, 4 July 1929, in Greenough, ed., *My Faraway One*,
    p. 454.

27 Stieglitz to O'Keeffe, 4 July 1929, ibid., p. 452.

28 O'Keeffe to Stieglitz, 27–30 June 1929, ibid., pp. 446–7.

29 Stieglitz to O'Keeffe, 24 June 1929, ibid., p. 441.

30 Stieglitz to O'Keeffe, 27 June 1929, ibid., pp. 445–6.

31 Stieglitz to O'Keeffe, 21 May 1929, ibid., p. 422. Stieglitz to O'Keeffe,
    21 June 1929, ibid., p. 438: '[Miguel] Covarrubias has made a drawing
    of you.'

32 O'Keeffe to Stieglitz, 25 July 1916, in Greenough, ed., *My Faraway One*,
    p. 15. Months after Pollitzer's fateful visit of 31 December 1915, O'Keeffe
    did write about her ambivalence: 'I wouldn't mind if . . . you had torn
    them all up . . . but I'm not always the same.' Ibid.

33 O'Keeffe to Stieglitz, 13 July 1929, in Greenough, ed., *My Faraway One*,
    p. 476.

34 Stieglitz to O'Keeffe, 1 July 1929, ibid., p. 449.

35 Stieglitz to O'Keeffe, 6 July 1929, ibid., p. 457.

36 Stieglitz to O'Keeffe, 11 and 7 July 1929, ibid., p. 468; p. 471 n. 117.

37 O'Keeffe to Stieglitz, 9 July 1929, ibid., p. 468.

38 Ibid.

39 Stieglitz to O'Keeffe, 6 July 1929, ibid., p. 461.

40 O'Keeffe to Stieglitz, 9 July 1929, ibid., p. 469.

41 R. Whelan, *Alfred Stieglitz: A Biography* (Boston, MA, 1995),
   pp. 512–13.

42 Strand to O'Keeffe, 11 July 1929, in Greenough, ed., *My Faraway One*,
   p. 474 n. 120.

43 Stieglitz to O'Keeffe, 15 July 1929, ibid., p. 480 n. 124.

44 B. Grad, 'Georgia O'Keeffe's Lawrencean Vision', *Archives of American
   Art Journal*, XXXVIII/3–4 (1998), p. 16 n. 17.

45 Stieglitz to O'Keeffe, 25 July 1928, in Greenough, ed., *My Faraway
   One*, p. 397. R. Fine and E. Glassman, *The Book Room: Georgia
   O'Keeffe's Library in Abiquiu* (Abiquiu, 1997), p. 44.

46 O'Keeffe to Stieglitz, 29 July 1929, in Greenough, ed., *My Faraway
   One*, p. 499.

47 O'Keeffe to Stieglitz, 29 July 1929, ibid., p. 501.

48 Grad, 'Georgia O'Keeffe's Lawrencean Vision', p. 15 n. 2. The painting
   was exhibited as *Pine Tree with Stars – Brett's, N. M.* in O'Keeffe's 1930
   exhibition, but after Lawrence's death on 6 March 1930 she changed
   the title to *D. H. Lawrence's Tree*, and still later to *The Lawrence Tree*.

49 O'Keeffe to Stieglitz, 2 August 1929, in Greenough, ed., *My Faraway
   One*, p. 505.

50 O'Keeffe to Stieglitz, 8 and 9 August, 1929, ibid., pp. 512–14.

51 O'Keeffe to Stieglitz, Stieglitz to O'Keeffe, letter, telegrams of 18–19
   August 1929, ibid., pp. 522–4.

52 Robinson, *Georgia O'Keeffe*, p. 348, citing Georgia to Betty O'Keeffe,
   24 January 1930.

7 The Great Depression: New York and Lake George

1 Esther Adler, 'The Problem of our American Collection: MOMA
  Collects at Home', in *American Modern: Hopper to O'Keeffe* (New York,
  2013), pp. 125–40.

2 S. D. Lowe, *Stieglitz: A Memoir/Biography* (New York, 1983),
  pp. 300–301.

3 Barnes to O'Keeffe, 11 March 1930, Presidents' Files, Albert
  C. Barnes Correspondence. The Barnes Foundation Archives, Merion,
  Pennsylvania. Reprinted with permission. Beinecke Rare Book and
  Manuscript Library, Yale University, Yale Collection of American

Literature, Alfred Stieglitz/Georgia O'Keeffe Archive (hereafter: Stieglitz/O'Keeffe Archive), MSS 85, Box 180.

4 E. Passantino, ed., *Eye of Duncan Phillips: A Collection in the Making*, Phillips Collection, Washington, DC (New Haven, CT, and London, 1999), p. 434.

5 Barnes to Stieglitz, 19 December 1930, Presidents' Files, Albert C. Barnes Correspondence, The Barnes Foundation Archives, Merion, Pennsylvania. Reprinted with permission. B. B. Lynes, *Georgia O'Keeffe: Catalogue Raisonné*, 2 vols (New Haven, CT, and London, 1999), CR 673. *The Wooden Virgin*, a painting of a 'santo' (after a wooden ritual icon O'Keeffe owned in 1929, created in New Mexico), was listed as no. 18 in the O'Keeffe exhibition of 1930 at An American Place. In a letter Stieglitz also referred to the Barnes painting as a 'santo' on receipt of the work in New York: Stieglitz to Barnes, 7 January 1931, Presidents' Files, Albert C. Barnes Correspondence, The Barnes Foundation Archives, Merion, Pennsylvania. Reprinted with permission.

6 Barnes Foundation Archives. Accession card, no. 1002: typed title 'Still Life'. The word 'Eggs' is pencilled in on the accession card, possibly *Still-life with 3 Eggs* of 1929, Museum of New Mexico, Santa Fe. See Lynes, *Georgia O'Keeffe*, CR 647.

7 Barnes to O'Keeffe, 21 March 1930, Presidents' Files, Albert C. Barnes Correspondence. The Barnes Foundation Archives, Merion, PA. Reprinted with permission.

8 Barnes to Stieglitz, 21 March 1930, by Western Union. Stieglitz/O'Keeffe Archive, Box 3.

9 Barnes to Stieglitz, 19 December 1930, Presidents' Files, Albert C. Barnes Correspondence. The Barnes Foundation Archives, Merion, Pennsylvania. Reprinted with permission.

10 O'Keeffe to Barnes, [28?] December 1930. Stieglitz/O'Keeffe Archive, Series VIII: Georgia O'Keeffe Correspondence, MSS 85, Box 180.

11 Dove to Stieglitz, 4 December 1930, Presidents' Files, Albert C. Barnes Correspondence. The Barnes Foundation Archives, Merion, Pennsylvania. Reprinted with permission. The 'phallic burst' referenced renewed criticism of O'Keeffe's *Jack-in-the-Pulpit* (1930) series, published in S. Kootz, *Modern American Painters* (New York, 1930).

12 O'Keeffe to Russell Vernon Hunter, late August 1931(?), cited in R. Robinson, *Georgia O'Keeffe: A Life* (New York, 1989), p. 359 n. 41.

13 Lynes, *Georgia O'Keeffe*, CR 722. *White Calico Rose* (alternative title: *White Rose, New Mexico*), ibid., CR 709–11. Exhibition checklist 1931, nos 12–13. Two versions of *Apple Blossoms* were on view, ibid., CR 700–701. *Black and White* and *Black White and Blue*, ibid., CR 728. Exhibition checklist 1931, no. 19. *Hills Back of Mabel's – Taos* (retitled *Sandhills with Blue River*).

14 Edna St Vincent Millay to O'Keeffe, 13 August 1931, O'Keeffe Correspondence Ser. VIII, Stieglitz/O'Keeffe Archive, MSS 85, Box 203.

15 O'Keeffe to Millay, undated letter (August–September? 1931], cited in N. Milford, *Savage Beauty* (New York, 2001), p. 340; Millay to O'Keeffe, 16 September 1931, Stieglitz/O'Keeffe Archives, MSS 85, Box 203.

16 G. O'Keeffe, *Georgia O'Keeffe* (New York, 1976), n.p (opposite no. 58).

17 Lowe, *Stieglitz*, Appendix II, p. 435: 127 photographs, including New York from high windows at the gallery and Hotel Shelton, portraits of O'Keeffe since 1922, and portraits of Dorothy Norman.

18 S. Greenough, ed., *My Faraway One: Selected Letters of Georgia O'Keeffe and Alfred Stieglitz*, vol. I: *1915–1933* (New Haven, CT, and London, 2011), p. 554. Cf also ibid., pp. 591–6: Stieglitz to O'Keeffe, 7–10 July 1931.

19 Robinson, *Georgia O'Keeffe*, p. 361.

20 O'Keeffe, *Georgia O'Keeffe*, n.p. (opposite no. 55). J. Weinberg, 'First Person: Me and Georgia O'Keeffe, *Chicago Reader*, archived edn XVII/20 (3–9 March 1988), www.chicagoreader.com. Weinberg travelled to Abiquiu to meet O'Keeffe in August 1976.

21 A. Douglas, *Terrible Honesty: Mongrel Manhattan in the 1920s* (New York, 1995), p. 34. R. L. Blaszczyk, 'The Colors of Modernism: Georgia O'Keeffe, Cheney Brothers and the Relationship between Art and Industry in the 1920s', in *Seeing High and Low*, ed. P. Johnston (Berkeley, CA, 2006), pp. 228–46.

22 W. Corn, 'Painting Big: O'Keeffe's *Manhattan*', *American Art*, XX/2 (Summer 2006), pp. 22–5.

23 H. McBride, 'Opening Exhibition of Murals at Museum of Modern Art', *New York Sun* (7 May 1932). D. Grafly, 'Murals at the Museum

of Modern Art', *American Magazine of Art*, xxv/2 (August 1932), p. 93.

24 A. Berman, *Rebels on Eighth Street: Juliana Force and the Whitney Museum of American Art* (New York, 1990), pp. 303–4. Stieglitz's letter, in the Whitney Archives, details strict payment terms between 1 July 1932 and 1 July 1933 for a total of $4,500 for the two paintings, *Single Lily with Red* (1928, Lynes, *Georgia O'Keeffe*, CR 633) and *The Mountain, N. M.* (1931, ibid., CR 790). *Skunk Cabbage* (1927, ibid., CR 612), now in the Montclair Art Museum, NJ, was later exchanged by the Whitney with the artist for the purchase of *Abstraction* (1926, ibid., CR 522).

25 Corn, 'Painting Big', p. 25 n. 3: O'Keeffe's letter of April 1929 to Blanche Matthias, where the artist expressed interest in 'painting it big'.

26 Lowe, *Stieglitz*, p. 320.

27 D. Deskey, 7 November 1978, cited in L. Lisle, *Portrait of an Artist: A Biography of Georgia O'Keeffe* (New York, 1980), p. 205. Robinson, *Georgia O'Keeffe*, pp. 370–79.

28 C. Tomkins, 'The Rose in the Eye', *New Yorker* (4 March 1974), p. 47.

29 Lynes, *Georgia O'Keeffe*, CR 812 and 814. O'Keeffe carefully drew, then painted, a small oil of the single blossom of *Bleeding Heart* as early as 1928 (ibid., CR 634–5); later, she made the large pastel.

30 O'Keeffe to Stieglitz, 17 November 1932, in Greenough, ed., *My Faraway One*, p. 662.

31 Greenough, *My Faraway One*, pp. 665–6.

32 Stieglitz to O'Keeffe, 19 January 1933, ibid., p. 672.

33 J. Quasha, *Marjorie Content: Photographs* (New York, 1994), pp. 83, 85: from the *Windows of Doctors Hospital*, winter 1933.

34 Frida Kahlo to O'Keeffe, 1 March 1933, Stieglitz/O'Keeffe Archive, MSS 85, Box 201.

35 Audio interview with Catherine O'Keeffe Klenert (1977), Laurie Lisle Research Documents, Archives of American Art, Washington, DC.

36 Robinson, *Georgia O'Keeffe*, p. 372.

37 E. A. Jewell, 'Another O'Keeffe Emerges', *New York Times* (29 March 1933).

38 Stieglitz to Barnes, 4 March 1933, Presidents' Files, Albert C. Barnes Correspondence, The Barnes Foundation Archives, Merion, Pennsylvania. Reprinted with permission; Barnes to Stieglitz, March 1933, Stieglitz/O'Keeffe Archive, MSS 85, Box 3.

39 D. C. Rich, ed., *The Flow of Art: Essays and Criticism of Henry McBride* (New York, 1975), insert after p. 244.

40 Stieglitz to Arthur Dove, 25 June 1933, cited in Morgan, *Dear Stieglitz/Dear Dove*, p. 277.

41 O'Keeffe to Stieglitz, 6 November 1933, in Greenough, ed., *My Faraway One*, p. 720.

42 O'Keeffe to Stieglitz, 27 July 1928, ibid., p. 399.

43 Lowe, *Stieglitz*, p. 328.

44 O'Keeffe to Jean Toomer, 2 January 1934, Beinecke Rare Book and Manuscript Library, Yale University, Yale Collection of American Literature, Jean Toomer Papers, James Weldon Johnson Collection (hereafter: Jean Toomer Papers).

45 O'Keeffe to Toomer, 7 January 1934, Jean Toomer Papers, Box 6. On 4 January 1934 O'Keeffe also wrote to Stieglitz: 'painting again and keeping the fires going', Stieglitz/O'Keeffe Archive, MSS 85, Box 88.

46 Jean Toomer Papers, Box 43, note for 'York Beach': 'Aloneness'.

47 O'Keeffe to Toomer, 7 January 1934, Jean Toomer Papers, Box 6.

48 O'Keeffe to Toomer, 10 January 1934, ibid.

49 Toomer to O'Keeffe, 21 January 1934, Stieglitz/O'Keeffe Archive, MSS 85, Box 216.

50 Stieglitz to Ansel Adams, 9 June 1934, in M. S. Alinder and A. G. Sillman, eds, *Ansel Adams: Letters and Images, 1916–84* (New York, 1988), p. 71.

51 O'Keeffe to Stieglitz, 5 March 1934, Stieglitz/O'Keeffe Archive, Box 88; O'Keeffe to Toomer, 10 January 1934, Jean Toomer Papers, Box 6.

52 Toomer to O'Keeffe, 4 March 1934, Stieglitz/O'Keeffe Archive, MSS 85, Box 216.

53 'Paintings by Women Artists Bought by the Metropolitan', *New York Herald Tribune* (26 March 1934).

54 Toomer to O'Keeffe, 10 April 1934 and 4 March 1934, Stieglitz/O'Keeffe Archive, MSS 85, Box 216.

55 O'Keeffe to Toomer, 11 May 1934, Jean Toomer Papers, Box 6.

56 O'Keeffe to Toomer, 7 June 1934, ibid.

8 Ghost Ranch

1 E. H. Colbert, *Digging into the Past: An Autobiography* (New York, 1989), p. 288.

2 J. Cowart, J. Hamilton and S. Greenough, *Georgia O'Keeffe: Art and Letters*, exh. cat., National Gallery of Art, Washington, DC (1987), p. 10.

3 L. Poling-Kempes, *The Valley of the Shining Stone* (Tucson, AZ, 1997), p. 158.

4 C. Tomkins, 'The Rose in the Eye', *New Yorker* (4 March 1974), p. 50.

5 'Georgia O'Keeffe Turns Dead Bones to Live Art', *Life* (14 February 1938), pp. 28–31.

6 M. L. Kotz, 'Georgia O'Keeffe at 90', *Art News* (December 1977), p. 42.

7 A. Barr, *Fantastic Art, Dada, Surrealism*, exh. cat., Museum of Modern Art, New York (1936), pp. 216–17. The other O'Keeffe work on view was *Black Abstraction* (1927), Metropolitan Museum of Art, New York.

8 J. J. Brody, *Pueblo Indian Painting: Tradition and Modernism in New Mexico, 1900–1930* (Santa Fe, NM, 1997), pp. 4–5, 121. Pueblo artists, trained in the revival of ancient kiva painting traditions at the School of American Research in Santa Fe, displayed their work as early as 1922 in the Southwest Indian Fair (p. 121), and in 1941 in *Indian Art in the United States* at the Museum of Modern Art (pp. 4–5).

9 L. Janos, 'Georgia O'Keeffe at Eighty-four', *Atlantic Monthly* (December 1971), p. 115.

10 *Georgia O'Keeffe: Exhibition Catalogue*, An American Place, New York (1939). Beinecke Rare Book and Manuscript Library, Yale University, Yale Collection of American Literature, Alfred Stieglitz/Georgia O'Keeffe Archive (hereafter: Stieglitz/O'Keeffe Archive), Box 118.

11 Daniel Catton Rich, interviewed by Perry Miller Adato, in *Georgia O'Keeffe: American Masters* (1977), documentary, PBS, Educational Broadcasting, broadcast November 1977.

12 E. Colbert, *The Little Dinosaurs of Ghost Ranch* (New York, 1995), p. 50.

13 Colbert, *Digging into the Past*, p. 293.

14 Colbert, *Little Dinosaurs*, p. 50.

15 'Science: Earliest Dinosaurs', *Life* (11 August 1947), pp. 49–52.

16 'Georgia O'Keeffe Turns Dead Bones to Live Art', pp. 28–31.

17 Georgia O'Keeffe, 'About Myself', exhibition statement, An American Place, New York, January 1939, Stieglitz/O'Keeffe Archive, Box 118.

18 O'Keeffe to Stieglitz, 25 August 1937, *Fourteenth Annual Exhibition of Paintings, with some Recent O'Keeffe Letters* (New York, 1937), p. 8, ibid., Box 118.

19 Barnes Foundation. Cézanne's *Mont Sainte-Victoire*, 1892–5 (BF 13). Two important examples of the Cézanne mountain were on view from the time O'Keeffe visited the Barnes collection in 1927.

20 B. B. Lynes, *Georgia O'Keeffe: Catalogue Raisonné*, 2 vols (New Haven, CT, and London, 1999), CR 1117, *Pedernal*, pastel on paper (1945, Georgia O'Keeffe Museum, Santa Fe), is one of many such examples.

21 K. Hokusai, *Fugaku hyakkei* (One Hundred Views of Fuji), 3 vols (1850–1910), in Fine et al., *The Book Room: Georgia O'Keeffe's Library in Abiquiu* (Abiquiu, NM, and New York, 1997).

22 Audio interview with David McAlpin (1977), Laurie Lisle Research Documents, Archives of American Art, Washington, DC. McAlpin recalled details of meeting O'Keeffe in 1928, and Ghost Ranch in the summers of 1935–7, where he had been invited by his Princeton friend Arthur Pack. Cf. S. S. Phillips, 'What Adams Saw', in *Georgia O'Keeffe and Ansel Adams: Natural Affinities*, exh. cat., Georgia O'Keeffe Museum, Santa Fe, New Mexico (2008), p. 156, for a different account of how McAlpin and Adams met at the cinema.

23 R. Robinson, *Georgia O'Keeffe: A Life* (New York, 1989), p. 425.

24 A. Adams, *Yosemite 1938: On the Trail with Ansel Adams and Georgia O'Keeffe*, exh. cat., National Museum of Wildlife Art, Jackson, Wyoming (2003).

25 Phillips, 'What Adams Saw', p. 157.

26 A. Adams and M. S. Alinder, *Ansel Adams: An Autobiography* (Boston, MA, 1985), p. 228.

27 Ansel Adams to Alfred Stieglitz, 10 September 1938, in M. S. Alinder and A. G. Stillman, eds, *Ansel Adams: Letters and Images, 1916–1984* (Boston, MA, 1988), p. 107.

28 Adams and Alinder, *Ansel Adams*, p. 228.

29 O'Keeffe to Ansel Adams, 8 July 1958, in P. Jennings and M. Ausherman, *Georgia O'Keeffe's Hawaii* (Kihei, HI, 2011), p. 25.

30 O'Keeffe to Stieglitz, 8 February 1939, in Jennings and Ausherman, *Georgia O'Keeffe's Hawaii*, p. 28.

31 O'Keeffe to Stieglitz, 17 February 1939, ibid., p. 7.

32 O'Keeffe to Stieglitz, Hana, 18 March 1939, ibid., p. 86.

33 Ibid., frontispiece; reprinted as 'Pineapple for Papaya', *Time* (12 February 1940).

34 O'Keeffe to Stieglitz, 15–17 February 1939, in J. Saville, 'Off in the Faraway: Georgia O'Keeffe's Letters from Hawaii', *Hawaiian Journal of History* (2012), p. 95. O'Keeffe's reference is to *Corn Dark*, 1924 (Metropolitan Museum of Art, New York), Lynes, *Georgia O'Keeffe*, CR 455.

35 Stieglitz to E. Arden, 20 July 1936. Stieglitz–Arden correspondence. Stieglitz O'Keeffe Archive, MSS 85, Box 3; payment received in November 1936. Letters exchanged between Alfred Stieglitz and Elizabeth Arden include details on the contract of $12,000 due for the mural, with subsequent payment schedule.

36 O'Keeffe to Stieglitz, 27 July 1940, and Stieglitz to O'Keeffe, 29 July 1940. See B. Lynes and J. Agapita Lopez, *Georgia O'Keeffe and her Houses: Ghost Ranch and Abiquiu* (New York, 2012), pp. 7–8.

37 Lynes, *Georgia O'Keeffe*, CR 1022–3: *Pedernal My Front Yard – Autumn*; and *My Front Yard – Summer*, Georgia O'Keeffe Museum.

38 Janos, 'Georgia O'Keeffe at Eighty-four', p. 117.

39 O'Keeffe to Patricia Jennings, 1 May 1941, in Jennings and Ausherman, *Georgia O'Keeffe's Hawaii*, pp. 75–7.

40 B. Lynes and A. Paden, eds, *Maria Chabot–Georgia O'Keeffe Correspondence* (Santa Fe, NM, 2003), p. 11.

41 B. G. Kelm and A. C. Madonia, *Georgia O'Keeffe in Williamsburg*, exh. cat., Muscarelle Museum of Art, College of William and Mary, Williamsburg, Virginia (2001).

42 M. Winn, 'Georgia O'Keeffe: Outstanding Artist', *Chicago Tribune* (28 February 1943), p. C4. Art Institute of Chicago, 'Largest Showing of the Paintings by Georgia O'Keeffe Opens', press release, 21 January 1943.

43 D. C. Rich, *Georgia O'Keeffe*, exh. cat., Art Institute of Chicago, Chicago, Illinois (1943).

44 Stieglitz to Chabot, 24 January 1943, cited in Lynes and Paden, eds, *Maria Chabot–Georgia O'Keeffe Correspondence*, p. 64.

45 Lynes, *Georgia O'Keeffe*, CR 1052, cited from O'Keeffe's Whitney notebook of 1970: 'This belonged to Frank Lloyd Wright and I tried to buy it back when he died, but they would not sell.'

46 D. C. Rich, 'The New O'Keeffes', *Magazine of Art* (March 1944), press release, Art Institute of Chicago, 21 January 1943.

47 M. Breuning, 'O'Keeffe's Best', *Art Digest* (1 March 1944), p. 26.

48 O'Keeffe, *Georgia O'Keeffe*, n.p.: 'Statement for 1944 exhibition at An American Place', An American Place, New York, 1944. Cf. Stieglitz/O'Keeffe Archive, MSS 85, Box 118.

49 Ibid.

50 P. M. Adato, *Georgia O'Keeffe: American Masters* (1977), documentary, PBS, Educational Broadcasting, broadcast November 1977.

51 L. Poling-Kempes, *Ghost Ranch* (Tucson, AZ, 2005), pp. 154–5, 157.

52 O'Keeffe to Maria Chabot, 16 May 1946, cited in Lynes and Paden, *Maria Chabot–Georgia O'Keeffe Correspondence*, pp. 360–61.

53 J. T. Soby, 'To The Ladies: Fine Arts', *Saturday Review of Literature* (6 July 1946).

54 N. Newhall to Ansel Adams, 15 July 1946, in *Ansel Adams*, ed. Alinder and Stillman, p. 175.

55 S. D. Lowe, *Stieglitz: A Memoir/Biography* (New York, 1983), p. 377.

56 R. Whelan, *Alfred Stieglitz: A Biography* (New York, 1995), p. 573. O'Keeffe to William H. Schubart, 4 August 1950, cited in Robinson, *Georgia O'Keeffe*, p. 464.

9 *Sky Above Clouds*

1 M. Brennan, *Painting Gender, Constructing Theory: The Alfred Stieglitz Circle and American Formalist Aesthetics* (Cambridge, MA, 2001), pp. 232–6. Brennan cites C. Greenberg on John Marin as '[one of] the greatest American painter[s] of the twentieth century', in contrast to O'Keeffe as a painter who created 'private fetishes with secret and arbitrary meanings'. See also C. Greenberg, 'Review of an Exhibition of Georgia O'Keeffe', *The Nation*, XV (June 1946).

2 H. McBride, 'O'Keeffe at the Museum', *New York Sun* (18 May 1946). 'Austere Stripper', *Time* (27 May 1946).

3 O'Keeffe to Edith Halpert, 10 September 1951, and 19 January 1955. Archives of American Art, Downtown Gallery Papers, Reel 5550. January 1955 letter cited in L. Pollack, *The Girl With the Gallery* (New York, 2006), p. 312.

4 B. B. Lynes and J. Lopez, *The Houses of O'Keeffe: Ghost Ranch and Abiquiu* (New York, 2012), p. 152.

5 S. D. Lowe, *Alfred Stieglitz: A Memoir/Biography* (New York, 1983), p. 346. Stieglitz stopped exhibiting his own photography after 1935, and showed selections of his own pieces one last time in a 'mixed-media group show', in 1941.

6 Interview notes for *Good Morning America* (ABC News, November 1976), Laurie Lisle Research Documents, Archives of American Art, Washington, DC.

7 Ibid., p. 30.

8 Marina Pacini, 'Interview with Mildred Hudson', *Nashville Number*, XVII (1992), pp. 12–13, Hudson attended the inauguration of the Stieglitz Collection at Fisk University in 1949.

9 Carl Van Vechten to Dr Charles S. Johnson, 10 January 1948, in B. Kellner, ed., *Letters of Carl Van Vechten* (New Haven, CT, 1987), pp. 234–5.

10 Audio interview with Catherine O'Keeffe Klenert (1977), Laurie Lisle Research Documents. The grave of John Robert O'Keeffe is marked by a simple stone in the Forest Hill Cemetery of Madison, Wisconsin; his death is registered as 'Killed in Action' at Heartbreak Hill, on 17 September 1951 in North Korea. My thanks to James Grandfield, USM, Ret., for this information.

11 Chabot telegram to O'Keeffe, 13 July 1946, in B. Lynes and A. Paden, eds, *Maria Chabot–Georgia O'Keeffe: Correspondence, 1941–49* (Santa Fe, NM, 2003), p. 366. O'Keeffe to Kiskadden, October 1951, Beinecke Rare Book and Manuscript Library, Yale University, Yale Collection of American Literature, Alfred Stieglitz/Georgia O'Keeffe Archive (hereafter: Stieglitz/O'Keeffe Archive), MSS 85, Box 198.

12 O'Keeffe to Edith Halpert, 8 August 1954, Downtown Gallery Papers, Archives of American Art (Box 25, Reel 5550), references *Red Tree – Yellow Sky*, Lane Collection, Museum of Fine Arts, Boston, Massachusetts. B. B. Lynes, *Georgia O'Keeffe: A Catalogue Raisonné*, 2 vols (New Haven, CT, and London, 1999), CR 1244.

13 Lynes, *Georgia O'Keeffe*, CR 1264, *Antelope with Pedernal* (1953).

14 H. Drohojowska-Philp, *Full Bloom: The Art and Life of Georgia O'Keeffe* (New York, 2004), p. 446.

15 C. Tomkins, 'A Rose in the Eye', *New Yorker* (4 March 1974), p. 64.

16 L. Messinger, ed., *Stieglitz and his Artists*, exh. cat., Metropolitan Museum of Art, New York (2011), p. 336. *Fourteen American Masters*, October 1958–January 1959 (no catalogue).

17 O'Keeffe to Claudia O'Keeffe, 16 April 1958, Claudia O'Keeffe Papers, Archives of American Art. O'Keeffe to Charles Wickham Moore, 9 March 1958, O'Keeffe Research Center Archives, Georgia O'Keeffe Museum Research Center.

18 O'Keeffe to Frances O'Brien, 12 October 1958, Frances O'Brien Papers, Georgia O'Keeffe Museum Research Center.

19 Daniel Catton Rich to O'Keeffe, 11 February 1960, Laurie Lisle Research Documents. Cf. B. B. Lynes and R. Bowman, *O'Keeffe's O'Keeffes: The Artist's Collection*, exh. cat., Milwaukee Art Museum (New York, 2001), p. 30: 'At the time of her death in 1986 . . . O'Keeffe owned more than one-half of the 2,029 known works of her total output.'

20 O'Keeffe to Rich, 2 February 1960, Laurie Lisle Research Documents.

21 Rich to O'Keeffe, 7 March 1960, Stieglitz/O'Keeffe Archive, MSS 85, Box 220. '43 Paintings to be Shown', *Worcester Telegram* (3 October 1960), p. 23.

22 D. C. Rich, *An Exhibition by Georgia O'Keeffe*, exh. cat., Worcester Art Museum, Worcester, Massachusetts (1960).

23 O'Keeffe to Maria Chabot, 17 November 1941 (written in flight), in Lynes and Paden, eds, *Maria Chabot–Georgia O'Keeffe*, p. 12.

24 Brandeis University Archives, Creative Arts Awards, Box 1, Correspondence, 1957–63.

25 Ibid., CR 1478, *Sky Above Clouds II*.

26 S. Hunter, *American Modernism: The First Wave*, exh. cat., Rose Art Museum, Brandeis University, Waltham, Massachusetts (1963).

27 E. Genauer, 'A Rear-mirror View of the Year', *New York Herald Tribune* (29 December 1963): 'The Rose Art Museum, normally dedicated to the last word, also decided that words spoken a little earlier might be worth listening to . . . a call of rebellion against the rebels.'

28 Lynes and Lopez, *The Houses of O'Keeffe*, pp. 38–9, show O'Keeffe in front of her finished painting in the garage, and the 2011 site.

29 M. Wilder, ed., *Georgia O'Keeffe*, exh. cat., Amon Carter Museum of Western Art, Fort Worth, Texas (1966), pp. 7–9, 22–3, 14.

30 P. Plagens, 'A Georgia O'Keeffe Retrospective in Texas', *Artforum* (May 1966), pp. 27–30.

31 E. C. Goossen, 'Georgia O'Keeffe', *Vogue* (1 March 1967).

32 E. C. Goossen, 'Introduction', in *The Art of the Real*, exh. cat., Museum of Modern Art, New York (1968).

33 K. Millett, *Sexual Politics* (New York, 1969).

34 Interview notes for *Good Morning America* (ABC News, November 1976), Laurie Lisle Research Documents.

35 Ibid.

36 J. Poling, *Painting with O'Keeffe* (Lubbock, TX, 1991), pp. 71–2, 67. C. S. Merrill, *Weekends with O'Keeffe* (Albuquerque, NM, 2010), pp. 39–40.

37 Frances O'Brien interviews conducted by Nancy Wall, 1986–7, Frances O'Brien Papers, Georgia O'Keeffe Museum.

38 Poling, *Painting with O'Keeffe*, pp. 17–16. See Lynes, *Georgia O'Keeffe*, CR 1624–31. *From a Day with Juan I* (1976–7), CR 1624, includes inscription, and the catalogue makes note of Poling's assistance.

39 Georgia O'Keeffe, *Plaintiff v. Doris Bry*, defendant. No. 77 Civ. 2576, U.S. District Court, 8 August 1978. 456 Federal Supplement, pp. 822–31.

40 O'Keeffe to Peggy Kiskadden, 3 September 1977, Stieglitz/O'Keeffe Archive, MSS 85, Box 198.

41 E. E. Asbury, 'Georgia O'Keeffe Dead at 98: Shaper of Modern Art in U.S.', *New York Times* (7 March 1986).

42 An O'Keeffe painting in the secondary market, the *Poppies* (1950), sold in 1973 for $120,000, setting a new sales high for an American painting at auction. See J. H. Merryman and A. Elsen, *Law, Ethics and the Visual Arts*, 4th edn (London and Boston, MA, 2002), p. 824.

43 K. McMurran, 'A $13 Million Lawsuit over Georgia O'Keeffe Highlights a Portrait of the Artist's Young Man', *People* (12 February 1979).

44 F. M. Biddle, *The Whitney Women and the Museum they Made* (New York, 1999), p. 255.

45 W. Corn, 'Telling Tales: Georgia O'Keeffe on *Georgia O'Keeffe*', *American Art*, XXIII/2 (Summer 2009), p. 60.

46 J. Weinberg, 'First Person: Me and Georgia O'Keeffe', *Chicago Reader*, archived edn XVII/20 (3–9 March 1988).

47 Lynes and Bowman, *O'Keeffe's O'Keeffes*, p. 34. O'Keeffe to Edith
    Halpert, 1952, Reel 5550: 'I have destroyed forty of my paintings . . .'.
48 M. L. Kotz, 'Georgia O'Keeffe at 90', *Art News*, LXXVI (December
    1977), p. 45.
49 J. Malcolm, 'On Photography: Artists and Lovers', *New Yorker*
    (12 March 1979), p. 118.
50 Merrill, *Weekends with O'Keeffe*, p. 4.
51 D. Johnston, 'Portrait of the Young Artist and the Young Man: Why a
    Once-impoverished Potter is Giving Up Georgia O'Keeffe Inheritance',
    Los Angeles Times (23 August 1987).

Epilogue: Ancient Spirit

1 J. Turrell, 'Signs Enough', in *Georgia O'Keeffe: Visions of the Sublime*,
   ed. J. S. Czestochowski, exh. cat., University of Michigan Art
   Museum, Ann Arbor, Michigan (Memphis, TN, 2004), p. 127.
2 Ibid., pp. 126–7.
3 O'Keeffe to Frances O'Brien, November 1949, and Abiquiu,
   7 February 1950, Frances O'Brien Papers, Georgia O'Keeffe Museum.
4 O'Keeffe to Frances O'Brien, 7 February 1950, ibid.
5 Frances O'Brien interviews conducted by Nancy Wall, 1986–7,
   Frances O'Brien Papers, Georgia O'Keeffe Museum Research Center.
6 Frances O'Brien to O'Keeffe, 27 February 1950, Georgia O'Keeffe
   Museum Research Center.
7 Interview notes for *Good Morning America* (ABC News, November
   1976), Laurie Lisle Research Documents, Archives of American Art,
   Washington, DC.
8 C. S. Merrill, *Weekends with O'Keeffe* (Albuquerque, NM, 2010), p. 124.
9 Rich to O'Keeffe, 4 May 1973; acceptance speech for Skowhegan
   Medal for Painting (in O'Keeffe's absence), 3 May 1973, Beinecke
   Rare Book and Manuscript Library, Yale University, Yale Collection
   of American Literature, Alfred Stieglitz/Georgia O'Keeffe Archive,
   Box 210.
10 T. Merton, *Woods, Shore, Desert: A Notebook, May 1968* (Santa Fe, NM,
   1982), pp. 35 and 36; Merton quote p. 57.
11 Merrill, *Weekends with O'Keeffe*, p. 68.

12 Ibid., p. 66.

13 G. O'Keeffe, *Georgia O'Keeffe* (New York, 1976), n.p. (opposite no. 102).

14 M. Tuchman et al., *The Spiritual in Art: Abstract Painting, 1890–1985*, exh. cat., Los Angeles County Museum of Art (New York, 1986).

15 S. Nesbitt, 'The anatomy of *Effigia okeeffeae* (Archosauria, Suchia), Theropod-like Convergence, and the Distribution of Related Taxa', *Bulletin of the American Museum of Natural History*, CCCII (2007).

Select Bibiliography

Archives

Archives of American Art, Washington, DC (Claudia O'Keeffe Letters, 1940–62; Downtown Gallery Records, 1949–55 [Edith Gregor Halpert]; Laurie Lisle Research Documents)

Barnes Foundation Archives, Merion, Pennsylvania

Beinecke Rare Book and Manuscript Library, Yale University, New Haven, Connecticut, Yale Collection of American Literature (Alfred Stieglitz/Georgia O'Keeffe Archive; Jean Toomer Papers; James Weldon Johnson Collection)

Georgia O'Keeffe Museum Research Center, Santa Fe, New Mexico

Museum of Modern Art Archives, New York

Whitney Museum of American Art Archives, New York

Catalogues of the complete works and selected correspondence

Giboire, Clive, *Lovingly, Georgia: The Complete Correspondence of Georgia O'Keeffe and Anita Pollitzer* (New York, 1990)

Greenough, Sarah, ed., *Alfred Stieglitz: The Key Set: The Alfred Stieglitz Collection of Photographs*, 2 vols (Washington, DC, 2002)

—, *My Faraway One: Selected Letters of Georgia O'Keeffe and Alfred Stieglitz*, vol. I: *1915–1933* (New Haven, CT, and London, 2011); vol. II forthcoming

Lynes, Barbara Buhler, *Georgia O'Keeffe: A Catalogue Raisonné*, 2 vols (New Haven, CT, and London, 1999)

—, *O'Keeffe, Stieglitz and the Critics, 1916–29* (Chicago, IL, 1989)

—, and Lynn Paden, eds, *Maria Chabot–Georgia O'Keeffe: Correspondence, 1941–49* (Santa Fe, NM, 2003)

Biographies, memoirs and autobiography

Drohojowska-Philp, Hunter, *Full Bloom: The Art and Life of Georgia O'Keeffe* (New York, 2004)
Hoffman, Katherine, *Stieglitz: A Legacy of Light* (New Haven, CT, 2011)
Lisle, Laurie, *Portrait of an Artist: A Biography of Georgia O'Keeffe* (New York, 1980)
Lowe, Sue Davidson, *Stieglitz: A Memoir/Biography* (New York, 1983)
Messinger, Lisa Mintz, 'Georgia O'Keeffe', *Metropolitan Museum of Art Bulletin*, XLII/2 (Fall 1984)
—, *Georgia O'Keeffe* (New York, 2001)
O'Keeffe, Georgia, *Georgia O'Keeffe* (New York, 1976)
Pollitzer, Anita, *A Woman on Paper: Georgia O'Keeffe* (New York, 1988)
Robinson, Roxana, *Georgia O'Keeffe: A Life* (New York, 1989)
Whelan, Richard, *Stieglitz: A Biography* (Boston, 1995)
Whitaker, Sarah Peters, *Becoming O'Keeffe: The Early Years* (New York, 1991)

Sources and theory

Brennan, Marcia, *Painting Gender, Constructing Theory: The Alfred Stieglitz Circle and American Formalist Aesthetics* (Cambridge, MA, 2001)
Brody, J. J., *Pueblo Indian Painting: Tradition and Modernism in New Mexico, 1900–1930* (Santa Fe, NM, 1997)
Corn, Wanda, *The Great American Thing: Modern Art and National Identity, 1915–1935* (Berkeley, CA, 1999)
Dell, Floyd, *Women as World Builders* (New York, 1913)
Douglas, Ann, *Terrible Honesty: Mongrel Manhattan in the 1920s* (New York, 1995)
Fine, Ruth E., Elizabeth Glassman and Juan Hamilton, *The Book Room: Georgia O'Keeffe's Library in Abiquiu* (Abiquiu, NM, and New York, 1997)

Lynes, Barbara, and Judy Agapita Lopez, *Georgia O'Keeffe and her Houses: Ghost Ranch and Abiquiu* (New York, 2012)

Selected exhibition catalogues

Bry, Doris, *Alfred Stieglitz*, Museum of Fine Arts, Boston, MA (1965)

—, and Lloyd Goodrich, *Georgia O'Keeffe*, Whitney Museum of American Art, New York (1970)

Coe, Erin B., *Modern Nature: Georgia O'Keeffe and Lake George*, The Hyde Collection, Glen Falls, New York (2013)

Cowart, J., J. Hamilton and Sarah Greenough, *Georgia O'Keeffe: Art and Letters*, National Gallery of Art, Washington, DC (1987)

Eldredge, Charles, *Georgia O'Keeffe: American and Modern*, Hayward Gallery, London (New York, 1993)

Georgia O'Keeffe: A Portrait by Alfred Stieglitz, Metropolitan Museum of Art, New York (1978)

Greenough, Sarah, and Juan Hamilton, *Alfred Stieglitz*, National Gallery of Art, Washington, DC, and Metropolitan Museum of Art, New York (1983)

Haskell, Barbara, ed., *Georgia O'Keeffe: Abstraction*, Whitney Museum of American Art, New York (2009)

Hassrick, Peter H., ed., *The Georgia O'Keeffe Museum* (New York, 1997)

Lynes, Barbara, ed., *Georgia O'Keeffe*, Fondazione Roma Museo, Kunsthalle der Hypo-Kulturstiftung, Munich, and Helsinki Art Museum (Milan, 2011)

—, ed., *Georgia O'Keeffe and Ansel Adams: Natural Affinities*, Georgia O'Keeffe Museum, Santa Fe, New Mexico (New York, 2008)

—, and Russell Bowman, *O'Keeffe's O'Keeffes: The Artist's Collection*, exh. cat., Milwaukee Art Museum (New York, 2001)

—, and Carolyn Kastner, *Georgia O'Keeffe in New Mexico: Architecture, Katsinam and the Land*, Georgia O'Keeffe Museum, Santa Fe, New Mexico (2012)

Messinger, Lisa Mintz, *Stieglitz and his Artists: Matisse to O'Keeffe*, Metropolitan Museum of Art, New York (New Haven, CT, 2011)

Pyne, Kathleen, *Modernism and the Feminine Voice: O'Keeffe and the Women of the Stieglitz Circle*, Georgia O'Keeffe Museum, Santa Fe, New Mexico (Berkeley, CA, 2007)

Rich, Daniel Catton, *Georgia O'Keeffe*, Art Institute of Chicago, Chicago, Illinois (1943)

—, *An Exhibition by Georgia O'Keeffe*, Worcester Art Museum, Massachusetts (1960)

Tuchman, Maurice, et al., *The Spiritual in Art: Abstract Painting, 1890–1985*, Los Angeles County Museum of Art (New York, 1986)

Turner, Elizabeth H., *Georgia O'Keeffe: The Poetry of Things*, The Phillips Collection, Washington, DC (1999)

Wilder, Mitchell, *Georgia O'Keeffe: An Exhibition of the Work of the Artist from 1915 to 1966*, Amon Carter Museum of Western Art, Fort Worth, Texas (1966)

Acknowledgements

My interest in the art of Georgia O'Keeffe deepened when I first read her letters to Anita Pollitzer, in the Beinecke Rare Book and Manuscript Library at Yale University. Many years of teaching a seminar on Stieglitz and O'Keeffe followed from my interest in O'Keeffe's first moves towards abstraction. I am indebted to my many students since, who proposed new research angles and, in debate and discussion, refined my thinking. From my later archival research, I learned that O'Keeffe herself had privileged the Pollitzer letters, sharing them only with chosen curators in the 1940s, and then denied her oldest friend Anita the right to publish excerpts from the letters. Against expectations, Miss O'Keeffe granted me permission in 1983 to publish a brief essay on the O'Keeffe–Pollitzer letters, three years before her death.

My work stands on the shoulders of many diligent and creative biographers and scholars who have plumbed the documented details of O'Keeffe's life, and notably those who captured the voices of O'Keeffe's world while she was still alive. I especially remember with gratitude the late William S. Pollitzer, who shared with me O'Keeffe's notes on his aunt's manuscript, *A Woman on Paper*, before its eventual publication. Another biographer, albeit in film, Perry Miller Adato, convinced O'Keeffe to work with her in the creation of a documentary, capturing O'Keeffe's voice and presence as a record for posterity. The award-winning documentary *Georgia O'Keeffe* debuted on O'Keeffe's 90th birthday in 1977.

Barbara Buhler Lynes and Sarah Greenough, in separate massive compendia, have published the foundational source material on the paintings, works on paper, Stieglitz photographs and the Stieglitz–O'Keeffe correspondence. Lynes has defined the research field on O'Keeffe's art for 25 years. Greenough, Curator of Photography at the

National Gallery in Washington, DC, has contributed immeasurably in cataloguing Stieglitz's corpus and then editing the correspondence. I acknowledge the generous scope of their publications, and the vital sources that these scholars provided for this book and for the wider field of American modernism.

Archivists and librarians at the Georgia O'Keeffe Research Center, notably Elizabeth Ehrnst, Eumie Imm-Stroukoff and Judy Agapita Lopez; the librarians at the Beinecke Rare Book and Manuscript Library; the Archives of American Art; the Barnes Foundation Archives; the Whitney Museum of American Art; and the Museum of Modern Art have all been key to my research. At the Yale Collection of American Literature at the Beinecke, I appreciated the advice of director Nancy Kuhl. Barbara Beaucar and Amanda McKnight, archivists at the Barnes, not only possess deep knowledge of the archival materials but welcomed my research and many questions.

My colleagues Karen Haas, Lane Curator of Photography at the Museum of Fine Arts, Boston; Cody Hartley, Director of Curatorial Affairs at the O'Keeffe Museum; and art historian Melissa Renn have kindly shared their expertise and provided most helpful direction. My former student Esther Adler, assistant curator of drawings at the Museum of Modern Art, ably shared her expertise during the 2013 *Hopper to O'Keeffe* exhibition.

Closer to home, I have been generously assisted by the private collectors who allowed me to study and reproduce works in their magnificent collections. My colleagues at the Rose Art Museum at Brandeis University, Kristin Parker, Deputy Director, and Chris Bedford, Lois Foster Director, made accessible the exhibition files from the 1963 and 1966 exhibitions involving O'Keeffe paintings. At the Brandeis Farber Library, Lisa Zeidenberg as well as archivists Anne Woodrum, Maggie McNeely and Director of Special Collections Sarah Shoemaker have unfailingly opened access to archival papers and photographs from our Carl Van Vechten Photographic Archives, the Native American Watercolors collection and the papers and documents of the university's 1963 Creative Arts Awards. Our Visual Resources Curator, Jennifer Stern, has been a constant source of helpful knowledge in securing images, and more recently Yi Wang provided more assistance. Several of my Fine Arts colleagues have been instrumental in answering questions and discussion pertaining to art making in the West, O'Keeffe in Isfahan, and the careers of women artists: Professors Talinn Grigor, Peter Kalb, Joe Wardwell and Aida Wong. My colleague Gannit Ankori quite simply made the genesis of this project possible, and to her and for her scholarship, I am deeply indebted.

The Theodore and Jane Norman Fund, administered by the Dean of Arts and Sciences at Brandeis, has been a generous source of support for travel to archives, and especially to the O'Keeffe Research Center, throughout this project. Earlier, a technology project from the Farber Library at Brandeis University funded an educational CD-ROM I created, 'O'Keeffe and the Southwest', and allowed for travel to the major O'Keeffe painting sites in New Mexico, including the Black Place, and a stay at Ghost Ranch.

My friend Janie Lindsay loaned me her grandmother's copy of Le Mirage, the West Texas State Normal College yearbook of 1918 that began the search for images in this book. This treasured resource led to many other acts of generosity. Thanks to author Natalie Dykstra for her close reading and expertise on biography. Thanks to my dear friend Sara Delano in Maine and to my cousin and friend, Amy McCrimmon Jackson in New Mexico, both of whom housed me during the research and writing trips. In addition, Sara Delano read the entire manuscript in various stages, with a sharp editorial eye.

To my children, Katie, Sam and Rebecca, I am so fortunate to enjoy the fruits of your distinctive, creative ways of thinking. You all contributed ideas and reactions that germinated in the book, but more than that, you endured the very long drives in New Mexico during long-ago summer vacations. Above all, to Martin, my husband, life partner and most stringent editor, words cannot express all I owe for the lively conversation and loving support that sustains my life and work.

Photo Acknowledgements

The author and the publishers wish to express their thanks to the below sources of illustrative material and/or permission to reproduce it:

Page 6: courtesy of Georgia O'Keeffe Museum (gift of The Georgia O'Keeffe Foundation – 2003.01.002), photo Art Resource, NY © Georgia O'Keeffe Museum; p. 13: photo © Presidents' Files, Albert C. Barnes Correspondence, The Barnes Foundation Archives, Merion, Pennsylvania; p. 14: Amon Carter Museum of American Art, Fort Worth, Texas; p. 20: courtesy of Georgia O'Keeffe Museum, Claudia O'Keeffe Papers (*RC-1999-001-151) – photo © Georgia O'Keeffe Museum; p. 25: photo © 2015 Georgia O'Keeffe Museum; p. 36: The Metropolitan Museum of Art (Alfred Stieglitz Collection, 1933), photo Art Resource, NY © The Metropolitan Museum of Art; p. 39: photo courtesy of the Library of Congress, Washington, DC (Records of the National Woman's Party Collection); p. 42: photo courtesy of Beinecke Rare Books and Manuscript Library, Yale University, New Haven, Connecticut (Georgia O'Keeffe/Alfred Stieglitz Archives, Yale Collection of American Literature); p. 51: The Metropolitan Museum of Art (Alfred Stieglitz Collection, 1950 (50.236.2)), photo Art Resource, NY © The Metropolitan Museum of Art; p. 53: The Metropolitan Museum of Art (Alfred Stieglitz Collection, 1969 (69.278.3)), image Art Resource, NY © The Metropolitan Museum of Art; p. 56: Georgia O'Keeffe Museum (gift of The Georgia O'Keeffe Foundation – 2006-06-0726), photo © Georgia O'Keeffe Museum; p. 59: Georgia O'Keeffe Museum (gift of The Georgia O'Keeffe Foundation – 2006-06-0748), photo © Georgia O'Keeffe Museum; p. 60: The Museum of Modern Art, New York – image © The Museum of Modern Art/licensed by SCALA/Art Resource, NY; p. 64: *Le Mirage* Yearbook 1918, Faculty page, private collection, Texas; p. 66: Amon Carter Museum of Western Art, Fort Worth, Texas; p. 75: National Portrait Gallery, Smithsonian Institution, Art Resource, NY © Aperture Foundation, Millerton, Connecticut; p. 78: The Metropolitan Museum of Art (gift of Georgia O'Keeffe, through the generosity of the Georgia O'Keeffe Foundation, and Jennifer and Joseph Duke, 1997 (1997.61.11)) – image © The Metropolitan Museum of Art; p. 81: The Metropolitan Museum of Art (gift of Georgia O'Keeffe, through the generosity of the Georgia O'Keeffe Foundation, and Jennifer and Joseph Duke, 1997 (1997.61.06)) – image Art Resource, NY © The Metropolitan Museum of Art; p. 83: The Metropolitan Museum of Art (gift of Georgia O'Keeffe, through the generosity of The Georgia O'Keeffe Foundation, and Jennifer and Joseph Duke, 1997 (1997.61.21)) – image Art Resource, NY © The Metropolitan Museum of Art; p. 92: from *Vanity Fair* (22 July 1922); p. 106: The Metropolitan Museum of Art (Alfred Stieglitz Collection, bequest of Georgia O'Keeffe, 1986 (1987.377.2)) – image Art Resource, NY © The Metropolitan Museum of Art; p. 111: private collection; p. 118: Georgia O'Keeffe Museum (gift of the Burnett Foundation) – photo Malcolm Varon 2001 © Georgia O'Keeffe Museum/Art Resource, NY; p. 121: photo Martin Newhouse; p. 122: private collection, photo Georgia O'Keeffe Museum/Art Resource, NY; p. 131: gift of The Georgia O'Keeffe Foundation (2003.01.017) © The Georgia O'Keeffe Museum, photo Georgia O'Keeffe Museum/Art Resource, NY; p. 138: Whitney Museum of American Art, New York: 32.36; p. 140: The Metropolitan Museum of Art (Alfred Stieglitz Collection (52.203)) – image Art Resource, NY © The Metropolitan Museum of Art; p. 143: from *Murals by American Painters and Photographers*, Museum of Modern Art, New York, catalogue (1932) – photo courtesy of Brandeis University Libraries; p. 149: photo © Beinecke Rare Book and Manuscript Library, Yale University, New Haven, Connecticut (Jean Toomer Papers, Yale Collection of American Literature); p. 155: Museum of Fine Arts, Boston (gift of the William H. Lane Foundation, 1990.432); p. 157: photo courtesy of Brandeis University Archives Special Collections; p. 166: Indianapolis Museum of Art, Indianapolis, Indiana, gift of Eli Lilly and Company, 1997.131 © Georgia O'Keeffe Museum/Artists' Rights Society; p. 169: Indianapolis Museum of Art, Indianapolis, Indiana (gift of Anne Marmon Greenleaf in memory of Caroline Marmon Fesler, 77.29) © Georgia O'Keeffe Museum/Artists' Rights Society; p. 176: Museum of Fine Arts, Boston (gift of the William H. Lane Foundation, 1990.433); p. 177: